The Country Kitchen

The Country Kitchen

Della Lutes

Introduction and Modern Recipes by
Mary Norwak

Bell & Hyman

First published 1938 by
G Bell & Son Ltd
This revised edition published 1985 by
Bell & Hyman Limited
Denmark House
37–39 Queen Elizabeth Street
London SE1 2QB

British Library Cataloguing in Publication Data
Lutes, Della,
The country kitchen.——Rev. ed.
1. Food habits——Michigan——History——19th
century
I. Title
641.3'009774   GT2853.U5

ISBN 0–7135–2567–3

Designed by Malcolm Harvey Young
Illustrations by Sylvia Gainsford
and Leon Olin

Typeset by Inforum Ltd, Portsmouth
Printed and bound in Great Britain at
The Bath Press, Avon

ISBN 0 7135 2567 3

Contents

Foreword
by Mary Norwak

Social history is a series of domestic links which form a chain across the centuries between the lives of our ancestors and ourselves. It is being increasingly recognized that the records of battles, treaties and revolutions merely note the landmarks of history, and that our understanding of past time is enhanced by knowledge of the way our forebears lived. Their houses, clothes, food, social pastimes and neighbourly attitudes may seem like the footnotes of history, but these small details of everyday life point the way to a clearer interpretation of great events.

When Florence White wrote her introduction to the 1938 edition of *The Country Kitchen*, the study of social history had not been fully developed. Herself a collector and recorder of old British recipes, she looked on Della Lutes' book as a mere collection of fifty-year-old recipes, and was content to interpret American vocabulary for British readers. Today, we are looking back on life as it was lived in the American Mid-West a hundred years ago, and can interpret links which lead us back to life in late eighteenth century England. 'Lijer, the father-hero of the book, was proud of his British ancestry, but had been born in America in the 1820s. He was fond of harking back to the old ways of cooking over an open fire, liked the idea of preparing Yorkshire Pudding under a joint of beef, and was fascinated by a recipe for cooking suckling pig, recorded by his wife's mother but taken almost word for word from Hannah Glasse's *Art of Cookery Made Plain and Easy* published in 1747. We are back two-and-a-quarter centuries ago linked by a recipe to Georgian England, pioneering America of the late nineteenth century, and our own times when we avidly collect old cookery books and study culinary traditions.

7

Della Lutes was just six years old when she observed the farming life of
Michigan in the 1880s. She was a natural reporter with an eye for telling detail,
and when she made her record in middle age, she used editorial skill in
extracting the essence of a story. She grew up in a house of gaiety and laughter,
where the kitchen was the centre of the home. The huge kitchen with its stove,
braided rugs, rocking chairs, clock and calendars seems timeless. The wood-
fired elevated oven with its reservoir for heating water was the pulse of daily life,
with the black iron tea-kettle simmering constantly, the winter snow being
melted for household washing, and mother 'Miry warming herself at the open
oven door. The author described the room as 'homely, cheerful and charming',
but it was a difficult place to work. The saucepans were black, ugly, heavy and
unwieldy, with dirt-collecting rolled rims; the deep frying pan on legs, known as
a 'spider', was a relic of open-fire cookery; the pie tins were well used and
seasoned; and the primitive sink was made of iron with splintery wood draining
boards.

'Miry could never rest from her labours, for every scrap of food had to be
preserved against hard times. There was a cellar, a root pit and a buttery in
which were stored barrels of pickles, jars of jams and bottles of sauce. There
were crocks of lard and sausages, pickled pigs' feet, barrels of salt pork, hams
hanging from the rafters. There were herbs and dried fruits, mincemeat, barrels
of beans, flour, buckwheat and cornmeal, two kinds of sugar and a pan of
broken honeycombs. Apples, potatoes, squash, turnips, cabbages and fruit
were kept right through the year, and even nuts were shelled and hung in bags
or buried in sugar buckets. On rare shopping trips, 'Lijer and Della would
barter surplus produce for salt cod, molasses, tea and green coffee beans,
pickled mackerel and tins of oysters, and the transactions took place over the
cracker barrel with a taste of strong cheese.

The seasons were marked, as they always are in the country, by social
diversions and appropriate foods. There were family birthdays, a donation
party for the minister's family, and a rare oyster supper which had to be paid for
with 'cash money'. There were regular church suppers, a Sunday school picnic,
the Fourth of July, Thanksgiving, Christmas and the Ladies' Aid dinner for
eight selected guests, memorably disrupted by 'Lijer and a skunk. A favourite
was the spring supper by the lake at the house of kinswoman Adelaide, a
memorable cook. She and Big Jim lived in an old log house, had trekked to
California and come home round Cape Horn.

Della loved this woman with 'the priceless disposition of time' who worked
hard yet always had the leisure to gather wild strawberries or morel mushrooms. She had no equipment but beautiful ingredients and above all she had
standards. 'She knew a good thing when she saw it, and she knew how to make

it,' said Della, and hers was 'the hand of a woman who cooked food as if she loved it.' The perfect epitaph for a true cook who rarely consulted a printed book, but culled recipes from newspapers and asked her friends for recipes or 'rules'.

Adelaide and the shrewder, quieter 'Miry worked for demanding husbands and ever-hungry children. Breakfast was served at 6 a.m. and was a huge meal of eggs, ham, salt mackerel, sausages, hot breads, doughnuts, pancakes, pounds of butter and gallons of milk. The children had to eat this meal too for they walked to school in all weathers, and were expected to do their share of the farmwork and household chores. Dinner was eaten at noon, and had to be a 'fillin' meal, mainly of pork or chicken, kept by all country families. Supper was a lighter meal taken around five o'clock, and bedtime was at eight, ready for a 5 a.m. start on the farm.

Readers of *The Country Kitchen* should be particularly grateful to 'Lijer Thompson, the author's father, because without this highly individual farmer there might have been no book. He was the reason why vast meals were cooked and why the household ran on traditional lines. He could be wildly generous but cunningly shrewd. He knew how to outwit his shiftless neighbours, but never forgot his great tribal family. He hated to go out on social visits, but always succumbed and then had to wait impatiently for his family. Unusually for a farmer, he was a keen gardener, but like all countrymen always wanted to outdo his neighbours and the preacher in the earliness of his produce. Everyone will recognize his kitchen muddle drawer in which everything he might need was stored, and his eternal hat which might be old or brand-new but always looked the same. This warm yet selfish and demanding man has his exact farming counterparts today.

The many dishes which were recorded also have their modern counterparts, and in preparing edited versions for today's use, I have enjoyed many familiar flavours and dishes. Like all natural cooks, the author's family were inclined to a 'bit of this and a bit of that', relying on good palates and family preference for that little extra something which distinguishes favourite dishes. All I have done is tidied up a few of the details and made sure that ingredients are available. *The Country Kitchen* is however so much more than a collection of recipes – as the author herself said of her life, it was 'nothing to make history, but good to live, good to remember.'

Mary Norwak 1985

9

Introduction to first edition
by Florence White

This book is not a mere collection of cookery recipes; it is a fascinating story of life as lived in a South Michigan farmhouse some forty to fifty years ago. The heroine is the wife and mother; the kitchen and storeroom are the hub of her universe. The events are noticed and recorded in the memory of her only child, an observant small person of six who has made of her childish recollections a very fine piece of literature. The descriptions and characterizations are perfect. ' 'Lijer,' her father, is equal to the best of any of Dickens' characters, whilst retaining the impress of his nationality. Most of his quaint expressions are untranslatable; he probably made them up as he talked. His wife 'Miry is lovingly depicted, and the child observer must have been a wonderful little girl to notice all she did and remember it. The characters that fill the rest of the picture, although secondary, are equally well drawn.

So much for the literary value of the book. It has, however, historical and traditional worth of no mean order. Beginning with 'Lijer's birthday on New Year's Day, when the author was only six, she takes us through a whole year of everyday doings, customs and cookery in this particular part of the world. It is a lively page of social history literally packed with cookery recipes and information that will be welcome to the enterprising English housewife, but, although the films have acclimatized a number of American expressions in England, there are still some that require a little explanation. On p. 22 reference is made to dill pickles, and the modern English housewife may not know what dill is. And that brings us to another interesting feature of the book: words used and dishes mentioned remind us of our relationship with our American cousins. We are apt to forget that before September 6th, 1620, when the *Mayflower* sailed from

11

Plymouth, the foundations of English and American cookery were the same. Amongst other cookery books dating from 1399 to the present moment, I have a copy of Gervase Markham's *English Housewife* dated 1660, which was first published in 1615, and I often think that some copies of the original edition must have been taken by the Pilgrim wives and mothers when they sailed in the *Mayflower*.

One word at any rate survives over yonder which is not in general use in England today. On p. 80 of *The Country Kitchen*, in a list of herbs and vegetables grown in the garden, we find scallion included. It is mentioned by Gervase Markham (in 1615), and Artemus Ward in his *Encyclopedia of Food*, published in New York, 1923, says: 'Scallion is a name applied to any onion which, because of age or other reason, has developed no bulb. It is also another name for the shallot.'

'Squash' is another American word he explains.

'Squash,' he says, 'is a term applied to the edible fruits of many varieties of gourds, found in divers sizes, shapes, and styles. The most famous of all is the *Pumpkin*. The others are classified are "summer" and "winter" squashes, the latter being generally of late autumn ripening.'

Summer squashes are chiefly of the species which include the true pumpkin and the *Vegetable Marrow*.

Winter squashes are generally larger, and firm and yellow in flesh, and are eaten ripe, both as a vegetable and in pies, etc., the seeds being removed before cooking. The pie is generally called 'pumpkin,' except in New England, where it may be frankly labelled 'squash pie.'

Molasses is also excellently described by Artemus Ward. 'It is,' he says, 'the syrup, or (as it is termed in the districts where it is manufactured), the "mother-water," that is separated from the crystals or grains of "raw sugar" in the process of manufacture. Its quality depends upon the character and treatment of the cane juice from which it is obtained.

'The best is that from sugar made from the first crops collected previous to the copious periodical rains which occur where the cane is cultivated. It is generally dark brown, but the choicest grades, those produced in St. Croix, Barbados, Antigua, Porto Rico and Louisiana, are of bright amber tint. Fine products are listed commercially by the name of the place of production; ordinary types are graded as "open-kettle," "prime," "good," "fair," "common," etc.

' "Blackstrap molasses," the poorest, is the final, or exhausted, molasses of raw sugar manufacture.'

For molasses, the English housewife should use Fowler's West Indian Syrup, which can be bought at any good grocers. It is very good indeed, not dark like ordinary black treacle, and not as thin and pale as golden syrup.

Dill is a well-known European herb much used in pickles in days gone by and today as an ingredient in popular remedies for flatulency.

John Evelyn, in his *Acetaria*, published 1699, gives the following recipe for 'dill and colly-flower pickle':

'Boil the Colly-flowers till they fall in pieces; then with some of the stalk and worst of the Flower, boil it in a part of the liquor till pretty strong. Then being taken off, strain it; and when settled, clean it from the Bottom. Then with Dill, gross pepper, a pretty quantity of salt, when cold add as much vinegar as will make it sharp and pour all upon the Colly-Flower.'

It may be interesting to some people to know that John Evelyn dedicated his *Acetaria* to the first President of the Royal Society.

Amongst the light puddings mentioned on p. 40 is 'Brown Betty' the name of which has been familiar to me since childhood. As *The Country Kitchen* does not give a recipe for it, here is a good one published in *Warnes' New Model Cookery Book* (edited by Mrs. Mabel Wijey. Published, London and New York, 1925).

Brown Betty Pudding

'For 5 or 6 persons.

'Time 3 hours.

'6 oz. of brown breadcrumbs, 4 oz. suet, peel of ½ a lemon, 2 oz of candied peel, 3 oz. castor sugar, 1 tablespoonful of brandy, ¼ teaspoon of grated nutmeg and powdered mace, 3 eggs, ½ pint of melted butter, 1 lb. apples, fingers of brown bread. Shred the suet finely and mix it with the breadcrumbs, nutmeg, mace, grated peel and half a lemon, cored and chopped apple and the sugar. Add the brandy and beaten eggs. Should the mixture be too dry add a little milk. Grease a mould or basin, put a round of bread at the bottom and line the sides with fingers of bread. Put in the mixture, cover with a scalded cloth and boil for 3 hours.'

This is an English recipe and the measures used are the modern English measures in use today. But it is important for anyone trying modern American recipes to remember that the American measures (U.S.A.) are different. We give 20 liquid ounces to a pint. In the United States the pint only contains 16 liquid ounces, and the American 'cup,' which is an American ½ pint, only contains 8. It is curious and interesting to note that the contents of a pint measure in England as given by Dr. William Kitchener in *The Cook's Oracle*, first published in 1817, is the same as the modern American measure (16 fluid ounces). Those who want to study this matter further for practical use today will find the subject of weights and measures in all the principal countries of the world dealt with very effectively in *Whitaker's Almanack* under the heading 'Weights and Measures.' For our present purpose, it is sufficient to say that when a cup is mentioned in this book, it means 8 liquid ounces. Also an American tablespoon only holds 3 teaspoonfuls of liquid, whereas an English tablespoon holds 4 teaspoonfuls. Staine's Kitchen Equipment Shop, Victoria Street, London, S.W.1 used to stock an American measuring cup and set of measuring spoons, all in aluminium, but I was lucky enough many years ago to have mine sent me as a present straight from the United States.

A cup of flour and other bulky food does not, of course, weigh the same as a cup of liquid, and I think it best to give here the table of measures printed in Mrs. Kander's Settlement Cook-Book, *The Way to a Man's Heart*, published in Milwaukee, Wisconsin, as this is not so far from South Michigan:

2 cups	1 pint
2 pints	1 quart
4 quarts	1 gallon
8 quarts	1 peck
4 pecks	1 bushel
1 peck potatoes	15 pounds
4 cups flour	1 pound
3 cups corn meal	1 pound
2 cups granulated sugar	1 pound
$2\frac{2}{3}$ cups powdered sugar	1 pound
$2\frac{2}{3}$ cups brown sugar	1 pound
2 cups solid butter	1 pound
2 cups solid meat	1 pound
9 medium sized eggs	1 pound
16 ounces	1 pound
2 tablespoons butter, sugar, salt	1 ounce
4 tablespoons flour	1 ounce

16 tablespoons	1 cup
60 drops	1 teaspoon
3 teaspoons	1 tablespoon
4 tablespoons	½ cup
1 cup shelled almonds	¼ pound
1 cup raisins	6 ounces

Anyone, therefore, using the following recipe in *The Country Kitchen*, 'Miz' Taylor's Cup Cakes' on p. 51, can be sure of accuracy if she uses this table of weights and measures:

'One cup of sugar, two eggs, one-fourth cup of butter, one-half cup of milk, a cup and a half of flour, 2 teaspoons of baking powder, a pinch of salt, and a teaspoon of vanilla. The butter and sugar were creamed, the eggs (beaten separately) added, yolks first and whites at the last. Milk and flour (into which baking powder had been sifted) were added alternately, and vanilla last. This was then poured into well-buttered muffin tins (floured) and baked about half an hour in the brown-paper oven, or, according to modern standards, 375 degrees.

'When these had been cooled, a round was cut off from the top, a cavity made and filled with lemon or orange custard; then the top was replaced and covered with a stiff icing. Over this icing – if you want your cakes to look as ours did – sprinkle some pink sugar.'

There are all sorts of little snags or pitfalls for English readers in the expressions used in *The Country Kitchen*, particularly when almost the same words, but meaning something rather different, are used. For example, muffins in U.S.A. are not the same as in England. I often get correspondents living in Canada and the United States asking me for recipes giving directions for English muffins, which they tell me are very different from the cakes called 'muffins' in America. Here our old friend Artemus Ward comes in useful again. Turning to the word 'Muffin,' in his *Encyclopedia of Food*, we find the following:

'In this country generally a small thick round, unsweetened "cake" or "biscuit" as "egg muffin," "corn muffin" and "bran muffin". The muffin most famous in literature is that of England, also round but larger and flattened, generally bakery made, of flour, milk, eggs, etc. Very light and spongy, eaten toasted and buttered as breakfast or tea. For toasting, the muffin is first slit around the edges and inwards, but not to the centre. After toasting it is pulled apart for buttering.'

15

Hickory nuts resemble walnuts. There are many varieties, of which the pecan is best known in this country, where it is now pretty generally sold. Where hickory nuts are mentioned in *The Country Kitchen*, the English housewife should substitute pecans.

Johnnycake, which is mentioned frequently in this book, is simply a popular name given in this district to corn bread (made with maize or Indian corn meal), eaten hot, split and buttered, made in shallow tins. When made in smaller tins, they are called 'corn muffins.'

A lady who spent her childhood in America says: 'Johnnycake was the common name for an excellent bread baked in shallow tins. We had a song for exercise, which I remember standing in the nursery and singing as we jumped in time, placing our hands simultaneously one before us and one behind our backs. The song was:

'Give me some Johnnycake, thick, thick, thick;
And a piece of butter, quick, quick quick.
Peter stands at the gate
With his knife and his plate
Waiting for butter to put on his Johnnycake
Come, Butter, come,
Come, Butter, come.'

Some people say this is an old churning song.

The American use of 'kettle' as the name of a big pan to use over the fire is interesting as a probable survival of the name of an old English utensil which is still in use, the fish-kettle. We also have an expression, 'Here's a pretty kettle of fish.'

Spider, which is represented in England by the modern term 'frying-pan,' is one that has a long handle. It acquired its name because originally it had four long legs, so that it could be stood over the embers of a fire made on the earth. It looked like a spider, and our forebears were exceedingly clever in giving articles of daily use picturesque names.

Soapstone is 'soft stone used in fireless cookers because it retains the heat, and the food in the pan above it goes on cooking for a long time, as distinguished from the hay-box cooker and food thermos, which are not cookers, but merely insulated articles for keeping food hot.'

Doughnuts are, of course, fried cakes, but there are others made and cooked in this manner in England. Both doughnuts and English fried cakes are examples of comparative cookery which in itself is an interesting study that has not yet been exploited, probably because, to get anything like satisfactory results, financial or otherwise, would entail too much work and expense.

Corned beef, mentioned in the recipe for a boiled dinner on p. 38, is salted beef. The word 'corned' originally signified meat preserved by dry salting – by being sprinkled with or imbedded in 'corns of salt' (i.e. coarse salt) instead of being preserved by brining – the Old English word 'corn' being largely synonymous with the 'grain' of Old French derivation – one spoke of a 'corn' of sugar or sand etc., as today one still says a 'grain' of sugar or sand.

The shank bone used in the preparation of the monumental vegetable soup is known here as the shin bone.

Cornstarch, see pp. 68 and 82, is what we know as cornflour.

'Pan-boiling' simply means cooking meat or fish in an iron frying-pan with little or no fat; 'broiling' is an old English word for which we have substituted grilling. A similar process which still exists in English country or camp kitchens is pot-roasting. This also, like the spider, is a survival from the days of the open fire on the hearth, and here with these old kitchen utensils we touch another line of research or study that might well interest the modern housewife, and that is the part that the improvement or adjustment of primitive kitchen appliances have played in the invention of modern labour-saving gadgets. The only question is whether in lessening work by mechanical means we have lost some of the picturesqueness of life. 'If the salt has lost its savour, wherewithal shall it be salted'! After all, half the spice of life lies in the struggle to overcome difficulties and to make the best of a bad job. Achievement may be more dull than the fight that has reached its end.

Anyhow, *The Country Kitchen* is full of gaiety and laughter, and I am sure no one can fail to enjoy it.

I

The New Year

Southern Michigan was largely settled by York State folks, and it would seem, a considerable extent by various branches of the Thompson family, judging by the number of relatives, near and distant, who sooner or later turned up at our humble farm home to claim kinship. Mostly they were cousins, nephews and nieces of my father, although two sisters, a little younger than he, lent a matriarchal air to the tribe. My mother's relatives, way off East, near Detroit, were at too great a distance for frequent visiting.

These two sisters, Aunt Sophrony and Aunt Hanner, widowed, lived together in the village of Millbrook some twelve miles from us. Aunt Sophrony was in no way beholden to Aunt Hanner (she'd have you know), for money invested in mortgages kept her well provided for, but it was Aunt Hanner's house, left her, tradition whispered, by a somewhat questionable husband whose name had long, long ago been linked with Louisiana lotteries. However came their means, here lived the two staid, plump, capable sisters who bowed only before the superior, masculine qualities of their brother 'Lijer. He was my father.

They were well along in years at the time of my earliest recollection, but both hale and full of vigour, which seemed characteristic of the Thompson breed. In fact, at the time of the particular incident I am going to relate, my father was celebrating his sixty-sixth birthday. I was then six years old, and while the events and occurrences here chronicled are clearly engraved upon my memory, the fact that I was an only child (the belated product of his marriage to my mother late in life) and that my elders conversed with me as an equal, and before me as if I were a stone wall, probably had much to do with my ability to recall scenes and conversations as I might not otherwise have done.

My father has been born on the first day of the year, a circumstance which accustomed our family to celebrate his birthday with such pomp and preparation as our simply country life offered.

'You'd have thought,' my mother commented somewhat testily, 'that nobody else was ever born on New Year's Day – way they act.'

Not all the relatives could forgather with us on this happy occasion, for they were scattered over the southern counties, and roads on the first of January were none too passable, but they were of a clannish nature and welcomed any opportunity for 'visiting.' And since visiting always included a feast of food as well as a flow of talk, consequent elaborate preparations had to be made. Sometimes my mother rebelled.

'Reg'lar gypsies,' she said, tartly. 'Always on the road.' Nevertheless she got on well with 'his folks,' and was indeed very fond of some of them. 'Lije's birthday, however, did sometimes rile her usually even disposition, since all the fuss and feathers so set him up in his own esteem that, as my mother said, he wasn't fit to live with for a week afterward. For not only did the relations, such as were within driving distance, rally to the celebration, but they never came empty-handed. They brought bags of apples, jugs or kegs or cider, spare ribs, squash, popcorn, mincemeat, preserves, socks (Aunt Sophrony always brought six pairs of socks she had knitted herself, a long, colourful scarf, mittens, and wristlets), and whatever other tributes and largess were part of their store. Aunt Hanner always gave him money. And for days thereafter he would gloat over these gifts and brag about what *his* folks thought of him. My mother's folks, although they boasted blood and heritage, did not give frequent evidence of their regard. Once in several years my grandmother or one of my mother's sisters would come for a visit and always brought substantial gifts of clothing and money, or some treasure from her household store, but these visits were far apart. Seventy-five miles by railroad was, in that day, no frivolous jaunt to be lightly taken.

Occasionally, after one of my mother's relatives had been staying with us (and especially if it was my Grandmother Bogardus, who was inordinately proud of mingled Huguenot and Anneke-Jans blood, and had been tactless enough to refer to such lineage), my father would suddenly go British and bring out documentary proof.

In a little worn leather wallet he carried a sheet of yellowed and badly creased paper which, in a fine goosequill hand, bore witness to the not unusual fact that Three Brothers Came from England, and settled – here, and here, and here. Few things gave my father greater pleasure than to bring out this old, worn evidence of honourable birth, and to discuss with Aunt Hanner and Aunt

Sophrony the antecedent marriages, births, and deaths, and the final pioneer move to Michigan.

You saw him sitting there in the front room of our small, unpretentious farmhouse, in a stout armchair of hickory, but the impression that remains is of his being enthroned on a sort of dais, his bald head shining from a recent scrub, his high white shirt collar overshadowed by the fringe of whiter hair. His feet were encased in cloth-top boots of fine leather and he wore a black alpaca coat. In his long-fingered, artisan's hands – never the hands of a farmer – he clasped a gnarled stick that he used as a cane – not that he needed a cane, but for the companionship.

You saw the gathered clan: men with rusty-black best coats and cowhide boots; women in dresses of cashmere, alpaca, or, in the case of Aunt Hanner, a black grosgrain with a lace fichu folded across her matronly breast and fastened with a huge cameo pin. Aunt Sophrony did not boast so fine a dress, but she had a dark green bombazine with many buttons in which we thought she looked exceedingly elegant. The younger women wore gayer gowns; a certain Amabel, I remember, on this particular occasion, wore a bright red merino trimmed in jet which was severely criticised by her elders as being far too gaudy for a married woman. All the skirts were full and long (it was after the day of hoops), and the basques and waists were bright with buttons and brooches.

Clustered about my father, they were, old and young, listening with respectful attention while he discoursed, after the manner of prophet and seer, of weather, crops, and family affairs. *His* family.

My mother did not keep a hired girl as did most of the women on big farms and with large families, but had in a neighbour woman to help at such times as this. Miz' Lury Lane was a youngish woman whose husband had been killed by lightning (his boots ripped right off his feet!), a woman amply formed, fond of food – and able to cook it – with a gossipy tongue and roving eye irritating to my Puritanical mother, but with a muscle well adapted to the subjugation of a kettle of potatoes. She had jet-black hair and eyes, she loved company – the more the better – and rejoiced in such affairs as called for a hand lavish with butter and cream.

Times when my father felt especially English there would be roast beef for his birthday dinner. This was not very often, owing, probably, to the fact that beef was not easy to obtain on the first of January. On one particular occasion, however, a neighbour's yearling heifer had broken her leg and had to be shot. My father bought a quarter of the beef, and on his birthday a huge roast, nicely ripened by hanging a couple of weeks or so in the woodshed, sizzled and hissed in the oven.

Much of the dinner, of course, had been prepared the day before. A great pan of beans was baked, nice, white, Michigan (or New York State) beans, soaked overnight, parboiled in the early morning with a pinch of soda, then washed in cold water and boiled again with a slab of salt pork and an onion, until the outer skin burst. They were then drained and seasoned with pepper, mustard, a little vinegar and brown sugar, turned into a heavy tin pan, with the pork, slashed across the rind into small squares, adorning the centre, and baked until the beans were brought to a mealy consistency suitable for slicing when cold. The water in which they had been boiled served as nourishing soup for that day's noon meal.

Pies, except mince, had to be made early on the morning of the day on which they were to be served, since my mother could not abide a soaked crust or a stale pie. Pumpkin pies were most in evidence, since this was my father's favourite – pumpkin custard with thin, golden-brown tegument over the top like cellophane covering for a pixie's bed.

Aunt Hanner told how when 'Lije was a very small boy he had set up a howl at the table because there was no more 'punkin pie,' whereupon Sister Sophrony had vehemently exclaimed, 'I wish't 'Lije had a punkin pie big's this table and he's right in the middle of 't.'

Miz' Lury Lane, who was somewhat acquainted with my father's prefer-
ences, having assisted at similar affairs, held something of the same opinion.
'The' ain't no use,' she advised my mother, mixing beaten egg, creamy milk,
and the freshly stewed pumpkin together, inspiriting them with a teaspoonful
of ginger and adding a dash of allspice and cinnamon, the whole consigned to a
waiting crust, 'in makin' any other kind o' pie's I can see. Give him his fill of
these and you won't need no others.'

'Well,' observed my mother with that dry tolerance in which she held many
of my father's whims, 'after all, there's goin' to be a few other folks here besides
him.'

Miz' Lury Lane stared at her in shocked surprise, for she, like most as the
women in his family, regarded my father's prejudices as inviolable. Nevertheless, mince pies were brought out of frozen storage for heating, and apple pie
added for those who preferred them.

The breads were given a fair start the previous evening and then baked on the
morning before the arrival of the guests. Yeast bread, 'salt-risin' bread,' and
'riz' biscuits,' filling the large, sunny old kitchen with a warm crusty fragrance
which, mingled with that of roasting meat and spices released from fruity jars,
teased the appetite almost beyond endurance. And into the kettles, timed to the
hour of need, went the potatoes, the onions for creaming, and the Hubbard
squash for steaming.

On special occasions when the parlour was opened and warmed for company to
sit in, we ate in the 'settin' room.' That is where the table was laid on this day.
And now came out the best cloth, a heavy linen woven by Aunt Sophrony in her
own young housekeeping days and which she had given to my father on a
previous birthday. The gold-banded china which Grandmother Bogardus had
brought my mother on her last visit, the best knives and forks (three-tined and
of steel) with ivory handles, and the goblets with the bell-flower pattern bought
exclamations of praise from Miz' Lury Lane.

'My!' she cried, holding a goblet up to the light. 'You cert'ny got nice things,
Miz' Thompson. I never see nicer dishes.'

The silver caster with its five bottles of etched glass (vinegar, mustard,
pepper, pepper sauce, and ketchup) had been shone to gleaming splendour and
occupied the centre of the table. Small cellars of heavy glass were at each place
for salt.

Flanking the caster and adorning the table here and there were dishes of
brandied peaches, apple jelly, grape jelly, dill pickles, mixed mustard pickles
and piccalilli, all in fancy dishes of glass or majolica. Mounds of bread and

rounded pats of butter lent substance to what might be called a preview of the meal to come.

My father wanted his potatoes (and it took a lot of them for such a cause) roasted in the pan with the meat, and on this particular birthday which I so vividly remember, he had, apparently feeling especially English, asked for Yorkshire pudding – and that it be also baked in the roaster. He had heard, he said (the inference being that such rumour had reached him through foreign – if not royal – kin), that if the pudding was put in the pan twenty minutes or so before the roast was done, it would be more richly flavoured than if baked separately.

'What you *really* ought to do,' he had informed my mother gratuitously, and with a slight pompousness of manner as of acknowledged vantage in such matters, 'is to cook the roast on a – grille or something, so the juice will drop down on to the pudding. Seems as if you could put it right on that rack in there – *ouch*! Dod-*blast* the thing!' Opening the oven door to demonstrate his theory, he had burned his fingers, and, alternately, blowing upon and wetting the afflicted members with his tongue, he glared about him in a rage of physical and spiritual hurt.

'Why,' he demanded, irately injured, 'couldn't you have *told* me the danged thing was hot?'

'Most folks'd *know* an oven door'd be hot when you're goin' to use it,' my mother told him mildly. 'And I can't try no such schemes as roasting the beef on a rack because the juice'd spatter all over the oven and smell to heaven. Go and put some yellow soap on that burn. It'll take the heat out.'

She did, however, accede to his request that the pudding be baked in with the roast.

When finally the dinner was an accomplished fact and all had been served, he enquired where the gravy was. He was particularly fond of roast-beef gravy. Upon learning that there was none, he sat, carving knife and fork erect in either hand, and stared at my mother in shocked amaze and rising choler.

'You can't have potatoes – *that* many potatoes – and a Yorkshire pudding big as a house,' my mother said with some impatience, 'all baked with the roast, and gravy too. They take up all the juice.'

'Well, why in tunket didn't you *tell* me so?' he demanded. 'What *are* you going to eat on the potatoes?'

'I didn't think you'd want anything on them,' she replied patiently, 'when they're baked right in the juice. But if you do, the's plenty of butter.'

My father snorted, but lowered his implements and bent to his dinner.

Finally, warmed and mellowed by a full pouch, they drew away from the table and disposed themselves as best they could to the comfort of their stomachs. My mother and Miz' Lury Lane withdrew to the duties of the kitchen, where, I once heard my mother say, she would rather be, after all, than have to sit around and listen to all the gabble about what a great man 'Lijer was.

Rendered charitable and generous by adulation, gifts, and much good food, my father grew expansive and longed to make suitable returns for all this hospitable observance of his birthday. To one he would give a two-quart jar of sauerkraut of his own making; to another a bag of hickory nuts or butternuts, a few ears of popcorn; and he had been known to take a can of berries off the cellar shelf, picked by my mother in the broiling sun and preserved over an equally broiling fire, and give them with gracious affability to some one of his favoured nieces who probably had twice the number of our own store.

Once in particular he overdid the approbational act and so incensed my mother that she threatened never again to officiate as cook and dishwasher while he sat in state and received the plaudits of an admiring audience.

My mother had a pet rocking-chair that she had brought with her to the late marriage with my father. It was a comfortable rocker, high-backed, cane-seated with gold stencils and nicely quilted cushions. It stood in a sunny window of the kitchen where my mother often rested or sewed.

One of the several nieces, and one whom my mother favoured least of all –

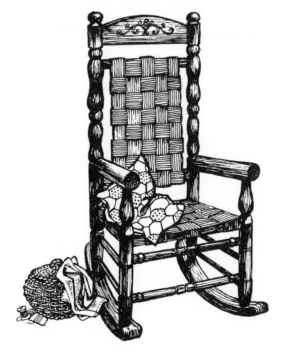

that Amabel of the red merino dress and greedy eye – expressed great admiration for this chair. She brought it into the sitting-room, sat in it, praised its comfort, its beauty, and wished she had one like it, but supposed she never would. She also patted my father's arm, leaned against him, bedazzled 'Uncle 'Lijer' with praise and flattery, until my mother said afterward she would have liked to put her outdoors.

When the clan was ready to depart, be-hooded, be-scarved, be-mittened, and be-damned – so far as my mother was concerned – what did my incomprehensible father do but come out of the house, bareheaded and smilingly wreathed in his own benevolence, carrying my mother's chair! To her shocked and angered astonishment he lifted it into the sleigh and said to Niece Amabel: 'There, Amy! There's your chair! You said you didn't s'pose you'd ever have one – but you've got it. Now set down in it and enjoy yourself.'

With a shower of hugs, kisses, and exclamations, Niece Amabel accepted her gift. To my mother she said, brazenly, 'I'm afraid you'll miss it, 'Miry, but' (quickly) 'if Uncle 'Lijer wants me to have it –' and off she went, sitting cosily in my mother's rocking-chair, sleigh runners squeaking, horses prancing, whips waving, mittened hands throwing woolly kisses to the patriarch standing with bare bald head in the winter twilight, while my mother flung her apron over her head and rushed into the house to give vent to her rage. I do not think she ever quite forgave him, even when a few days later he brought her another chair which he claimed was larger, stronger, and handsomer, for which he had swapped a barrel of cider and a shoulder of pork.

Later he had the grace – and the effrontery – to carry the new chair to Amabel and, with her will or without it, effect a change and restore my mother's rocker to her. But I do not remember that Amabel was ever again invited to our house.

My father's birthday ushered in the new year with such a crescendo of excitement as it would have been difficult to equal in succeeding events, especially in a community where homes were more or less isolated. Nevertheless, following hard upon the heels of this jovial occasion was another annual occurrence to which the whole family looked forward in eager anticipation. This was the arrival of the new almanac.

Every home of any consequence whatever boasted two books of a certainty. Some doubtless had more – few had less. These were the Almanac and the Family Bible, their relative importance in the order named. For while the latter, it seems safe to state, was perused with a vastly higher percentage of generality and zeal than is the case today, the former was *conned*.

For the almanac in the days of my childhood was a most important piece of literature. In fact, it was the most important, the most highly regarded piece of literature that came into our house. And it was free – ours for the asking. All you had to do was to go into the drug store and ask for it. And not just one almanac could you have, but two or more, depending upon the number of drug stores in your town, or the variety of remedies sponsoring these compendiums of information carried in any one store.

You never asked for two almanacs of a kind – at least you didn't if you belonged to my father, who witheringly denounced such greediness. This especially riled him when for any reason he had not been able to make his own application soon enough, and the entire supply of one of his favourite kinds would be gone.

'Hogs!' Succinctly he designated one family that flaunted in his indignant face *three* copies of the same book – so the children could have some to play with! When *he* had not been able to get one. 'But,' he added grimly, 'I'll get one of 'em yet!' And he did.

Covell was this family's name, and they were distinguished in the neighbour-hood for general shiftlessness and a pernicious habit of borrowing, accompa-nied by a coveniently lax memory in returning.

My father formulated his plan, but volunteered no information except to request that the first time any of the Covells came borrowing they were to be accommodated if possible.

Such demands were usually within the simple means of my mother's stores, but there had been occasions when their wants amounted to what in our family were counted as luxuries, as, for instance, chocolate, vanilla beans, or a little pink sugar for the frosting of a cake. In general, however, their needs were such as even a reluctant neighbour could hardly refuse – saleratus, cream of tartar, 'an 'east cake.' Or Mr. Covell had sudden use for a tool which he knew my father to possess. At any rate the Covells were certain to come borrowing, and my father's chief concern now was lest the Covell children should destroy or debase the coveted books before he could carry out his plan. But luck – or justice – was with him. Within a day or two after the vaunted possession had been proclaimed, a Covell youngster came to the door, tin pail in hand.

'Ma-says-can-you-lend-her-a-cup-o-m'lasses-she-wants-t'make-m'lasses-cookies.'

Since this was the third cup of 'm'lasses' the Covells had 'borrowed' within the month to make 'm'lasses' cookies, and none returned – nor ever would be – my mother met the demand without alacrity. My father's requests, however, were few, with reason generally behind them, and wisdom lay in compliance, so the cupful was liberally, if grudgingly, poured into the pail.

My father made no comment, nor did he yet give any intimation of his purpose. But that evening, after the corn was shelled for the morning feeding of the fowls, the apples brought up for later consumption, and the kindlings placed ready for the early fire, he put on his shabby overcoat, pulled a disreputable old fur cap down over his ears, wound a knitted scarf about his neck, drew woollen mittens on his hands, lighted a lantern, and offered the terse information that he was 'going over to Covell's.'

The distance between our house and Covell's dilapidated farm was probably about a quarter of a mile, and the roads were drifted full of snow, but in an incredibly short time my father returned, a smug grin on his face, a crafty gleam in his shrewd eyes, and the coveted almanac in his capacious pocket. This in an illy concealed triumphant manner he slapped down upon the table, then removed his cap, scarf, coat, and mittens. He pulled off his felt boots and shoved his feet into his old carpet slippers, thrust a stick of wood into the stove, drew his armchair comfortably up to the table where we ate our three daily meals, and on which in the evening stood the reading lamp and where sat my mother with her sewing.

Years of experience had taught her that confidences were best gained through silent, if watchful, waiting. And so, beyond a 'Bad walking?' on her part, and a comprehensive 'Unghrrh!' on his, no amenities were exchanged until his spectacles had been properly adjusted, the lamp pulled a half inch or so nearer, and the almanac ostentatiously opened. Then, shifting contentedly in his chair, his countenance still moulded into the cat-and-canary expression, he remarked affably:

'Well, I got it!'

'So I see,' my mother agreed dryly. 'How'd you do it?'

'Borrowed it,' he replied smartly, and with obvious satisfaction in his achievement, 'off'n Covell!'

'*Borrowed* it!' echoed my mother in surprise, for one of my father's most vigorous detestations was the borrower. 'Then you'll have to return it!' Disappointment clouded her voice, for if my father should feel that his honour as a borrower must be vindicated by an immediate return of the book, he was quite capable of packing off with it before its contents could be assimilated by the remainder of the family.

'Return it?' My father lifted shaggy and exaggeratedly astonished eyebrows. 'Of course I'll return it – when he's returned all the molasses and sugar and eggs and everything else they've borrowed in the last year – the ole shitepoke!'

And so, satisfied with the manner of justice to be meted out to the offending Covells, he settled himself a shade more comfortably in his chair, took an apple from the dish, bit into it with relish, and turned to his book with the air of a man deserving of rest and quietude.

The almanac was to us a compendium of information and entertainment. In it was humour – jokes that are today revived from some old crumbling file to provoke laughter for radio audiences and column addicts; pictures no less entertaining to us than are the Gluyas Williamses of the present strip. In one of these a very rotund gentleman stood in the centre of a tailor's shop coatless and vestless, but with trousers bulging fore and aft and a collarless shirt, being measured for a suit of clothes. The agile tailor was depicted as holding one end of the tape measure in his own hand and offering the other end to his patron, an anxious and troubled look upon his face. The caption read: 'Will you please hold this, sir, while I go 'round?'

There was humour for you! Not too subtle, not too plain. We understood it. We gloated over it. We studied it, speculated on it, repeated it time and again.

In it were also historical data. 'Benedict Arnold, born January 14th, 1741.'

'Who was Benedict Arnold, Pa?'

'He was a traitor to his country.'

'What's a traitor, Pa?'

'A traitor's a thunderin', dod-gasted, stinkin' rascal – *oughta* been shot! Don't ask any more questions.'

There was astronomical, phrenological, and physiological information in its pages. A disembowelled gentleman with attractive and stalwart legs straddled the first page, seemingly nowise disturbed by his apparently critical condition. That he was surrounded by creatures of a presumably savage nature, and crustaceans of questionable value, as well as being in imminent danger of death by archery, gave him neither apprehension nor alarm. Speculation on this one page alone afforded hours of concentrated application. With the ram, the goat, and the bull, we had first-hand acquaintance. The fish, too, were amongst our familiars, although we knew them by the homelier titles of bullhead, bass, and perch rather than *pisces*. As for the other objects illustrated, 'cancer' was a word with which we were somewhat familiar, since some of our more conservative neighbours would not touch tomatoes on account of how Ob Hutchens, who ate them, had developed this dread disease.

'Gemini' bore close resemblance to a term often used by my father in moments of stress, but one would hardly have expected to come upon it in a book of such cultural quality as the almanac was supposed to be.

There were also prescriptions, remedies, antidotes, most of them relating to that particular nostrum which, as we now say, 'sponsored' the book. There were recipes, household hints, even poems. But most especially were there forecasts of the weather, admonitions relating to planting, harvesting, even to social engagements.

When the annual Church Supper was under consideration, for instance, the almanac was consulted before the date was set. 'Better wait till after the tenth o' January – says "storm over the Middle West." When's the January thaw? Le's see – 'leventh to fourteenth. The roads is always cut up then.'

'Here – look. From the twenty-first to twenty-fifth – "clear and cold." Why ain't that a good time?'

'Wa-al, if 't ain't *too* cold.'

Our house did not boast a dining-room. Usually we ate at one end of the large kitchen – the end where two windows let in a stream of sunlight. The kitchen was a large, exceedingly pleasant room. The floor was bare except for braided rugs before stove and work table, with another at the sunniest window where stood my mother's rocking-chair and sewing basket. I do not remember much about the walls except for the huge map of the world hanging behind the table where we usually ate, and across from where I sat. A map on which I learned my letters and across whose green waters and pastel lands I journeyed countless miles in silent dreams.

On another wall was the shelf upon which stood an eight-day steeple clock which my father religiously wound each Sunday morning before breakfast. On a nail underneath hung the almanacs, Ayres' and Hostetter's, by which weather was foretold, seeds sown, crops reaped, and on the margin of whose leaves vital statistics were often recorded.

Our cooking was done on an 'Elevated Oven,' so called, I suppose, because the oven was above the stove surface as in most oil and some gas ranges of today. But since the stove itself was lifted high from the floor on long curved legs somewhat resembling the 'Queen Anne' of later furniture, the name was well taken. I do not know the principle on which that elevated oven was heated, since wood was our only fuel, but I can certify to the quality of the cooking, for the very walls of the kitchen were permeated with odours of roast meat, salt-rising bread, spice cake, gingerbread – a whole roster of fragrant memories, tantalising to the nose and stimulating to the palate. The elevated oven gave way in a few years to the newer-fashioned kind of stove, which, as I remember seeing my mother bend above it (being a tall woman), must have been, like almost all kitchen equipment of that and a considerable later time, too low for comfort or convenience. The elevated oven had at least the virtue of possessing height.

Cupboards held dishes and cooking utensils and a generous-sized 'butt'ry' contained ingredients for cooking, dry groceries, and the best dishes.

In such a room as this, inconvenient, poorly equipped for the work to be done in it, arranged with absolutely no thought to saving steps or labour, freezing cold in winter until the morning fire was lighted, hot in summer until the stove was allowed to cool off in late afternoon, but homely in comfort, with cheerful,

29

even charming atmosphere – here was cooked the food which, as I think about it, still makes my mouth water.

With the year well begun in renewal of family ties and family affection, and with the future reasonably well in hand through the prophetic pages of the almanac, we were established for the remainder of the winter. With a big cookstove in the kitchen, however, warming both that room and a bedroom opening off it, a chunk stove in each of the other rooms and plenty of fuel in the woodshed; with woollen, fleece-lined, and knitted garments for both under and outer wearing; and with cellar, root pit, and 'butt'ry' stocked against the inroads of lusty, wind-whipped, drift-whetted appetite, we faced the blustering days to come without dismay.

II

Winter Wears On

'As the days begin to lengthen, then the cold begins to strengthen.' That was in the almanac. We stay closely housed. There is little to be done outside except chores. Cows are milked, horses bedded and fed, all animals kept warm and comfortable. The barn smells agreeably of hay and grain and of animal flesh. The sound of munching hay and moving feet is pleasant and reassuring. The fowls venture but seldom outside their coop. Warmed water, warm meal mash with a little red pepper in it, and shelled corn are given them night and morning. The water in their drinking pans freezes in between.

The woodboxes are kept filled. Snow is melted on the stove for washing, and the clothes freeze into rigid effigies the moment they are hung out. My mother wrings her chilled fingers and sits for a moment to warm her feet and knees at the open oven door before going out again. Sometimes, hooded and mittened, I go with her to bring in the clothes, and we laugh at my father's stiff-legged, straddling underdrawers. We pile them on the table, and, as they meet the warmth, the air of the kitchen is permeated with the purest fragrance in the world – the odour of absolute cleanliness.

It is too cold for a little girl to go to school over drifted roads so I stay happily at home and play house in a corner of the warm kitchen with corncobs, broken dishes, and a docile cat. I do not care much for the china doll with the chilly chignoned head that Aunt Hanner once brought me.

Evenings, my father makes things out of wood, hickory wood that he has been seasoning through the year – axe helves, hoe handles, and such. He makes shavings on the kitchen floor too, thin little yellow curls from his plane, tiny chips from his drawknife, and dusty scrapings from the pieces of glass with which he smoothes the wood. Sometimes my mother complains about the dirt.

'Well,' argues my father defensively, 'it's clean dirt. If you never have anything worse'n *that* to bother you, you'll be lucky.'

My mother contends: 'I don't see why you can't clean it up yourself. It's your dirt, if it *is* clean.'

'Cleaning up,' states my father positively, 'is a woman's job. I don't ask you to meddle with *my* work, and I won't meddle with yours.' An argument that seems sufficiently reasonable – or sufficiently arbitrary – to close the matter.

These are the days, too, on which we have good, sustaining food. One of my father's favourite dishes is soup. Now, 'soup,' as it was understood in my family, was not a liquid whose only purpose is to prepare the stomach of the meal to follow. Soup *was* the meal.

This was true of bean soup, potato soup, or pea soup, but it was particularly true of vegetable soup. To this day I do, and as long as I am able to handle pot and pan I shall continue to, make a vegetable soup as nearly like that my mother made as one hand can cut and contrive like another. Twice at least during the coldest months of the year I make it, and my mother made it even oftener – as often, in fact, as she could get a shank bone.

For, say what you like, the ideal vegetable soup must be made with a shank bone – the shank of a beef critter. For a shank bone is the only bone of any consequence that has marrow in it, and it is the marrow that gives that peculiar richness, body, and flavour which a true vegetable soup should have.

The bone must be cracked in order to get the value of the marrow. So, in case you should be inspired to try your hand at making a good, stout, sustaining soup for a winter's day, the kind that will warm you to the core and stick to your ribs until time for the next meal, go and buy a shank bone of a size according to your family, and ask the butcher to crack it.

Wash and dry the bone and put it in a good-sized kettle of cold water. Enough water to cover the bone completely and some to spare.

Set it where it will cook slowly. Of course if you had a good old-fashioned wood stove you would put the soup kettle on the back griddle to simmer, but if you must struggle along with a gas or electric range and other folderols of an effete generation, turn the heat low and let it slowly cook.

Now, prepare your vegetables, and believe me this is going to be a *vegetable* soup. Again you will proportion your vegetables to the size of your family, but this is what I do: I use a six-quart kettle and cover the bone with about four quarts of water. (It is a good-sized bone.) As this boils away I add *hot* water to keep the amount of stock about the same.

Then I take onions, potatoes, carrots, celery, in reasonable proportions, but not stinting on the onions, and *one* parsnip; peel, wash, and chop them together to make about a quart of the mixture. I add about a cupful of shredded cabbage, and around an hour and a half before dinner time I put these all into the kettle together with a cup of washed barley. Then I add a sprig of parsley if I have it, and season it with salt and pepper to taste.

Continue to boil slowly until the vegetables are done and the meat falls from the bone, adding water as necessary.

I read the other day in some of the numerous admonitory columns regarding polite usages that a soup in which either meat or vegetables were left at serving was in bad taste and poor manners. It said you have to *eat* such a soup.

Well, you do. You eat it with a spoon and you taste it, going down. You even have to chew it a little. First, a cautious experiment of the tongue, exploring temperature and taste: hot, smooth, unctuous, with the rich flavour of marrow and the age-old wisdom of salt, it meets approval and is commended to all the outlying areas of sapidity and relish, and to that arbiter of savoury sense, the palate.

Then, our gustatory soul satisfied with tentative essay, we meet substance – just enough resistance to halt the course of action and give the ravished senses time to speculate on varied savour. We meet:

Potato: bland, amiable, and homely; an honest vegetable, giving honour where honour is due – in an honest soup. *Cabbage*: so revered by the Egyptians for its stimulating qualities as to warrant a temple built in its honour. *Parsnip*: the faint, sweet, fragrant flavour of which lends romance to the dish. *Onion*: humble kindred of the lily clan, rooted from oblivion by Alexander the Great and bestrewn by him, along with learning, to the civilised world, thus lending a touch of wisdom and sophistication to the whole. And *barley*. Barley lends a slight viscidity to the broth, a holding property superior to rice, and a rich quality to the dish, completing and fulfilling its nutritive mission to mankind. The carrot is an innovation of later date. In the culinary prime of my mother's day, carrots went, if anywhere, to the cattle – a gain to the latter, but a loss to us.

This, then, was the soup that once warmed the hearts of a homely farmer and his humble family in Southern Michigan. And this is the soup that I still set before a more modern but none the less appreciative family who can – if they wish – listen to the Philharmonic concert as they eat. This, I think, was the soup of which the Mock Turtle sang:

> 'Soo-oop of the e-e-evening,
> Beautiful, beautiful Soup!'

And this, doubtless, is the soup for which the historic narrator stole, from the marauding Welshman, a marrowbone. And although my father was an honest man, if filching from a Welshman was the only way in which he could have got a marrowbone, I should not have liked to be responsible for his probity.

And I leave it to you to judge whether a three- or four-course dinner following upon the heels of *this* soup would have been required, appreciated, or even eaten.

This soup *was* the dinner. No Melba toast accompanied it, nor any croûtons, crackers, or other supplementary starches. The starch was in the soup.

It was served in a huge china tureen and ladled into soup plates of generous size. It was 'eaten' with a spoon, but whether from the side, tip, or whole spoon I do not remember. I only remember that it was – and is – *licking good*!

An amusing incident relating to this particular brand of soup, as well as to my father's disciplinary disposition, comes to mind.

Whatever mail we had – and it was exceedingly limited in quantity – came through the Jackson Post Office. Any neighbour going to town gathered up all the mail belonging to those along his homeward route and distributed it upon his return. The onus was not great.

Our next-door neighbour, Si Covell, one day late in February brough a letter from Aunt Hanner, saying that she would like to dispose of her Jersey cow, that she and 'Phrony had decided they were too old to bother with milking, and if my father wanted the cow he could have her for fifteen dollars, but she wanted to get rid of it at once.

Now fifteen dollars, although certainly a modest price for a Jersey cow ('She's prob'ly going' dry,' commented my mother shrewdly, 'and she don't say anything about her age'), is not plucked from even the prosperous farmer's purse at the end of winter without due consideration. And my father simply didn't have it. As for asking Aunt Hanner to trust him, this was utterly out of the question.

'If you can't pay for a thing, don't buy it,' was my father's tenet, a principle in which he was staunchly supported by my mother. 'It ain't goin' to be any easier when it's half wore out or dead.' And asking favours of a relative was doubly obnoxious. No, if he could not figure out some way of paying for the cow, they would not take her. So for a whole day the matter was under consideration. There was hay to sell, but the price was low and no immediate buyer at hand. A couple of hogs might be spared, but what would Aunt Hanner want of hogs?

'I'll tell you,' exclaimed my mother with sudden inspiration. 'I've got something Hanner wants, and it's worth fifteen dollars if it's worth a cent.'

My father's eyes followed her briskly retreating form with doubtful interest. What could *she* have that was worth fifteen dollars – to anybody?

In a short time she returned bearing a huge folded bundle, which when spread out showed a beautiful hand-woven coverlet of blue and white with deep fringe. Into the border was woven a date, 1796, and the name of the weaver, my great-great-grandmother. It was a masterpiece of skill, and would be worth, at the present time, several hundreds of dollars. In thinking of it now I could consign that cow to my father's blasphemous 'tunket' with relish and gusto.

'I showed this to Hanner once,' said my mother, 'and she was green with envy. She said she'd give anything in the world for one like it – but there *ain't* another like it, and never will be.'

Enthusiasm for the cause, deflated by contemplation of matchless beauty and workmanship, ended in falling tones, flat, and final.

'But –' My father, fingering the fringe reverently, hesitated. 'You don't want to let that go. You – you *had* that –'

'We need the cow, don't we?' My mother briskly dismissed sentiment with countered need. 'If she's a good cow the butter'll help – and we got the hay. We'll look her over before we swap.'

So the matter was settled, and the very next day, unheralded, we set off in the pung – the sleighing still being good – for Aunt Hanner's.

After due examination of the creature under discussion – which proved to be young, full milched, and in good condition – the coverlet was brought forth, unwrapped, and spread before the popping, covetous eyes of the aunts.

Being something of a connoisseur in old furnishings (the day of 'antiques' had not arrived), it is safe to say that Aunt Hanner knew the value of the coverlet. At any rate she was not long in giving gracious consent to the bargain, and lugged her precious new possession off to try it out on the spare bed.

Of course we stayed to dinner. In fact they were about to set dinner on the table when we arrived. It was merely returned to the stove to await consummation of commerce.

When, finally, we were summoned, there were, at each place, large plates of soup with the huge white china tureen before Aunt Hanner.

'If we'd known you was coming,' apologised our hostess, 'we'd of had something else. Still, I know you like soup, 'Lijer.'

My father, prospecting with fastidious spoon, did not reply. Nor did he eat.

The soup – a thin and flavourless liquid floating an occasional segment of onion, revealing in its depths a too generous amount of sliced potato, and claiming its origin by massed hunks of so-called 'soup-meat' – was not up to his standard of soups.

My mother, sensing cumulative resentment at such defamation of one of his favourite dishes, kept up an almost hysterical flow of trifling talk, but not sufficient to stem entirely the impending clash.

'Well, 'Lijer,' observed Aunt Hanner, a trifle warmly, 'I thought you liked soup.'

35

'So I do. So I do,' admitted my father, eyeing the dish before him with bleak disfavour. 'Guess folks don't raise any barley around here, do they?' The enquiry was put amicably enough, but the inference was clear.

'If you mean why didn't I put any in the soup,' replied Aunt Hanner with asperity, 'it's because I happened to be out. I thought I had some rice, but last minute I found I didn't, and 'Phrony and I both had colds –'

' 'Twouldn't have saved it,' my father told her with brotherly frankness. '*Nothing* could have saved it – the way it was begun. What else you got?'

Sniffing, but with apparent tolerance for the older brother's sovereign position, Aunt Hanner removed the plates and brought in an Apple Dowdy, on which, with plenty of cream flavoured with nutmeg and sugar, my father was able to subsist until he could get home.

'You acted awful about that soup,' my mother told him, on the way. 'You could have eaten a little of it – 'twouldn't have killed you, and you prob'ly hurt Hanner's feelings.'

'Any woman,' replied my father sententiously, ' 's lived as long as Hanner Bates has and can't make a veg'table soup better'n that ought to have her feelin's hurt. But,' he added, with that air of the determined disciplinarian at which my mother's heart always sank, 'I'm going to learn that woman how to make vegetable soup if it's the last thing I do.'

My mother evinced no great curiosity. What he would do, he would do. They were *his* folks – let him do what he pleased. And, as she watched the gentle yellow cow being led to her new quarters, there was a certain thin set to her lips, and a far, nostalgic look in her eyes that even a small child, with a prophetic love for the old and beautiful, recognised as tribute to the loved and lost treasure.

In about two weeks my father came home from one of his infrequent visits to town with a can of oysters and a shank bone of beef.

'The oysters is for us,' he said, 'tonight. The shank we're goin' to take to Hanner.' My mother looked her surprise.

'Tomorrow. We're goin' to stay all night, and on Sunday you're goin' to show Hanner how to make a veg'table soup. She can't learn no younger, and I'd hate her to die thinkin' swill like that was *soup*.'

It is hardly necessary to add that Aunt Hanner, irascible and touchy as she often was, accepted her favourite brother's missionary intent and my mother's embarrassed apologies in the best of grace – gave unstinted praise to the result, and presented my mother with a five-dollar gold piece. 'I'm so tickled with my coverlet,' she said warmly, 'I couldn't rest without you havin' a little more for it.'

Stricture of tears prevented my mother's speaking, but whether because of

the unexpected kindness, or for a passing vision of her loved counterpane, I do not know.

My father, warmed by the bestowal of favour, and completely satisfied with a dish of what he considered his own concoction, rose from the table and announced that he'd go and hitch up the horses so we would get home before dark. His womenfolks, accustomed through long experience, did not try to dissuade him. He brought the sleigh to the door and we were duly packed in with old comfortables and buffalo robes.

'You got your pay *that* time, all right, Hanner,' he called gaily to the women standing in the doorway. 'I wouldn't trade that soup for your danged old cow at *any* price.'

Perhaps, in passing, a word is due to the Apple Dowdy which Aunt Hanner had served, since its appearance drove the blackest clouds from my father's face and in some degree compensated for the fiasco in soup. Aunt Hanner may have been just an average hand at soup, but she was a master at Apple Dowdy.

Apple Dowdy is not a dumpling, a pudding, or a pie – deep-dish or otherwise. It is just a dowdy – sort of common, homely, gingham-like, but it has character.

To make it you peel and quarter firm tart apples, and you lay them in a deep earthen pudding dish. (The dowdy would probably reconcile itself to a glass baking dish if it had to.)

You fill the dish with apple, and over this sprinkle light brown sugar, the amount depending upon the tartness of the apples and the size of your dish. Add a slight scattering of nutmeg, a little less of cinnamon, a dash of salt.

Now, with generous judgement, cut some slivers of butter over the whole, say about a teaspoonful to each serving. Then add half a cup of warm, not hot, water.

Make a rich baking-powder crust. (One cupful of flour, two teaspoonfuls of baking powder, two tablespoonfuls of butter, one-fourth teaspoonful of salt, and half a cup of milk.) Roll this out to three-fourths of an inch in thickness, cut a dido in the centre – you know, a big S with eyelet holes slashed alongside – and lay the crust over the apples, pinching it to the edge.

So far, so good, but the proof of the dowdy is in the baking. It must be baked in a *slow* oven (300–350 degrees) at least three hours. When done it will be delicately brown on top, a rich fruity red on the inside, and delicious withal.

Serve it as Aunt Hanner did, with thick cream slightly sweetened and flavoured with nutmeg.

The boiled dinner was another stand-by of our winters, and one, to my mind, still to be recommended even in these days when temperature-controlled furnaces and air-conditioned houses so temper the wind to the lamb whose shearing goes to pay for it that such heartening food is less essential.

As the vegetable soup calls for a shank bone, so the boiled dinner demands a piece of lean, firm corned beef and a lesser chunk of salt pork. The combined flavour of these two meats lends to the vegetables marinating in their juices a succulence that I have found in no other. The end of a smoked ham bone offers a fairly satisfactory variety in my own family, but in my father's home a boiled dinner meant corned beef and cabbage, with the salt pork for flavour, and potato and turnip for body.

A boiled dinner in Southern Michigan differed from its counterpart in New England by the absence of beets. To have added this vegetable to the dinner would have been to affront the eye with a discolouring tint, and to offend the taste with a foreign flavour. Even as an accompaniment we did not consider this vegetable necessary. Beets were all right in their way, especially young and tender beets from the garden in their season, but they did not belong to our kind of boiled dinner.

To get the full flavour of your meats, the corned beef should be put in cold water and set on the back of the stove (or, if again hampered by modern devices, over the lowest possible heat) to simmer. It should never be brought to a high rolling boil.

A three-and-a-half to four-pound piece of beef should be allowed to cook slowly for three hours; the pork, of which one pound will be plenty, for half that time. Excess fat or scum should be skimmed off as it rises.

Now the manner in which my mother cooked her cabbage was apparently all wrong, according to present nutritive standards, although there is something, perhaps, to be said for the cabbage. It is now possible to get new cabbage before the old has felt its age. But when we made a boiled dinner in February or March – or any other time as long as the cabbage lasted – we had to use the *old* cabbage, cabbage that was buried out in the root pit. Maybe it needed to be cooked longer than the younger, but at any rate it was cut into quarters and simmered along with the meats for an hour or more. And I should like to make an interpolation right here to the effect that that cabbage taken out of the root pit had a flavour to it that no new, or other, cabbage fresh from its stalk ever had. And this is no illusory sentiment, or memory complex either, as I am sure anyone will testify who has poked the snow and straw away from a pit to haul forth the cold, hard, firm, and earth-flavoured potatoes, turnips, celery, cabbage, or carrots so preserved. There is a nutty flavour to them, a sort of aged-in-the-earth flavour that freshly picked vegetables do not have. Even the stalk, that hard, white, solid centre to which the leaves are attached, when dipped in salt and gnawed – raw – had a fine, homely tang remembered with pleasure.

The turnip – or 'beggie,' a yellow and more delicately flavoured member of the turnip family which we preferred, and properly known as rutabaga – was sliced to the thickness of about one-half inch or less, and put in with the cabbage. Yellow turnips are a little slower to cook than white. Poatoes were put in last.

Onions my mother considered superfluous to a boiled dinner, and so do I. They lose their own individuality in the lustihood of other and more legitimate ingredients, and contribute nothing of value to the plate. Personally, I like to add a couple of parsnips, but this must be a matter of individual inclination, for both odour and taste of this vegetable are offensive to some. To me it adds a slight sweetness and special flavour which are pleasing.

In serving, the boiled dinner was placed all together on a huge platter, cabbage in the middle garlanded by the other vegetables, the whole garnished by thin slices of beef and pork alternating.

With this dinner was served a dish of mixed mustard pickles or horse-radish. Bread and butter, of course, ubiquitous, omnipresent, supported the vegetable content, and a light dessert followed – an apple dumpling, perhaps, Brown Betty, or a custard.

Corned-beef hash was a natural sequence to the boiled dinner. Now corned-beef hash, rightly made, is a dish fit for kings, but it needs a craftsman's hand to preserve it from the ranks of the trite – or worse.

The first mistake made by many is to overproportion the potatoes, thinking to economise by sacrificing quality to quantity. There should be an equal amount of chopped meat (previously freed of fat, skin, and gristle) and chopped potato.

A second mistake is to chop meat and potatoes together. To do this is to create a gaumy mess uninviting and unappetising. And both meat and potato should be chopped fine – but not mashed or pulverised. On the other hand, chunks of either are repulsive. It remains, therefore, to determine exactly the right degree of fineness for both and then to mix them together with a wide fork. Now moisten the whole with just enough top milk or cream to hold the ingredients together, but never enough to make a sloppy conglomeration. Season with salt and pepper, and place in a heavy aluminium or steel (or iron spider if you can get it) frying pan in which a generous amount of butter has been brought to smoking heat (but not browned). Stir it with a wide fork until well blended, then spread it over the bottom of the pan and let it cook slowly. Do not put it over a hot flame to scorch before being cooked through. It should brown slowly, taking anywhere from half to three quarters of an hour, depending on the amount.

When it is browned on the bottom and slightly crisped, fold it over and lift to a platter. Poached eggs may be placed around it, making a heavier meal, and the whole garnished with a green – cress, parsley, or strips of pepper.

The next event of importance to our opening year was the arrival of the seed catalogues. Even lacking the extravagant colour content of similar books of today, these, as they were stripped of wrappers, offered exciting adventure into the land of promise.

For days – and evenings as well – my father pored over these catalogues. It was his custom to make out, first, a list of everything he would *like* to get, which included pretty much everything in the book. Then, appalled by the sum total of such extravagance, he would, with regret, cut out all the extras, the new, untried, interesting things, and content himself with familiars, adding just a *few* of the improvements on old friends. This list he and my mother would discuss at length.

'Better put a few more onion sets'n we did last year, hadn't we, 'Miry? They didn't seem to carry over, way they ought to.'

'If you set out a million they wouldn't carry over. I wish't you'd put in an extra row of beets, though, for greens.'

'I'm goin' to put in some of these new early peas. I'd like to have some a *lee-tle* before the Fourth, if I could.'

'What you want is to be sure to get some before anybody else, that's all.'

'I always have. But the preacher had some almost early as I did last year, dang him.'

'Maybe they grow quicker if they're sprinkled with prayer.'

'Maybe. But I'll take my chances on an earlier kind and some good manure.'

And so on until, hewed and whittled down to meet the limited budget, the list was finally made out in my father's fine flourishing hand, the money order bought, and the letter sent.

Then came the suspense of waiting. Two weeks – three weeks – and finally, late in February, it would arrive, that eagerly awaited package pregnant with flavour, colour, taste, odour, nutriment, in little bags and envelopes, labelled with names lovely to the ear.

My father kept his seed packets in the wide deep upper drawer of an old cherry bureau that stood in the sitting-room, along with fish-hooks and lines, husking pins, bits of leather, straps, buckles, padlocks, and heaven knows what. It was a fascinating drawer to peek into, but a source of irritation to my mother. Once in a great while, and always in his absence, she would clean it out – gather up stray seeds and organise the heterogeneous mess into some kind of order, only to stir up a hullabaloo infinitely worse to bear with than the drawer itself.

'How in *tunket*,' my father would storm, 'do you suppose a man's going to *find* anything when you go and litter it all up? I don't poke around in *your* bureau drawers, do I? Now, let's understand *this*: you leave my things alone and I'll leave yours. *I* have to know how to find things once in a while if you don't!'

III
'For All Good Things'

In the days of which I write, we were all more or less poor together, compared, that is, to the luxury in which many people of today live, and still proclaim their poverty. But nobody, so far as I can recall, ever starved or froze or even felt the pinch of dire necessity. We were cold, we ate a lot of cabbage, potatoes, salt pork and beans, but we didn't *know* we were so badly off. We saw no life of luxury or ease by which to contrast our situation. And so we went along under the delusion that we were often having a good time. We knew nothing of Higher Education, Woman Suffrage, Communism, or Realism, although most of the time we were pretty well on a level with the last. But we believed in God, and some of us believed in the devil. We sang 'Rock of Ages' for other reasons than the harmony. And we sort of looked after each other. If a neighbour got sick, other neighbours went in and took care of him. If he died, his friends and relations washed and dressed him in his best and carried him to his last resting place. Sometimes they even looked in on him afterward and read his epitaph. They didn't begrudge the time or effort. When one amongst us had hard luck, like losing a cow or horse, or even a farm, the neighbours got together and made up a little purse, or even shared their own small homes. We didn't talk or think much about being our brother's keeper, but in a way we seemed to think we were.

The minister, however, was one for whom everybody had to have a little thought. His salary was generally around three to five hundred dollars a year. Eight hundred was a *big* salary, and when he got that much he could jolly well look out for himself. But the man that tried to live and bring up a family on three hundred (and house) deserved sympathy – and got it. He got more.

42

Once a year, and perhaps in some communities twice, the minister's family was given a donation party. As I remember it, this was sponsored by the Ladies' Aid and usually occurred sometime in March, when what stores he had were pretty depleted and it would still be some time before he could realise anything on the garden that went with his house.

Now, a donation party was not by any means an organised affair. Nobody found out what the minister's family needed because what they might need nobody else could give. So the date was set, word sent around by children, hired men, or the dressmaker, and announced at Meetin'. The party took place after supper so the guests would in no way diminish the store.

Each one took what he or she happened to have most of and could best spare. One farmer might take a bag of potatoes. Two, or even three, might be of the same mind. A peck of beans would furnish substantial meals well into the summer. Beans are wholesome, filling, and cheap. If an army can march on beans, why not the hosts of the Lord? And a good solid slab of salt pork, brine-encrusted, stacked up against the beans, was suggestive of considerable sustenance. A bushel of 'beggies' was all that another might have to offer. In March, cabbage was no longer plentiful and onions were sprouting. The green shoots, cut off well into the solid part, and chopped up with vinegar, pepper, and salt, made a not-half-bad relish, but they were pretty well past the cooking stage. The minister's family would have to do without.

Sauerkraut, however, was plentiful and ripe. A covered tin pail, nosily inspected by some curious guest, exhaled an odour that caused exclamations in varying degree of shock. An odour quickly suppressed. It had no place amongst the more polite occupants of the table where it sat: a pan of raised biscuits, loaves of bread, a crock of butter and another of lard, jars of canned fruit, glasses of jelly, pickles.

Sometimes a farmer would take a few bags of grain to mill, and share part of the resulting grist with the minister – wheat flour (not too 'refined'), buckwheat flour, or corn meal.

Occasionally the contributor would go to town and buy a few pounds of sugar or groceries to 'donate.' Why this generous spirit could not as well have dropped a silver dollar (which made a nice ringing sound against other coins) into the contribution box on Sunday and let the minister buy his own groceries is one of those mysteries of the charitably inclined mind into which one probes with futility.

In certain instances of which I know, the minister stealthily loaded up the boot of his old top buggy with surplus provender, took it to the next town, and swapped it for something more urgently needed.

It was a custom also for the minister and the treasurer to appraise the value of

the donations and credit the amount to the Ladies' Aid. And there *have* been instances where it was credited against his meagre salary!

The donation party was often a bitter pill for the minister to swallow. He would like to have thought of himself as a professional man earning his keep, however small, and being paid like any other labourer. The donation party put him in the class of the present-day welfare dependent, but there was nothing he could do – or say – about it, and doubtless the members of his flock never even dreamed that their generosity left a little mark of hurt pride.

Occasionally some understanding mother smuggled in a bundle of clothing outgrown by her own children, but this must be handled with utmost tact.

'You won't be offended, Miz' Wheaton, now, will you? These are just a few things Willie and Eva've outgrown an' seein' they're just a year or so older'n yours – I hope you *won't* take offence.'

Miz' Wheaton assures her she will not, but an astute eye catches a little tightening of the lips, a slight chill in the averted eye. Food – yes. The donation of food is an accepted custom amongst the indigent profession. But *clothes*, other people's left-over hand-me-downs – this is another matter. To accept from the largess of a man's parishioners, a proportion, as it were, of their wealth, is one

44

thing – a sort of tithe. But to be given something for which his family has no longer any use, something worn and discarded, *old clothes* – that is another. Even a minister's wife has her pride. The children are shabby – no doubt. Bodies must be warmed as well as fed, but there is a price. Fortunately for us of today whose needs are often no less than were those of yesterday, we have learned, through suffering, that there is such a thing as sharing without endangering self-respect.

The minister's children stand anxiously near, their eyes popping, their nostrils dilating, their mouths watering. How long, oh, how *long* before the 'comp'ny'll go' and they can have a bite!

The neighbours visit; the men, congregated restlessly near the door, talk of the weather. Sun's getting pretty high now – thaws some every day. Eaves drip – icicles fall. Well, it won't be long now. Ain't been a hard winter – saw a woodchuck yest'day. Crows cawin'.

The women, centred about the minister's wife, talk of spring sewing – Miz' Lou Esty, the seamstress who goes from house to house, is here, and gives account of her itinerary for February and March. She also deals with the absorbing subject of sleeves – basques, dolmans, width of skirts, gores and gussets. Mrs. Wheaton shows them the rag carpet she is making for the parsonage. Offers of rags follow and are accepted with gratitude and pleasure. It makes a difference whether old clothes are given to put on your back or on your floor.

Finally, the restive males begin to look significantly at their womenfolks and hitch their chairs uncomfortably. The minister takes a hint.

'Friends,' he says in his deep and properly ministerial voice, as he rises, 'I want to tell you how much we appreciate this evidence of your great kindness. Shall we kneel down and extend our thanks for the spirit of brotherly love that prompted these generous gifts?'

'Huh!' says my father tartly as he tucks the buffalo robe around my mother's knees and his own, with me huddled snugly between. 'I bet he'd rather a *cussed* a little. *I* would – folks come polin' out a little grub and standin' around grinnin' as if they'd laid an egg.'

The church supper was another means designed to help meet the startlingly small salary of the minister, who usually held Sunday morning services in the church at the nearest community centre, and then, to earn a few dollars more, travelled to outlying communities where a meeting was held in the afternoon, in a church if there was one, otherwise in the schoolhouse. The supper was given in each of these neighbourhoods, price probably twenty-five cents, the food having been contributed. It was one of the chief social functions of the year.

Occasionally this supper took the form of a box social. Each woman or girl packed a box with suitable food for two people. Wrapped in white tissue and tied with ribbon, they gave promise, and when piled together on the table offered a pleasing lottery to the men whose duty – and, in most cases, pleasure – it was to buy them unsight, unseen.

Sometimes, this took the form of an auction when, if the best cooks could be spotted, certain boxes brought in a most satisfactory return. The older boys often took a girl, the engagement made, perhaps, weeks beforehand, at Meetin', Spellin' school, or a neighbourhood dance. Sometimes they tried to get their girl to describe her box, but this was not considered fair play and only such as were desperately in love succumbed.

Men, too, would often try to identify their own wives' cookery, being sure then of something good, for, while most of that community were excellent cooks, there were some whose contributions were not sought.

Gallantry played its part. 'Well, if I can't get hold of my own woman's cookin', I'd be tickled to death to get yours, Miz' Bouldry. That fig cream cake you make is enough to make a man drool just to think of it.'

The Covells – that irresponsible family distinguished for general shiftlessness, but with several pairs of eyes ever alert for the beneficences of a kindly Providence – always attended church suppers *en masse*. Mr. Covell, of course, had to buy a box, but it was the custom to provide a generous supply of free food for the children, so the Covells went forth fortified by a lean stomach and a fat appetite.

'I fed 'em light on purpose,' Mrs. Covell would say blithely, marshalling her brood towards the table prepared for the children. 'Now girls' – the Covell children were all girls – 'you set to and eat your fill. It's free, you know, so make the most of it.'

It was Mrs. Covell's duty, also, to provide a box, and since this was likely to be an unwrapped shoebox of worn and battered appearance, tied with a string, the men were reasonably aware of its parentage – and consequently skilful at evasion. For Mrs. Covell was known as a 'greasy cook,' and no one ever partook of her meals a second time if he could help it.

The trouble in evading Mrs. Covell's contribution was that Mr. Covell also knew his wife's handiwork and took this welcome opportunity to accomplish a change in nutriment by arriving early and grabbing off, the moment the boxes were put up, *any* box but his wife's. Therefore, by the simple process of elimination, Mrs. Covell's box was always left, and, as in the game of Marching through Jerusalem, the one left out had to take it.

And this might not have been so bad – there was food in the pantry and the men were not stupid – but the rules of this particular form of entertainment provided that the purchaser of a box must share it with the woman who prepared it.

My father, after one sharp and bitter experience, utterly refused ever to attend another box social. He was not particularly socially-minded anyway, except with his own clan, and hated what he called 'cutting up.' He was reserved, given to silence, and shy. He did not like mixing in crowds and always got back in a corner, acting, my mother said, 'like a clam with its mouth shut.'

On this one particular occasion, having followed his usual conservative custom, he found himself with Mrs. Covell's box, and Mrs. Covell herself, on his hands. He cast an appealing eye at my mother – in telling of it later she said he 'looked like a calf that knew it was going to have its throat cut.' But she told it with an air of gusto and a wicked light in her eye that hinted of appreciation unworthy of the theme.

'She led him off in a corner,' my mother related with relish, 'like leading a bull into a boxcar. He balked every step of the way – but he went. He said afterwards that when she lifted up the box cover (*he* wouldn't) and he took one look at what's inside, his stomach turned right square over. Two greasy pieces of cold sausage, coated with lard, two slabs of grey, sour-looking bread, two pickles, two friedcakes. The smell, he said, when the box was opened – sausage, pickles, and friedcakes that had been cooped up together since the middle of the afternoon – was enough to knock you down.'

At the moment, however, my mother was eating her supper across the room with the minister, when she saw my father jump up as if he had been stung and come barging across the room straight to her. And before he got halfway there he began to boom, ' 'Miry – for gosh sakes, 'Miry, get up! We've got to go home!'

My mother rose in alarm and so did the minister. 'What's the *matter?*' she asked him, but he had her by the arm and was marching her out, looking neither to left nor to right, making neither excuse nor explanation except to say, loud enough for everyone to hear, 'I plum forgot to milk – I was that anxious to get to the social.'

My mother, to whose skirt I was by that time clinging, stopped dead in her tracks and looked at him in dumb amazement. He was not a man for practical joking and he did not look ill. And he had *hated* coming to the social.

'Come along,' he scolded. 'Get your things on and *come*. I got to go home and milk.'

My mother knew he had milked. She had taken care of the milk herself. And my father did not lie. Still – *he had lied*. And now he added another lie.

'I've got a fresh cow and I got to go home and milk her.'

Nothing would do but we must go home. My father had the horse and sleigh

47

at the door by the time my mother and I had our wraps on. My mother was ready to die of shame and she was so mad she shook.

' 'Lije Thompson,' she said when we were under way, *'you're a liar!'*

'Yes,' said my father truculently, 'and what if I be? I'd ruther tell a *dozen* lies than eat that stuff.'

'Well,' said my mother angrily, 'if you're going to lie, you might at least tell something folks'd believe.'

'No,' declared my father stonily, 'I don't tell that kind o' lies.'

The men, Mother said afterward, couldn't get over laughing about it. They admired his courage. The women didn't blame him either. They thought he was smart. They all knew cows didn't freshen in February. But Mother said she was so ashamed of him it made her sick. She said he could have stood it once. Father said maybe he could – if he'd had to. But he didn't have to. And he never went to another box social.

In general, however, the women took great pains with their boxes. There was excitement in the thought of a chance partner. The girls didn't like it so well because they wanted to choose whom they'd eat with. But with the older women almost anyone would be – well, different.

Cold chicken was one of the most popular of box contents. Not pressed chicken, or chicken salad – women didn't mess up their chicken in ways like that. It was good enough just plain cold. You disjointed and cooked the chicken (a last-spring *chicken*) slowly in a small amount of water, with an onion and a bay leaf and salt and pepper at the last, until it was done. Then you took it out, let it cool, and fried it in butter until slightly brown – just enough butter so it wouldn't stick.

Only the white meat and drumsticks were put in the box. The dark meat – upper thigh, neck, back, and liver – was used for the children. Nice, thin slices of bread and butter (yeast bread – my mother said salt-rising bread wouldn't stand being shut up) and either sweet cucumber or watermelon-rind pickles in a little jar went into my mother's box. And cake. Most always everyone put in two kinds of cake. For one my mother made a marble cake – a cake you almost never see nowadays, probably because it's a little trouble to make.

For this a rich white cake batter was mixed; three-fourths of a cup of butter, two cups of sugar, four eggs, one cup of milk, three cups of flour, four teaspoonfuls of baking powder. When this mixture was beaten to the right consistency (eggs added one at a time to creamed butter and sugar), one-third was taken out and to it was added one-fourth of a pound of grated bitter chocolate, one teaspoonful of cinnamon, and one-fourth teaspoonful of cloves.

Then, into a deep buttered cake tin a layer of the white batter was poured, then a layer of dark, alternating until all the batter was used, leaving white on

48

top. This required baking forty-five minutes in an oven that would just turn a piece of white writing paper to a nice delicate brown. That was the way we tested the oven.

The fig layer cake for which Miz' Bouldry was famous deserved its popularity. A white batter, doubtless similar to that used for the marble cake, was baked in layers, but it was the filling that gave it distinction. One-fourth pound of figs, one-fourth pound of seedless raisins (chopped), one-half cup of water, and one-third cup of sugar were cooked together to a rich syrup. A heavy frosting was made by beating the whites of four eggs to a stiff froth. To half of this the figs and raisins and the small amount of syrup were added, and this was placed between the layers. The remainder of the egg whites, flavoured with vanilla and sweetened, covered the cake.

Then there was jelly cake – a sponge cake baked in a thin sheet, spread with currant jelly, rolled, and dusted with powdered sugar.

Many of the recipes used by the farm women of that time would appal the average housewife of today whether of country or town, in the lavish use of eggs, butter, and cream. Every farmer raised all the fowls his own family could consume and some to spare. The market, however, was limited and prices low. Butter and eggs were exchanged for groceries, but ten cents a dozen was a fair price for eggs, and I have seen butter sold for twelve cents a pound.

There was a certain 'cream cake' of which my father was very fond, and which my mother often made for supper when company was coming. This called for four eggs (beaten separately), one cup of sugar, one cup of flour, one-fourth cup of butter (creamed with the sugar), one-third of a cup of milk, three teaspoonfuls of baking powder, and one teaspoonful of lemon juice. This was baked in layer tins and put together with a cream made of one cup of thick sour cream, one cup of sugar, one-half cup of hickory-nuts meats rolled fine. This was mixed, boiled, and spread between layers. The cake was then frosted with white of eggs and sugar.

Of course every storeroom or attic had its supply of nuts. We should as soon have thought of buying apples as nut meats. 'Going nutting' was one of the seasonal ceremonies, as distinctive and certain as gathering greens in the spring. My father, mother, and I, followed, preceded, and circumambulated by the dog, Shep, devoted several Sundays to this delightful ceremony throughout October, after the first heavy frost.

On our own place were several hickory-trees – shagbarks. (And, although I have lived in New York State a number of years, and am devoted to it – flora, fauna, scenery, and people – I have never been able to overcome a feeling of irritation at hearing upstaters speak of hickory nuts as 'walnuts.' As if a hickory

nut could grow on a walnut-tree! They simply refuse to recognise the hickory-tree, and what their forebears made ox yokes, axe helves, and flails of, I cannot think. Certainly not 'walnut!')

There were both walnut (and I *mean* walnut) and butternut-trees along the roadside, and hazel brush grew everywhere. The shucks from the shagbarks dropped off in neat brown sections, but both walnuts and butternuts had to be shucked when first gathered. If the shucks dried on, it was impossible to remove them, and the nuts were harder to crack. Removing the shucks from the nuts, however, was no easy task, and hands and clothing were likely to be stained with an almost indelible brown. In fact, housewives used these husks, or the green nut itself, as well as the leaves, to dye carpet rags.

Hazelnuts, growing in clusters, were easier to shuck. When all were done there was a rich store of all four kinds either hung in bags from the rafters of the attic so mice, rats, and squirrels could not get at them, or hidden in large wooden sugar buckets. The tin can had not yet invaded our homes to any great extent.

There, however, was the required ingredient for our hickory-nut cake, walnut cake, and for butternut candy; also for many a winter night's or Sunday afternoon's entertainment. The sound of a hammer clopping against the upturned edge of a flat-iron was as familiar to our ears during the winter season as the chonking of apples.

The box social was still popular when, ten years later (for I must have been about six at the time my father put a quietus upon our attendance at this particular social function), I began teaching country schools. And what limited memory I have of the earlier affairs is, perhaps, mingled with and coloured by those of a later period. And since we 'have our hand in,' as the excellent cooks of that day used to say, in the matter of cakes, I should like to recall one more recipe, and one that I can recommend if you should suddenly decide that a box social might be 'something new' by way of entertaining friends bored by the modern cocktail party.

These were quite simply called 'Miz' Taylor's cup cakes,' but if pigs is always pigs, it by no means follows that cup cakes are always cup cakes.

Miz' Taylor's recipe called for one cup of sugar, two eggs, one-fourth cup of butter, one-half cup of milk, a cup and a half of flour, two teaspoonfuls of baking powder, a pinch of salt, and a teaspoonful of vanilla. The butter and sugar were creamed, the eggs (beaten separately) added, yolks first, and whites at the last. Milk and flour (into which baking powder had been sifted) were added alternately, and vanilla last. This was then poured into well-buttered muffin tins (floured) and baked about half an hour in the brown-paper oven, or, according to modern standards, 375 degrees.

When these had been cooled, a round was cut off from the top, a cavity made and filled with a lemon or orange custard; then the top was replaced, and covered with a stiff icing. Over this icing – if you want your cakes to look as ours did – sprinkle some pink sugar – if you can find it!

Beguiled by the memory of those cakes which were star features of the box socials, we have for the moment lost sight of the church supper and its twofold object: a focus for community sociability and a means of replenishing the pastor's slender purse.

Such efforts were by no means confined to the box social, which was but one variant of the occasion. Sometimes, but not frequently, it took the form of an oyster supper, but because oysters had to be paid for, cash money, and the usual viands were contributed, the difference in profit rendered the former less popular.

Few if any of the country or small-town churches were equipped with means for serving a supper, or even boasted any room in which such an affair could be held. The supper, therefore, was given in whatever public building might be available, at the home of the pastor (he thereby benefiting by any surplus quantity of food) or at some private home accommodated to the purpose. After the supper was eaten games were played – Whirl the Platter; Spat 'em In, Spat 'em Out; Marching through Jerusalem – the minister looking benignly on from the seat of honour, flanked by deacons, trustees, Sunday School teachers, and other persons of importance.

As the time for parting drew near, the acknowledged singers of the neighbourhood gathered about the organ and led the soaring melody of such appropriate airs as 'Shall We Gather at the River,' 'Sweet Hour of Prayer,' and finally the Doxology, in which due recognition of present blessings was given.

My father did not much like church suppers, no matter what form they took. In fact, he was quite plainly and sometimes belligerently averse to going away from home at all, especially at meal time. He liked his own home food, his own chair, his feet under his own table. He enjoyed having his relatives come to visit him, and once in a while on Sunday he enjoyed visiting them, but he wanted to start early and he never wanted to stay long. The morning chores out of the way, his toilet made – consisting of a shave, his bald head scrubbed until it shone ruddily like a polished Baldwin apple, a clean shirt, black tie, best trousers, and cloth-topped boots – and his breakfast eaten, he was all set to go.

'How long 'fore you'll be ready?' he would demand of my mother as he rose from the table.

'Well, I've got the dishes to wash and get us ready,' Mother would answer, meaning herself and me. 'Take about an hour maybe.' She always gave him at least an extra thirty minutes more than she expected it to take, in order to avoid as much champing at the bit as possible.

'An hour! What 'n tunket you want to take an *hour* for to wash up a mess of dishes and change your dress? I could wash up them dishes, and more too, in fifteen minutes.'

'S'pose you take right hold of 'em then,' my mother countered amiably. 'You do the dishes and I'll go get ready.'

Since my father, to my almost certain knowledge, never washed a dish in his life, the challenge was unnoticed other than by a grunt of derision. What he would do would be to go to the barn, hitch the horse to the buggy or sleigh, drive up ostentatiously and noisily to the stepping block, and then call out, 'Hey, 'Miry! You 'most ready?'

As long as she could avoid it, Mother would pay no attention. If, within a few minutes, she did not appear at the door ready to go or to reassure him, he would get out, hitch the horse to the post, and, pushing his old felt hat (for he never seemed to have a new one, whatever the date of purchase) back on his head, come, stomping and fuming, inside.

52

'What in tarnation Tophet you *doin'?*' I can hear him cry. 'You been *two* hours now, and you ain't ready *yet!*'

'You look at the clock,' my mother would advise him. 'It's just exactly twenty minutes since we got up from the table, and if you'll go out and keep still I'll be out. I've got to feed the cat and –'

But what minutiæ of detail still remained to her list of duties were lost to his ears. He would take me by the hand, hustle my stumbling feet to keep stride with his own, and hoist me to the seat. Then he would put his hands behind him, bend his head forward as if searching the ground for reasons for such unconscionable delay, and pace back and forth from horse block to door, pausing an instant at the latter for sounds of approach.

When, finally, my mother did appear, a rather dusty black hat or bonnet on her head, coated and gloved, she, impatient at finding him rampant and chafing on the step, would exclaim:

'What you in such a hurry for anyway? We're just goin' visitin', ain't we?'

'I want to get started,' he would argue earnestly, 'so's we can get home. *I* got chores to do.'

Inasmuch as no powers of persuasion ever put forth during his lifetime, so long as I knew him, could induce him to remain more than an hour after dinner had been eaten, unless it was an all-night visit, there seemed no immediate likelihood of stock or fowl going too long unattended. The controversy, however, was a ritual, seldom varied, never missed.

I remember one particular instance where a church supper was to be held at the town hall some five miles away, when my father's stubborn disinclination to go from home very nearly redounded to his own grief. He had absolutely refused to go. It was along the first of March; the roads had thawed and fozen, then snow had fallen until neither wheels nor runners could make headway, and he declared that neither he nor his horses were going to be dragged out in such weather.

My mother, however, had been asked to contribute a pan of scalloped potatoes and a couple of pies, and nothing my father could say would deter her from responding to what she considered her duty.

'I'll send 'em a couple of dollars,' my father volunteered, 'and that's more than the stuff's worth. *Take* two dollars out of the ho'ses to go over there. Say nothing of *me.*'

'How'll you send it?' enquired my mother tersely.

'Some tarnation fool'll be goin' over,' returned my father sententiously. 'Bouldrys, likely.' (The Bouldrys lived half a mile beyond us on the east.) 'Can't keep some folks to home.'

'Then I'll go along with the Bouldrys,' replied my mother calmly, and proceeded with her baking.

Now a pan of scalloped potatoes, as it came from my mother's oven, was something that would have drawn a man of less epicurean tastes than my father from wherever he might be, so was his nose tickled by its aroma.

For such purpose as this she used a four-quart milk-pan. The potatoes were sliced almost precisely to an eighth of an inch in thickness, crisped in ice-cold water, and then drained on a clean thick cloth. Over a layer of these in the bottom of the pan, butter was thickly dotted, salt and pepper shaken, followed by a thin drift of flour. This was repeated until the pan was full. Then fully a quart of half milk, half cream was poured over the whole, and the pan set into the oven to cook slowly until the potatoes were done, and the top encrusted in golden brown and richer bronze.

This was one of my father's best-loved dishes, but to whet, tease, and harry the poor man's sweating palate even further, she had at the same time made two luscious mince pies, unusually large in size, and seeming to excel all others in steaming savouriness.

Close at hand stood my father, his eyes hankering with desire, his face long and doleful.

'Couldn't you've made an *extry* dish of potatoes,' he said wistfully, 'see's I wasn't goin'? Or anyway another pie?'

'I just didn't have time,' my mother sweetly regretted, as she swathed the dishes in towels to keep them hot. 'There's the cold beans left over from yesterday, and some eggs I hard-boiled. You can get the bread out of the crock, and the butter's in the cupboard. And there's some sauce –'

'Ain't you even goin' to *set the table*?' he demanded incredulously. For my mother to go and leave him alone at meal time under any circumstances was unbelievable enough, but to leave him to set his own table was simply unthinkable.

'I'll get myself and Delly ready,' my mother said, 'and if I have time before the Bouldrys come along I'll set it.'

'They may not go,' argued my father, casting a hopeful eye at the betowelled pans. 'Jim Bouldry ain't no fool about *his* ho'ses, either, if his womenfolks is.'

'They're going,' my mother assured him cheerfully. 'The hired man went over to town this afternoon – I forgot to tell you. He said they'd be along.'

My father took a few uncertain steps toward the door, hesitated, came back.

'What time *is* this tarnation-fool supper?' he wanted to know.

'Six o'clock,' said my mother, glancing at the clock. 'It's pretty near five now. They'll be along any minute.'

Another turn to the door and back – clump, clump!

'Well,' he stood over the table and glowered, 'seein's you seem to have time enough to get up something to eat for everybody else but *me*, I s'pose I'll *have* to go along, or starve.'

He went along.

The back of winter is now broken. And high time! The vegetable pit is pretty well depleted. What few cabbages are left must be used soon. The turnips are almost gone. Onions are on the verge of decay. Only potatoes, a few Hubbard squashes, and some apples are left in the pit.

But the sun swings high and to the north. The snow is going. Crows caw. Grass shows faintly green on the south side. And my father takes a basket and spade into the garden. Presently he returns with a mess of parnips and a few roots of horse-radish.

Parsnips were never, in those days, gathered in the fall as other root vegetables were. There was a superstition to the effect that they were not fit to eat, in fact were poisonous until after they had been frozen in the ground.

The fact is that they keep better frozen in than pulled. They are not a 'keeping' vegetable. They wilt and wither, and if pulled in the fall must be buried in earth to keep at all fresh.

Dug in early spring, however, after a long season monotonous in diet, they came to us with a sweet, earthy taste that was refreshing and good. We, you see, took the offerings of the seasons as they came. We were obliged to, and while I would not forego the present opportunity of adding a scallion to my supper in January, or a parsnip to my stew in December, I doubt if we get the same titillation of the senses – taste, sight, and smell – from an everyday acquaintance with all the fruits of the varied seasons that we did when we had to wait for them.

When parsnips were finally available, we ate them in a number of different ways. Buttered for one, which must have been a favourite way, or at least a familiar dish as long ago as when, sometime early in 1600, the phrase, 'Soft words butter no parsnips,' came into existence. They were peeled and throw into cold water to prevent discolouration, sliced once in two – if not too large – lengthwise, put into salted boiling water, and cooked until tender, then drained and put in a hot dish, sprinkled with pepper, dotted generously with butter, and set in the oven to melt the butter.

Fried: Boiled in the same manner and then drained and fried slowly, first on one side and then on the other in butter, to a golden brown. Not hurried.

Creamed: Cut in small chunks, steamed, and then dressed with a hot cream sauce, butter, salt and pepper.

But a parsnip *stew* was best of all. Judging, however, by the dearth of recipes

in all the modern cookbooks that I have at my command, I must assume that parsnip stew is none too highly regarded by present-day cooks. Why, I cannot understand, unless it be that parsnip stew is an old-fashioned dish and there is hardly room for such with all the appetisers, *hors d'œuvre*, *canapés*, and other fancy doodads that are supposed to whet a man's appetite, whether there is anything worth while to satisfy it afterward or not. In the day of which I speak, an appetite was whetted by work and weather, and all we asked was good, solid, tasty food to satisfy it.

And so I must rely on my memory and my own culinary ability to revive a dish that, to my way of thinking, is one of the tastiest of the early spring – parsnip stew.

First, a few small pieces of lean salt pork were put into an iron kettle with a covering of water and allowed to cook until partly done. Parsnips, to the desired quantity, were cleaned and cut in cubes, together with about half the quantity of potatoes. When the pork had cooked perhaps half or three-quarters of an hour, the parsnips and potatoes were put in, and no more water added than just barely to cover; a lid was fitted over the pot and the whole cooked slowly, hardly more than simmering, until nearly done. Then the lid was removed, the water allowed to evaporate, and meat and vegetables were stewed and frizzled together to a browned delectability.

With johnnycake, perhaps an omelette, or a dish of scrambled eggs now that the hens were being more prolific, some pickled peaches, pears, or water-melon rind, this provided a meal that savoured of spring and satisfied to some extent our natural craving for a change of food.

Horse-radish was another harbinger of spring, the first green thing to shove its rapier blades above the chilly earth. A few weeks later the lacquered emerald leaves would find their peppery way to the simple planning of our menus as 'greens,' mixed with the milder-flavoured narrow dock which, with other edible weeds grew outside the pale of their more civilised relations.

In the first pale days of early spring, however, its part was merely to lend zest as a relish to the diet. Washed, scraped, and grated – with salt, vinegar, and sugar added, and conserved in a glass jar – it was ready to be used on baked beans, salt pork, or corned beef.

When the snow is gone and the roads somewhat settled so one can ride seven or eight miles in a lumber wagon without being jolted out by the roadside, my father and I go to town. He has several bushels of potatoes more than he will require for seed and is taking them in to exchange for groceries and meat. There are also crocks of butter and lard, and a basket of fresh eggs which my mother wants traded for unbleached muslin, calico, thread, and other notions. The weather has been so severe and the roads so bad that trade (we didn't call it 'barter,' but that is what it amounted to) has been delayed and our stores are low.

It is still cold, although by the time we reach the town around eleven o'clock the sun is high, water is dripping from the eaves of houses as we pass, the horses steam, and my woollen dress, coat, and hood, together with the fleece-lined underwear, white ruffled drawers, knitted woollen stockings and petticoat, which are underneath, have become almost unbearable.

My father drives up in front of the store and hitches the horses to an iron railing before it. He lifts me down – and I could not have been more than six at my earliest remembrance of going to town with him – takes me by the mittened hand, and we go across the wooden sidewalk, up the steps, and inside.

Of course, memory of later visits to this same store may colour the earlier vision, but at least my earliest recollections very clearly picture the interior of that general emporium which catered to a variety of human needs. To me it seemed the epitome of plenty and luxury. The eye was thrilled and the nose teased by diversity of both the strange and the familiar. As we entered, there stood on one side of the door a large open barrel of chowchow, yellow with tumeric, pungent with mustard and spices. Across from it on the other side was a keg of sweet pickles, also open. In the first a long-handled spoon stood ready for use and in the second a fork, although this seemed a rather futile suggestion, since practically every customer dipped in a finger, even poking about to ensure the preferred morsel.

Beyond these a counter ran down one side of the room, and a glass showcase displayed more delicate goods on the other side, such, for instance, as jars of stick candy – cinnamon, peppermint, wintergreen, and horehound. Also Jackson balls and candy hearts. Behind this were shelves on which were stored overalls, wampuses, shoes, bolts of calico and muslin, and, a little farther down, dishes and glassware, most of which would today bring ten times what it did then. On the top shelf were wash bowls and pitchers, and chambers.

On the counter amongst other things – and best remembered by me – was a large round cheese box with a wire mesh cover, and inside, with the cheese, a long and very sharp knife. Just in front of it stood a barrel of crackers.

It was my father's custom (and that of other farmers as well), after greeting the storekeeper, to step to the cheese box, take the knife, and cut for himself a generous wedge of cheese with a smaller one for me. Then he would dip into the barrel for a handful of crackers and stride back to where some upturned boxes and a nail keg made seating accommodations beside the pot-bellied, rusty stove at the back of the store. There the storekeeper would join us and he and my father would discuss the price of groceries, potatoes, butter, eggs, and the terms of trade. From him, too, my father would glean news regarding the state of politics and national conditions generally.

Parching with thirst I have sat for an hour or more, itching and burning with the heat from the often red-hot stove, not daring to unbutton my coat or remove my woollen hood, munching dry crackers and strong cheese, forgotten by my father and unnoticed by anyone else.

My eyes, however, feasted happily upon unaccustomed sights. Huge slabs of salt cod hung from the ceiling, probably dusty and fly-specked and exuding a tang which contributed to the growing anguish of thirst. A barrel of molasses, one of vinegar, and another of kerosene made a sort of barricade at the back of the room, each bolstered up sufficiently high to allow the setting of a jug under the spigot. Their mingled odours were characteristic of the place.

Kegs of salt mackerel sat one upon the other along the wall, and the barrels of brown sugar and white sugar (called, I believe 'coffee sugar,' being a creamy white and not granulated) kept company with the crackers. Large caddies of tea – lacquered in mysterious characters and ornamented in gold design straight from China – with burlap sacks of coffee – the green, unroasted bean from some other far-off country – sat on the floor, open.

On the shelves, too, behind the counter, were tins of oysters – narrow, flat

58

tins that held such succulent flavour, such delectable morsels of savouriness, as made your mouth water just to look at them. Maybe – *maybe* – if the eggs and butter and lard came to enough and to spare, maybe my father would buy a tin to take home! At the thought of that possibility I could even forget my thirst in blissful anticipation. I floated on the thought of that first heavenly aroma as the tin is punctured, the further tormenting fragrance as the stew heats, and the final swooning delight in the hot, redolent fumes from the soup plate under my nose.

The prayer is answered. Not only do we march triumphantly out the door with our tin of oysters, but my father carries a kit of mackerel, a slab of cod, and a large wedge of cheese.

'Say, Simson, last cheese I got here – just 'fore Christmas – 'member? Well, by cricky, the dang thing like to got home 'fore I did.'

Mr. Simson, the storekeeper, laughs. 'Pretty strong, was it?' he says.

'Strong!' echoes my father saltily. 'I tell you it *walked*!'

'Well,' admits the storekeeper mildly, 'I *did* have a cheese in 'bout that time 't was pretty lively. Could you use it?'

'Not 'nless we made hash of it, and my wife said she's ruther mix potatoes 'th her meat than cheese.'

They laugh. 'Skippers' in the cheese were not an altogether unknown occurrence, it would seem. It was well to look before leaping, especially in the dark.

Mr. Simson and my father carry in the potatoes, the crocks, jars, and baskets. They carry out packages of tea, a sack of coffee, bags of sugar.

I twitch at my father's sleeve. 'Get me a stick of candy, Pa?' He glances down at me in surprise. Almost he has forgotten my existence. Reminded, however, he smiles, pats my head, and tells the storekeeper to mix up a few sticks. There is a candy apple on the shelf which I would give my soul to possess, but when little girls are allowed to go to town with their fathers they do not tease. Emboldened by the paper sack which has been thrust into my hands, however, I pull again at my father's sleeve and whisper, 'Can I have a drink, Pa?' My father repeats the request, and the storekeeper leads the way to a little cubbyhole where a tin pail of water with a tin dipper in it sits on a bench. I drink – copiously. My father drinks – both of us leaning over the pail and then returning to it the remaining contents of the dipper.

And now, our groceries safely stored in the wagon, we go across the street to the drug store, where my father will lay in his store of supplies – rock candy and rye – with which to supplement the roots and herbs he will later gather to make his yearly antidote to disease – spring bitters.

'Have a little chewing tobacco?' The drug-store man offers a tin can. My

60

father shakes his head. He does not use tobacco and he does not drink. His eye lights on some small ornamental cakes of soap in the showcase. 'I'll take one of those,' he says, and later he presents it to my mother by sticking it under her nose. It is Colgate's Cashmere Bouquet and it smells sweet.

The drug store is a lovely place. In the front window are two beautiful coloured-glass bottles of great size. You can see them far down the street. Inside is an odour like that of the long, thin bottle which someone gave my mother and which they said had once held Attar of Roses. There are clear square-cut glass bottles of perfume in the case with glittering stoppers. There are boxes of cigars, baskets full of sponges, and on the shelves countless bottles wrapped in yellow, green, and blue papers – Dr. Pierce's Favourite Prescription, Peruna, Lydia E. Pinkham's Vegetable Compound, but there are no ugly posters cluttering wall or window.

One more errand before we start – we stop at the butcher's and my father buys a big piece of beef. The butcher throws in some suet, a shank for soup, and some bones for Shep. Ah-h! Soup with plenty of meat in it! Beef stew, probably with dumplings, and roast beef with browned potatoes and gravy. I think how pleased my mother is going to be and long to get home.

On our way out of town we meet a funeral. My father pulls the team to the side of the road, removes his hat, and holds it against his heart. I look around and see other men standing, also with their hats in their hands. No one moves. Respect is shown the dead. The black, sleek horses with proud heads handsomely tasselled in black plumes are held severely in check by the driver of the hearse, sombre and grave. The procession moves past at a snail's pace. It is gone, and we are on our way.

The horses jog forward eagerly, the harness making a pleasant creaking sound as they strain through mud and rut. The wheels turn – turn. My father's voice sounds oddly distant: 'G'lang there, Tom, lazy old puppy, you!' But Tom does not accelerate his pace appreciably and the whip remains stiffly upright in the socket. My father never uses a whip. He accuses Ned as well as Tom of laziness, incompetence, stubbornness, and other qualities of character incompatible with efficiency and speed, quite without effect. They plod homeward with steady, if measured, tread. I watch their well-rounded rumps rise and fall, rise and fall – rise – my head grows unaccountably heavy and rests against my father's arm. He pulls me to a more comfortable position and the next thing I know I am being lifted down by my mother and Shep is leaping against me and yelping a crazy welcome.

My legs are stiff. I am cold. But the kitchen is warm. I can see the fire shining through the open hearth of the stove. The teakettle sings, the lid dances, a fine graceful flow of steam rises toward the ceiling and flattens at the top. Something smells good. Something warm, fragrant – *johnnycake*!

'Get your things off, childie – supper's ready.' My mother is making milk gravy. She is taking up the potatoes with their jackets on. The fried ham, pink and not too crisp, is being kept warm in the oven. There are freshly baked beans and chilli sauce, and mashed turnips. On the table are a sour cream pie and Dutch cheese.

'Seems good to get home,' observes my father contentedly, helping himself lavishly to the gravy while my mother peels and mashes my potato. Not that I cannot do it myself, but because I have been away. We might have been gone a year. 'Supper looks good, too.'

'Well,' concedes my mother, not without pride, 'I thought maybe you'd be hungry.'

IV

The Simple Epicure

In the days when men wrested almost an entire living from the soil, there was little talk about dieting, and little need of it. People, old and young, worked and walked and had small occasion for reducing girth and girdle. They ate strong food, and bread was believed to be the staff of life. Flour was not as yet too refined, and milk, or the water in which potatoes had been boiled, was used as liquid, lard from the crock as shortening, and the whole, when baked, provided a rich, luscious, and nutritious food from infancy to old age.

My father did not like yeast bread, however, and would not eat it. He said there was nothing to get your teeth into, and that it wasn't for for a dog. My mother said, be that as it may, she was not going to feed it to the dog; that she liked it, that I liked it, and she was going to make it. To which my father replied that she could make it if she wanted to, and eat it, too, but as for him he wanted salt-risin' bread and he wanted it fresh.

So twice each week the big elevated oven yielded three fat, brown-crusted loaves of salt-risin' bread, along with an equal or greater number of loaves in which yeast cakes were the leavening power.

My mother never became quite reconciled to what seemed an unnecessary demand. She thoroughly disliked making salt-risin' bread. It was temperamental, required longer 'raising,' and took more time to bake. On one occasion my father, grown unusually testy from argument, clumped about the kitchen waving his arms, shouting, 'Jumpin' Christopher! What's your time *for*? I don't ask much of you, do I?'

This superfluous question my mother met with an enigmatical silence doubtless harder to bear by one of a controversial nature than argument, but

63

nevertheless she continued to make salt-rising bread.

Three loaves went into the oven at about nine o'clock, and although my father, from long years of anticipatory watchfulness, knew to a moment the hour of their consignment and the length of time it took to bake, he would invariably appear at the kitchen door within fifteen minutes to ask, 'What time do you think it ought to be done?'

Mother would reply, 'Oh, in about an hour, I guess. But you can't cut it when it's hot, you know' – being perfectly well aware that when it was hot was exactly when he did want to cut it, and would.

A fat-cheeked old silver watch that kept him company throughout his life apprised him of the time, but he never waited for the hour to expire. Within the half he would again appear at the door, eager and expectant.

'Bread done yet?' Craftily he would peer past her toward the oven as if he never quite trusted her computation of time.

'Mercy, no,' she would reply leniently. 'I've only just put it in.'

He had various ways of employing himself during the last few minutes of waiting. In the winter he would fill the woodbox to overflowing, or he would shell corn for the hens, an occupation generally accorded to the leisure of evenings, but sometimes anticipated in order to provide an excuse for a position near the oven door. In summer he would go to the garden, pick two or three crisp young cucumbers, throw them into a pan of cold water, and demand testily to know whether that bread wasn't done *yet*.

To satisfy him my mother would open the oven door a crack and peer inside, only to close it again with the verdict, ' 'Bout fifteen minutes more,' delivered in a professional tone.

'Jiminy *Christopher!*' The explosion was mild in word but electric in effect. 'Can't you hurry it *up*? You want some more wood?'

'No,' Mother would reply to both enquiries, 'the fire's all right and if you'd eat yeast bread it wouldn't take so long. You can't hurry salt-risin' bread.'

Then my father would snort and clump his feet down hard, and say he didn't see why she didn't bake it every day and then a man could have it when he wanted it, fresh.

No matter where he happened to be at the time, he seemed to know the moment the bread came out of the oven, if indeed he was not on hand. My mother tried to insist that the bread should be turned out upon a clean towel and covered with another until it had cooled at least a little – but this was beyond my father's endurance. The only concession he would make was a sufficient time to peel the cucumbers that were cooling and put them lengthwise on a plate with a salt-cellar. This, with another plate filled with huge slices of hot bread generously buttered, was then carried out to our accustomed position on the back steps, where he and I would feast our corporeal selves on the nutty richness of salt-risin' bread, and stock our souls with memories against another day.

I regret that I cannot give my mother's rule for salt-rising bread, but I can quote one that was printed by the *Detroit Free Press* in 1881 and is probably similar to hers. 'In the evening scald two tablespoonfuls of corn meal, a pinch of salt and one of sugar with sweet milk and set in a warm place until morning. [With the charming insouciance of old-time recipes this does not state how much milk, but I should judge it means just enough to make a mush, perhaps a cupful.] In the morning scald a teaspoonful of sugar, one of salt, half as much soda, with a pint of boiling water; add cold water till lukewarm, then put in the mush made the night before and thicken to a batter with flour; put in a close vessel and set in a kettle of warm water (not too hot); when light mix stiff [presumably with flour], adding a little shortening; mould into loaves and let rise again. Then bake.'

This rule does not say at what particular time the decidedly unpleasant odour peculiar to this kind of bread made itself known, but I am sure it was there when the 'empt'in's' were uncovered in the morning. In all my two hundred cookbooks I have not been able to find a satisfactory recipe for making salt-rising bread.

When it came to doughnuts my father was quite content with my mother's product, but he liked these, too, hot from the kettle, and insisted on a fresh batch three times a week with no impairment to digestion.

My father called them 'friedcakes.' That was what *his* mother had called them and that was what they were. He said he didn't know what a doughnut was, and he didn't care. Friedcakes were what he wanted, and friedcakes were what he would have. Moreover, he had to have them fried in a certain iron kettle, huge, heavy, and unwieldy. Unknown to him my mother once bought a lightweight, clean-looking kettle of granite-ware to take its place. When, however, he came in and saw the cakes sizzling about in this alien pot, he threw what is vulgarly known as a fit.

Who in tunket, he stormed, ever heard of such a thing as using anything but an iron kittle for friedcakes? He picked up one of the cakes, perfect in contour, light as a thistle, golden brown in colour, bit into it with pursed lips, and threw it down a contemptuous verdict.

Not fit to eat! What could she expect, coming out of that liver-coloured contraption? *Where was the kittle?*

You fry cakes, Mother told him, in the *lard*, and it don't make any difference what the lard's *in* so long's it's hot enough.

Father snorted and waved his arms. She needn't tell him, he shouted, that

65

she could fry cakes in that thing. She had only to *look* at them to see. He demanded the *kittle*. He said *he* would get the kittle. He got the kittle and banged it down on the stove.

My mother sought to calm him. She urged him to try another of the cakes and expressed herself as willing to wager that he could not tell the difference.

Tell the difference! he roared. Of course he could tell the the difference. They tasted of that stuff on that tarnation pot she was cooking them in.

She pointed out that this could not be so, as this was a granite surface and nothing could come off it. Father insisted that there was a decided taste of tin or something, but followed the first sample with another and another, doubtless to verify his original opinion. He had never expected, he grumbled, in *his* time, to eat such friedcakes. They might as well as thrown to the hogs. My mother remarked tartly that it looked as if there wouldn't be many to throw, but she apparently did not consider the battle worth waging, for she went back to using the iron kettle and used it as long as I can remember – but not the same kettle.

A little while after this the iron kettle was knocked off the table and cracked. Mother said it was an accident and she was sorry, but it couldn't be helped. Anyway she had the granite kettle, which would do quite as well, but Father declared he would get another iron kettle before the sun had set. He dropped everything, hitched the bay mare to the buckboard, and took me with him. He stopped at all the near-by farmhouses and asked if they had an iron kettle to sell. Some of the women were willing to part with one (doubtless in the hope of acquiring one more modern), but none of them was what Father wanted. Some were too large, some were too small; one that otherwise might have done had a chip in the rim; another had a slightly cracked ear which endangered the safety of the handle. No slightest flaw escaped his eye.

We stopped at two secondhand stores (there were no antique shops then) and at the junk dealer's, but nothing would suit. The perfect kettle was not found.

On the way home somebody told Father about an auction that was to be held on the morrow where there would be a lot of household goods. So, as soon as an early breakfast was over, he hitched up the bay mare and we set forth. The auction was some eight miles away over a dirt road. (As if all roads were not of dirt, in that day!) The sand on this particular road, however, was unusually deep and the day was hot. We proceeded slowly while Father perspired and the horse lathered. Father took off his alpaca coat and vest and opened his shirt collar. When we came to a stream he drove through it on the shallow side of the bridge and let the mare stop to drink. He said it would soak up the fellies on the wheels as well. After we had driven through he told me to get out and pick some elderberry leaves and wet them in the stream. He put these inside his hat and I picked some more, wet them, and stuck them in the bridle to keep the flies away from the horse's head.

Eight miles was a goodly journey in those days over a dusty road, but we reached our destination shortly after the auction had begun. My father immediately began to prowl among the junk which was gathered on tables, benches, and on the grass. There were several kettles, but again none suited him. Vexed and disappointed, he turned away, and was making toward the buggy when a leather-faced, horny-handed stranger approached and said he'd heard my father was looking for an iron kettle. Father said he was.

'I got one over to my house,' said the stranger, 'that's had more friedcakes cooked in it'n you e'd put in a haystack. House's just down the road a step. Come down, I'll show you.'

We followed him down the dusty road, his bare feet plopping in the dust, fringed overalls flapping about his thin, dirt-encrusted ankles.

'This-here kittle,' he volunteered, 'was my mother's and her mother's afore her, and just as good today as 't was then. Hain't no wear-out to it. My first womern set store by it, and fried a million cakes in it. But this-here one –' A flip of the hand, significant expectoration of tobacco juice expertly aimed at a ragweed taller than its thousand mates along the road, and scornful lift of moustached lip (badly discoloured) gave mute commentary on the housekeeping standards of this-here present 'womern.'

'C'min.' He pushed open the dilapidated door of what was clearly the most desolate, rickety, junk-strewn excuse for a house that ever disgraced a town ship. 'Womern's up t' the auction,' he explained. 'I'll get the kittle.'

Rattling and banging about amid the general débris in some outlying district he designated as the woodshed, he came back triumphantly bearing an exact replica of the late lamented article for which we were seeking a duplicate.

'Thar she is!' He set the kettle down on a cluttered table and, giving it a hasty brush with his sleeve, stood off to observe the effect of this miraculous consummation of a desire.

My father clutched the kettle, struck it resoundingly with a knife which he picked up from the table, listened critically, and nodded his head. He inspected the rim for nicks, the ears for cracks, and the handle for balance. His investigation seemed to give him complete satisfaction.

He enquired, tersely, the price. The owner, shifting ballast to the other jaw, hitched his overalls a notch higher, squinted speculatively at his customer, and said with equal brevity, 'Fo' dollars.'

My father took a worn leather bag from his pocket, counted out four silver dollars, and handed them over. He took the kettle carefully in hand, bade the man good-day, and we started back to the scene of the auction, where our horse was tied.

As we were about to climb into our buggy a slatternly woman approached.

'Got that kittle from the ole man, didn't you.' Which was a statement rather than an enquiry. 'How much d'ja pay for it?'

'I paid four dollars,' my father said shortly, his voice edged, and his eyes sharp with suspicion.

The woman gave a toothless chortle, flinging her sun-bonneted head back upon a dirty throat. 'He sure stung you good, mister,' she said with obvious amusement. 'He snatched that-thar kittle out'n the pile of junk over thar' – gesturing toward the auction – 'when he hearn you was lookin' for one. Paid fifty cents for it.'

My father made no reply, but set the kettle carefully in the buggy and bade me, curtly, to climb in. So far as I know, he never related the terms of transaction to my mother, nor did I.

As for desserts, we probably missed something, judging by the myriad varieties advertised in full page, spread, and column of magazine and newspaper, and lauded by air, platform, and print. But we did not know it, and although our choice was limited the quality was unexcelled, except the one instance, so far as I was concerned, of my father's favourite, which was known as a 'minute pudding.' This seemed to consist of flour being slowly sifted by the fingers of one hand into a kettle of boiling milk while the other hand diligently stirred – all, however, to small purpose, for the result was a lumpy concoction which was served with sweetened and flavoured cream in a certain small white pitcher which had purple lustre flowers on its fat cheeks. I have never seen or heard of a minute pudding in my later life and shall feel no regret if I never do.

There was another pudding, however, that I tasted first upon a Sunday visit to my Aunt Hanner. This, when carefully unmoulded from the good-sized coffee cups in which it had been cooling in the springhouse, proved to be a rich, yellowish preparation, semi-globular in shape, fine of texture, perfect in consistency, and also served with cream, sweetened and flavoured with vanilla.

Experience of later years taught me that this delicious dainty was no less but certainly more than what is called by the commonplace name of 'cornstarch pudding,' although I have never since tasted a cornstarch or other pudding that could compare with it. I have myself tried many recipes, some of them my own, in quest of the ideal, but apparently the ingredients are not the same; the cream is not as rich, the eggs are lacking in quality, or perhaps it is that the technique is not – and can never be – the same. However, or whatever the reason, Aunt Hanner's cup pudding, as she called it, was a dessert unsurpassed to my virgin palate, and in my memory of sweets.

68

Interspersed with the pies of the early season (which we had in plenty) was strawberry shortcake. Now strawberry shortcake, as my mother made it, was no mean matter of one small, rangy biscuit split apart and sparingly smeared with a little strawberry juice.

My mother made strawberry shortcake in a small dripping pan and of a very rich biscuit dough. (Four level tablespoonfuls of butter to the regular rule of two cups of flour.) When this was baked to flaky perfection it was turned on to a platter and split in two. The top half was laid aside and the bottom part lavishly spread with butter. Over this the berries (already crushed in a blue and white porcelain bowl) were thickly poured. Then the top half was laid over this (still piping hot), fulsomely buttered, while the remainder of the berries completely canopied the whole. The juice ran off and made a crimson lake on which the shortcake rested. It was then set in the oven to 'ripen' for a few minutes. A pitcher of cream on the table acted as accompaniment for those who wanted it.

When we had shortcake we had but little else, nor needed more. Here was a dish complete in itself, perfect in quality, adequate in quantity, and presenting a feast sufficient for gods or epicurean man.

69

Neither my mother nor her contemporaries had recipes as a recipe is counted today. They had 'rules,' but many of their rules were in their fingers and eyes. They had 'heaping spoonfuls' and 'heaping cupfuls,' 'pinches of salt,' 'lard enough to make a short crust.' But when they got through, the approach was such as not many of today's 'experts' can approach.

My mother's apple pie was beyond description. The crust was flaky, crisp, and tender. She used lard, and she mixed this with the flour until it 'felt right.' And she knew to a nicety when it did feel right. She poured in water from the teacup, or the dipper, or whatever was at hand, but she never poured too much or too little. She laid on to the lower crust a bed of sliced apples to exactly the right height for proper thickness when the pie was done. It was never so thick that it felt like biting into a feather bed, nor so thin that your teeth clicked. It never ran over, and it had just the proper amount of juice. She sprinkled sugar over it with neither mete nor measure, and allspice or cinnamon from a can. But when that pie was done (crimped around the edges and golden brown on the humps, with an 'A' slashed in the top crust) it was a masterpiece of culinary art. With the edge of the oven's heat taken off, but never allowed to chill, and a goodly piece of cheese from the neighbouring factory lying alongside, here was a dish which the average citizen of any country rarely meets. For not one woman in ten thousand can make a good apple pie, and if I need witness to corroborate my statement, there will indeed be clouds of such, darkened by frustrated desire.

Another of the beloved memories of the good things with which my mother coddled her family was tarts. Tarts! Little crinkly-shelled pastries, so tender that a touch might sever one of the pale, amber lobes; so crisp that one swift bite might send the whole sweet structure crumbling in the mouth.

Tarts were made in patty pans – little fluted pans into which the very short crust was pressed and baked. When cooled it was filled with currant jelly, or strawberry jam. And not always were tarts saved for the end of the meal. One, at least, we had, when first they came out of the oven. Maybe two. My father did not care for them. He said there was nothing to get your teeth into. But I loved them. And my mother made them – just for me.

My father was very fond of buttermilk, but he wanted it as cold as he wanted his friedcakes hot, a feat difficult to achieve with no means of cooling except to set the pitcher in a bucket of water drawn from the well, and especially since he was impatient of waiting for the buttermilk to cool as for the bread to bake. Mother churned three times a week, and Father insisted on her using an old-fashioned stone churn with wooden dasher. My mother wanted one of the more modern barrel churns, which required less effort and brought results in less time, but my father's mother had used the dasher type and one of his chores in boyhood had been to manipulate the dasher. Sentiment therefore clung to the stone churn, but I never noticed that sentiment urged him to revive the boyhood occupation for old time's sake.

'You can't make the same kind of buttermilk,' he argued, 'from any of these newfangled dinguses that you can from the old churn, and I want my buttermilk the way I've always had it.'

'You waste more butter in this churn,' Mother told him reasonably. 'The new kind doesn't leave so much butter in the milk.'

'Well,' said Father irritably, 'what are we after? A little more butter or good buttermilk? We'll have butter enough anyway.'

Once when Father was growing difficult because the buttermilk did not cool quickly enough, Mother put some ice in it. He did not see this done, but when he was handed a glass of the beverage to drink, he tasted it, licked his lips, and eyed Mother with bitter suspicion.

'What the – what in *tunket's* the matter with this buttermilk?' he demanded. 'It tastes like *swill*!'

'I put some ice in it,' Mother admitted. 'You been hollerin' so to have it cool, I couldn't do anything else.'

Father looked at her a full minute, his eyes cold, his cheeks red. Then he set the glass down on the table, walked out, and did not return until called for dinner.

On summer days when there was no fresh buttermilk, my mother would make switchel. This was concocted by taking the coldest water that could be drawn and adding a certain amount of vinegar, sugar (or molasses), and ginger to taste. This was put into a brown stone jug, corked, and carried to my father and any helpers he might have in the hayfield. The gurling sound of this beverage tumbling its way from the wide-lipped mouth of the jug to a tin cup was a pleasantly teasing one, and the flavour of switchel, while I have not felt impelled to test the recipe in order to lend authenticity to my tale, was, according to my memory, a not altogether unpleasant substitute for the average throat wash of today.

V

Old Wart

Many of my father's most trusted friends were to be found in his garden, and these he greeted on his early morning rounds with grunts or grin or glance as he met them, each going about the business of his day.

One of the most valued of these was Old Wart, a huge and very earthy toad who invariably appeared along with other indications of spring, and approximately in the same place, where the rhubarb thrust its crinkled rosy nose through mellow soil, and where a little later would be copious shade and moist earth.

From what amphibian resort he came and to what like retreat he kicked his backward way when frosts approached, heaven – and he – only knew. But year after year, as regularly as winter released its hold upon the earth and sap rose in the trees, Old Wart appeared.

By rights I suppose the garden belonged to Old Wart before it did to us, because he was there before us, but at any rate we discovered him – or rather my father did, and in what was, to Old Wart at least, a rather astonishing manner.

To enlarge his garden my father in one year of my earliest remembrance ploughed up a row of rhubarb, horse-radish, sage, and other perennials which occupied a strip of land between the garden proper and the meadow. This new ground, he said, must be ploughed early and deep. And in ploughing deep, amongst the upturned sods and clods of earth, there was hove into the light of day a very large and very dead-looking toad, gaunt and thin, whose encrustations, ridges, furrows, and lumps gave evidence of great age.

'Well,' said my father, halting his sweating horses and poking the supine

72

creature with his boot, 'kinda overslept, didn't you, Old Wart?'

Old Wart (for by that name he thereafter was known) blinked at him with beady, resentful eyes – and not without justification, for the waking had been abrupt – but stood his ground. The ploughshare had tossed him wide of the furrow, and there he sat, squatting on his papery haunches and staring at the huge creature whom he considered a brash intruder.

After a day or two Old Wart disappeared. Gone, my father said, on his yearly pilgrimage to the swamp that lay in the middle of the meadow where the hylas were already piping their reedy lay. There, my father said, he would perform his amphibian duty toward his kind and return when that was done.

It was some weeks before he returned, but on one fine morning in early May, there he was, at the edge of unfolding rhubarb leaves, squatting like some old beneficent Buddha on his earthly stool. But now, while he was still '*Old* Wart,' he was no longer thin and dry, nor had the appearance of a frost-stripped leaf appearing out of season. The moisture of the swamp had loosened and softened his skin. A generous diet of early and succulent insects had filled his sides, and doubtless the satisfaction to be derived from renewed acquaintanceships and family affiliations had something to do with his complacent appearance. But he was a cumbersome creature at best, and of so earthy a hue that an unwary foot was likely to stumble against his corpulent form. Old Wart, however, was one of the meek who expect to, and therefore do, inherit the earth, and he assumed his heritage would be recognised and respected, which it was.

My father was never a profane man, but he did have certain words and phrases peculiar to his use which seemed to stand him in good stead when in need of explosive media. 'Tarnation old fool coot' was one of these, with some personal addenda always seemingly remote from any reasonable application. So, if Old Wart happened to waddle his clumsy way too far out into the path and was avoided only by agile and dexterous action, my father would address him something thus:

'Get out of the way, you tarnation ole fool coot! Who do you think you are? Go-*lier*?' But the admonition was made with a tolerance bordering on affection, and the toe that poked him back to safety was shod with kindness. For Old Wart, in the warranted belief of my father, was a friend and benefactor as he sat there like some corpulent old brown god of the garden, his bellows-like sides heaving in the heat of the day, his beady eyes never seeming to look to right or left, but ever alert for the unwary insect that came his way. A darting flame of his long extensible tongue, a gulp, and one more contribution had been made to Old Wart's apparently justified expectancy of longevity.

You almost never saw him move, his attitude seeming to be that of the *boulevardier* who sits him down in some favoured spot, sure that all whom he

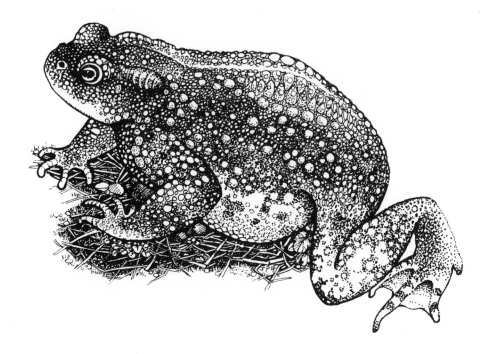

wishes to see will sooner or later pass him by. Still, he did move. In the morning you met him taking, as you might say, an eye opener from the dew on rhubarb leaves. Sometimes in the heat and glare of noon he would startlingly greet you with a knowing stare from the deeper shade of the currant shrubs, and, as shadows lengthened and you bent amongst the strawberry leaves for a basin of berries to accompany your supper of bread and milk, there, suddenly, would be Old Wart taking a nightcap of gnats, mosquitoes, or midges.

Old Wart was overseer of the garden, and my father felt that it was in able hands, for while there were others, like the Stri-pud family, for instance, who had their own chores to do by way of ridding the earth of moles *and* toads, and the robins and jays who, in spite of much maligning, *did* earn their salt – and cherries – these came and went, but Old Wart was, so to speak, resident boss. The garden was his domain and there he stayed from frost to frost. And – believe it or not, it still is fact – he *knew* my father. Knew and trusted him, and – this my father declared – followed him about! Not, as I have said, that his manner or time of locomotion was made obvious to heedless man, but my father would be here – and here, of a sudden, was Old Wart. My father went there, and likewise, after an interval, there came Old Wart. My father *said* he would come in answer to a call, but, with something of the contrariness of human nature, he would never evidence such intelligence at times when my father would have liked to show him off.

I had never in my life any reason to doubt the integrity of my father's word, but, also, I never actually saw Old Wart tagging him about as I have many times seen a gangling-necked, bow-legged, half-feathered, adolescent gosling that, unmothered, attached itself to him and followed where he went, waddling at his heels and piping some strange language comprehensible to his own kidney perhaps, but to no other unless it was my father, in the high-pitched, cracked, changing voice peculiar to transient youth.

The Stri-pud family came up out of the meadow a little later, perhaps, than Old Wart. Their eggs were laid in the warm stretch of sand that bordered the meadow and their young were introduced to the variance of life amongst the piles of stones that were mute evidence of earlier days of hand-callousing labour. There they stretched their lovely sinuous lengths, or curled themselves into braided mats of beauty in the sun. If Old Wart was static in his natural pose, the Stri-puds were fluid. They were here, there, gone. You encountered them one morning as you pulled roseate stalks of rhubarb from blanched sockets, and not five minutes later they slid out from under your very hand as you about to pluck a slender cucumber from the parent vine. Of course they had the advantage of Old Wart in numbers and in lack of individuality. They were like the twin sisters I used to know in school who so closely resembled one another that, when the teacher called on one, whichever felt she could answer the question best rose and took it. But they had their uses and my father would countenance no slaughter of the innocents in the garden variety of snake.

He allowed no casual traffic in his garden anyway. He was proud as Lucifer of his fruits and vegetables, and loved to show them off, but all tours were personally conducted. He went first, pointed out the way that was likely to cause least damage to tendril and leaf, calling attention to the triumphs of his horticultural skill in what he attempted to make a modest manner, and the guest followed, stepping cautiously and close in the wake of his guide.

'Sunday dinner' turns my thoughts to that one which was almost standard-ised in the home of my childhood, and is very nearly so in my own: an old-fashioned dinner of fricassee chicken, biscuits and gravy, mashed potatoes, boiled onions. That was the kind of dinner most favoured for the Sabbath day by my father and still favoured by my own family. I have never seen any reason for trying to improve upon it.

Now while, as a matter of habit and custom, we say 'fricasse of chicken,' it is, in fact, fricassee of fowl, for a *chicken* means a fowl under a year old, and has not the ripeness of flavour of one a year old. Even a plump, two-year-old hen properly cooked will have a richer flavour than a chicken. But *do not let the butcher cut it up for you*! He will take a cleaver and ruthlessly chop through bone and joint, leaving jagged edges and uncouth ends. Learning to unjoint a fowl is not a difficult job, and the satisfaction of being able to cut with scientific precision through skin, flesh, and cartilage to the point where bone is fastened to bone only by ligament and gristle is sufficient to pay for perfecting the technique.

Once disjointed, wipe each separate part with a clean damp cloth. *Do not throw it into a kettle of water and let it soak.* This is but to dissipate its flavour uselessly. Put the pieces of fowl into a small amount of boiling water and let them cook slowly (not at a top boil) until the meat is tender. This should take about an hour and a half with a year-old fowl. When the chicken is done there should be only a small amount of strong broth left – a pint or so. Take the pieces of chicken from the water and drain in a colander. Dust each piece lightly with flour and fry in a spider in which butter is melted to the sizzling point. Bacon fat is sometimes recommended, but you should remember that bacon will flavour the chicken. It is not advisable to use it.

Each piece of chicken should be browned and turned as it browns. The outside should not be allowed to get hard or crisp, but should be brought just to that delicate shade of amber that indicates perfection.

Place the pieces of fowl on a hot platter or serving dish and set where it will keep warm while the gravy is being made (and while the baking-powder biscuits (page 133) are taking on the last golden-brown flush in the oven.) Skim off any surplus grease if the fowl was very fat.

To make the gravy, add three level tablespoonfuls of butter to the fat in the pan after the chicken is fried, and let it come to a bubbling heat. Now stir into it four tablespoonfuls of flour and mix until smooth and a delicate brown. Stir in the broth in which the chicken was boiled. And a half cup of cream, season, and pour over hot split baking-powder biscuits.

Mashed potatoes were (and are) the proper accompaniment to an old-fashioned chicken dinner. Now, mashed potatoes may be one of three things: the usual soggy mess you encounter at most hotels and public eating places; a little better quality met with in the home of the average cook; or a light snowy *drift* of nutritive substance melting to the tongue, sweet to the palate, welcomed by the stomach, and cherished in memory.

To accomplish this miracle, a good quality of potato must be chosen – of the later fall and winter varieties, and ripe. New potatoes should never be mashed. The potatoes should be peeled as thinly as possible and thrown into cold water; then into boiling water and boiled until quite done, but not broken. They are then drained through a colander, and put back into the kettle in which they were boiled, and which has been wiped dry. With a wire masher, press them free from lumps. An old-fashioned wooden masher is too severe in action, reducing the potatoes to pulp.

When the potatoes have been mashed, add one teaspoonful of melted butter and one tablespoonful of cream to each cup of potato – adding each gradually, with salt and pepper to season. Then with a wire whisk, or wooden spoon, beat them until they are light as a feather, white as a drift of snow, and as tempting as the apple was to Eve. Pile them in a serving dish, *loosely*, not packed or patted down with a spoon; dib a dab of butter here and there, sprinkle them gently with paprika, minced parsley, or chopped chives, and set in the oven for not longer than five minutes, or until the butter has melted. And if anyone thinks this amount of valuable space and number of words an extravagant tribute to pay to the dish in question – then he has never so much as made its acquaintance.

My father was especially fond of mashed potatoes, but there was always an argument when he came to eat them.

'Pass the butter, 'Miry.'

'You don't *need* butter for your potatoes, 'Lije. There's half a cup o' butter and as much cream in 'em.'

'Well, what if the' is? I can't *see* it, can I? I want to *see* my butter.'

'There's butter on top, melted right into 'em. You can see that.'

'I can't either. Not if it's melted. Pass the butter.'

So, no matter how much butter or cream might have gone to the foamy content of the dish, my father plastered the outside thick. My mother always threatened next time not to put any in when the potatoes were mashed.

'What's the matter?' my father would want to know. 'We *got* butter, ain't we?'

So the argument came up, died down, and appeared again rhythmically with the return of the dish. It was not the amount of butter used that my mother contended, it was the dressing of a dish already properly prepared – an offence to her culinary art. He could sink in butter for all she cared, but enough was enough.

My father's fondness for butter was something like that of the Irishman who once worked for us. He slapped a great chunk on to a piece of cheese and said, 'There, domn you! Ye nivver should a been separated!'

In the spring of the year it was the small, round, delicately flavoured new potato over which the luscious chicken gravy was poured. Scraped, never peeled, boiled to tenderness but never to the breaking point, a dish of new potatoes (my father's favourite was Early Rose) was a fitting accompaniment to the chicken dinners.

At this time of year, too, boiled onions gave way to asparagus – creamed asparagus (sparrow-grass, to us). I do not know whether people today really do not care for creamed asparagus, or whether a side dish and spoon are so hopelessly out of date that the proper-minded modern housewife doesn't want to be caught dealing in the fashions which seemed good to her grandmother. Whatever the reason, it seems a pity that a vegetable so greatly improved by a few spoonfuls of cream and a little butter should so almost universally be sent to the table in long, dejected, tasteless stalks.

Peas, too, in my early home were, and in my home today are, given the same delicate attention and their flavour thereby extended to the dressing; and they are *never* submitted to the indigity of having baking soda added to preserve the colour. Cooked as they should be with the smallest possible amount of water, they will retain their colour.

One or the other of these succulent fruits of springtime, as well as a dish of green onions and radishes, lent an altogether different air to the chicken dinner than that given in late summer by summer squash (fried) or in winter by boiled onions.

My father grew vegetables and fruits as other men paint pictures. From the day when the first seed catalogues were found in the post office along in February, he planned, devised, forecast. He had the vision of his garden first in his mind, perfect and true, and then he plied his brush with practised hand. Scarlet, crimson, and madder he brought to life in radishes, tomatoes, beets. His eye pleasured in the blue-green of cabbage and cauliflower; in the rich orange and yellow of carrot and pumpkin; in the rhythm of line found in a crookneck squash, and in the feminine grace of an ear of corn. So far as his own hand could govern, the canvas followed the vision, but he was ever at the mercy of the elements.

Yesterday I saw acres and acres of young green vegetables being watered by an elaborate system of sprays and pipes, and I thought with heartbreaking sympathy of my father's utter dependency upon the caprices of the indifferent old woman of the sky. One incident in particular impressed upon me, as a child, the hazardous measures with which the farmer has to cope, and also the dangers that may be incurred by human meddling with divine affairs.

Upon the strawberry bed on which my father had expended considerable money and immeasurable love and care, we depended for ready money in the spring. There had been a long period of drought, an exigency not infrequent in the Middle West, and one which had doubtless influenced the home atmosphere, but which had made small impression on my young mind. A Sunday

School picnic was pending for the morrow, and, as I had never attended such a function, there was no place in my excited ego for consideration of natural or unnatural exigencies, since there were rumours of unlimited gallons of lemonade, fields of frosted cakes, and – *probably* – whole freezers of ice cream! The picnic, however, was contingent upon the weather. If it rained there would be no picnic, if it did not rain there would.

Being ever of a helpful and something of an executive nature, I proceeded on the afternoon of the day before the great event to a pile of lumber out behind the barn, where I was wont to bring my tribulations before the Lord, and there, in the proper attitude of supplication, I besought Him 'please not to let it rain tomorrow!'

The request was many times repeated lest the ear of the Lord should momentarily be turned upon some other of His – although of course more trifling – chores. Then, full of complacent faith and smug anticipation, I returned to the house.

Almost simultaneously my father entered by another door. His face, usually set in competent, if not always tranquil lines, was drawn with anxiety and concern.

'If it don't rain by tomorrow,' he said miserably, 'there won't be a single berry to pick. And there ain't a sign in the sky.'

Stricken with compunction (for well I knew why there was no sign in the sky!), a flood of guilty reckoning flaming through my soul, I fled to the lumber pile, sick with fear. *What if the Lord, my prayer annotated and pocketed, ready for the morrow's dispensation, had gone to some distant part of His domain where I could not reach Him?* With fearful apprehension I envisaged the enormous Figure striding across the firmament, robe tails flying, and only a broad, enigmatic back set toward a little frightened child of earth. Feverishly I clasped my small hands and desperately I besought Him to disregard my former plea. Earnestly I commended to Him my father's need, and humbly I tendered my sacrificial desires upon the altar of filial necessity.

Anxiously then we watched the sky, my father and I, until dark. Not a mackerel scale; not a cloud as big as your hand to mar the azure planes; not so much as a hair from the mare's-tail that presages storm.

'It *might*,' said my father with enforced hopefulness, 'be a weather breeder.' But early bedtime came and which prayer had found its final way to the divine ear was still unknown.

The next morning, however, we woke to the sound of a steady drumming on the roof. Not a brief shower that might bring relief to the berries and still clear off in time for the picnic, but a sod-soaker, such as the Little Shepherd of Kingdom Come had once invoked in like straits. There would be no 'ice-cold lemonade, made in the shade, stirred by an old maid,' no loaves of luscious gooey cakes, no rare ice cream. But there would be berries! And also there would be no further presumptuous interference on my part with the complicated machinery of celestial plans.

The gathering of the first fruits of the garden was a sacred rite. A small, home-made forcing pit and a cold frame expedited the growth of plants for later development, such as tomatoes, cabbages, cauliflower; but scallion bulbs (we called them 'scullions') and radish seeds were committed directly to the earth at the first warm caress of the spring sun, and in an amazingly short time my father would come strutting into the house bearing a few small scarlet globules of crisp and succulent flavour, and a dozen or so slender shoots of green – the first radishes, the first green onions of the season.

These, the first oblation to the epicurean gods, were not, as you might suppose, laid aside to be eaten at the next meal. No. To have so delayed a treat would have seemed to him a wanton disregard of the beneficence of nature. They were washed, trimmed, and eaten then and there with a proper accompaniment of bread baked in an elevated oven and butter churned on our own back stoop by means of stone churn and wooden dasher. A little salt in the hand, a thick slice of fresh, moist, odorous bread generously spread – and a seat

in the shade. These were to my father, who ate with eyes and nose as well as with teeth, tongue, and palate, the simple joys that kept him from undue repining.

Next in the halting procession of contributory offerings from a slowly yielding earth was rhubarb. Slender, almost translucent pipes of rose colour blanching to snowy white where stem meets the parent root; mere rods of tart juiciness held upright by a deeper fibrous body that melts to pulp at the mere hint of heat.

Cut into short lenghts, *unpeeled*, covered with a small amount of water, stewed for ten minutes or less and generously sweetened, the first rhubarb of the season is to the digestive tract of winter-logged inner man what a good hot bath with plenty of healing soap is to the outer after a bout with plough and harrow. Even the tongue and teeth have a scrubbed feeling after a dish of early rhubarb.

Some cooks make the mistake of peeling even the first young tender stalks of rhubarb. As the stalks grow older, tougher, and more fibrous this may have to be done, but never while yet crisp and rosily fresh. The skin is a mere wisp of coating and should be left intact to lend colour and flavour to the sauce.

After this the procession moves a little more rapidly. Radishes and scallions have already been noted, a little out of turn, but proper planting of the seed of one and bulbs of the other will keep a succession of them moving from garden to table from the first crop until supplanted by their fast-appearing followers.

Peas, for the small gardener, are probably the most costly of all crops to raise, since they require considerable ground and bear but one good crop. But he who grows a garden for the pure pleasure of it will plant one row of the earliest variety just for the joy of providing with his own hands the traditional 'green-peas-and-new-potaters' dinner for the Fourth of July. After this patriotic rite is observed, the vines can be pulled and the ground planted to turnips for the equally traditional boiled dinner of early fall.

A bed of asparagus, however, like the bed of strawberries and the row of perennial herbs, sage, savoury, thyme, sweet marjoram, and bay (names with which to conjure magical delights), was one of the thrifty farmer's friends, each of which we welcomed in its season with a joyousness of which the market buyer cannot conceive.

In honour of cherry pie a special eulogy should be written, one not restricted to the limitations of page or space. The sensitive hand of a Gauguin is required to portray the bowl – a bowl of Old Staffordshire in flowing blue, into whose heavenly depths the luscious crimson of juicy fruit was pitted. And only the epicure in taste and touch can gauge for you the exact amount of sugar which will temper the acid and still leave free just the right tartness to tingle the palate and tease the tongue.

My mother, however, knew her cherry pie. She compounded a mixture of flour, lard, and water, rolled it into a nicety of depth, neatly fitted it to a tin, and filled it not quite to the top with cherries reeking of crimson juice. A second crust embellished with an embroidered scroll was laid over the top, pinched down around the edges to melt with its mate, and the whole brought to a state of consummate perfection in an oven of slow-baking temperature. Served, not warm, never chilled, but just *fresh*, a cherry pie like this was without doubt one of the items of those Olympic feasts which gave rise to the phrase 'foods for the gods.'

A cherry pudding the way my mother made it (and the way I still make it) is another celestial dish. It sets as lightly in its repository after eating as ever it did in the steamer where it was cooked. And this is the way it is done: If you are using canned cherries, put them to drain in a small sieve over a bowl so the juice may be preserved. If fresh cherries, have a pint, when pitted, and sprinkle with sugar. Make a batter by mixing one cup of milk, two cups of flour into which you have already sifted two teaspoonfuls of baking powder and one-fourth teaspoonful of salt, one beaten egg, one cup of sugar, and two tablespoonfuls of melted butter (and give your hand plenty of licence with the butter).

Butter individual pudding dishes, and put two tablespoonfuls of cherries into the bottom of each dish. Cover with batter two-thirds full, and bake in a moderate oven for half an hour – or until a straw (or cake tester) thrust into the batter comes out clean.

For the sauce you take the drained-off juice of the cherries and put it into a double boiler; add a third of the amount of water and an equal amount of claret wine and thicken it with a very little cornstarch. If the juice was unsweetened, add sugar to taste. Cook until of a creamy consistency and then beat in one-half cup of thick cream. If fresh cherries are used, stew a pint of cherries in one-half cup of water and one-half cup of sugar, drain, and use the juice. Remove the puddings from their baking dishes on to serving plates, upside down, and pour the sauce over them.

I should add with all haste, and in order that my mother's spirit may continue to rest in teetotal peace, that the claret is my own innovation. Fresh fruit juice as God made it was good enough for her.

Until now the garden has been like some dainty hesitant maid, coyly proffering an occasional delicate gift with one shy timorous hand while mysteriously withholding the other behind her back. Her limbs are as yet a bit angular, but promising in their sweetly generous proportions a rounded fulfilment for the future. Her face is mistily veiled, the petal-like lids of her azure eyes hardly lifted to reveal the abundant promise of riches beneath her gentle breasts. Her lips are rosily parted in the eager delight of one who is about to confer beneficent gifts, and her breath is fragrant with the musk of warm rain on parched earth and fresh-turned sod, the bouquet of unfolding frond and throbbing sap.

But now, as the hot sun of early summer pours his fecund rays upon her receptive form, she becomes the pregnant woman unfolding from dawn to dawn the gracious promise of fruition. Her limbs fill into rounded and ample curves; her breasts swell with nourishment; her eyes glow with secret knowledge, and her lips are curved with the fulfilment of life.

And at her feet, oblivious of the mutability of time, unmindful of the mysteries of genesis, fertility, procreation, or consummation, sits Old Wart. Insensible to the whisper of lengthening root and creeping tendril; deaf to the sound of rustling leaf and bursting bud; blind to the emerald of pod and ear, the pumpkin's gold, the egg-plant's purple silk, the crimson cheek of the once-despised 'love apple'; intent only upon his one employment, the protection of his domain from malevolent intruders, Old Wart squats, unmindful of sound, sight, and smell, on his earthy haunches the season through.

VI

Outdoor Cooking and Eating

Amongst the many nieces, great-nieces, and nephews belonging to the tribal Thompson family was Adelaide. Adelaide was married to Big Jim, a huge, ungainly, awkward mastiff of a man with a leathern face carved into lines of tolerance and kindliness. He had a voice like his favourite hound, deep and wistfully musical. He used it not too often, but he spoke to effect. His boys never had to be chided twice, although it is doubtful if he ever reproved them and certainly he never punished them. He never had to.

There were four boys ranging in age from twelve to seventeen: William, the eldest – his father called him Will-yum; Gabey – I suppose his name was Gabriel, although so far as I know no one ever reminded him of such cruel fate; Philly – Philatus to his father – and Dan'l. And one puny, pindlin' little girl whose name was Cora. They called her Cory. She was just my age. They adored her and literally humoured her to death.

I loved to go to Adelaide's, and so did my father and mother. And it is to the credit of Adelaide's perennially youthful spirit that even at the time when our visits to their home made the deepest impression on my mind – between the years of six and eight – she never seemed more in years than one of her own roistering brood.

Adelaide's was a noisy place, but it was what my father called 'a good noise.' There was never any bickering, wrangling, or quarrelling. Big Jim would not have had it. He was a peaceful man himself, and one who loved peace. He had no objection to 'boy-noise' so long as it was good-natured, and would sit at evening with his chair tilted back against the house watching them wrestle and jump and pitch horseshoes with a grin of pride and pleasure on his leathern face.

84

Adelaide, with Big Jim and their five children, lived on a farm at a considerable distance from ours. It took a long time to get there and we did not go often. We started right after an early dinner and we got there just in time for my father to join in the preparations for the special kind of impromptu supper we found nowhere but here, and we stayed all night. Saturday night it was, and the first of these annual visits was so arranged as to fall after the spring planting was done, and before the first haying. In other words, and to be a little more specific, when bullheading was at its height, my father being especially partial to this particular fish. The second of these yearly visits was made to coincide with the first maturing of early sweet corn. The chores, on these occasions, were left to the hired man or an accommodating neighbour.

In the very earliest of my recollections, Adelaide and her family lived in a log house, one of the last, my father said, to stand in a country which had, not many years before, known only such crude dwellings. Big Jim and Adelaide had, in their early married youth, been amongst those adventurous souls who had trekced the long dusty trail to California in the hope of gleaning some remnant from the earlier 'rush.' They had gone in a covered wagon and come home around the Horn. Adelaide still had some mysterious and exciting seashells

which, if you had never heard the sea and believed what you were told, plainly translated to your landlocked ear the roar and beat of surf. They had gone in the first year of their marriage, and when they came back three years later they brought with them in the form of riches two little boys one year apart in age.

Apparently Big Jim had also met with some other measure of good fortune, for upon their return he bought what was then an extraordinarily large amount of land – some eight hundred or so acres on which was a log house. Since this was habitable, Big Jim had devoted his energies towards developing his fertile acres into fields of hay, grain and corn, orchards, and fodder for his many head of stock, until his larger family literally overran the two rooms, lean-to, and loft of the log house. Then he built a huge, square, unutterably ugly structure on the rise of ground beyond where the other stood, but this was not until after we had savoured richly of the simple life as Adelaide devised it within the log-and-plaster walls where three of her five children were born.

The big house, spacious though it was – with a front parlour for which Adelaide could never find any use beyond the storing of food and household effects, which, as Big Jim's fortunes grew, he lavishly bestowed – never had the charm of the old one. This little old log house had a fireplace. A fireplace that burned great logs and often, at a sudden gust of wind, sent both sparks and smoke out into the room. A fireplace that, as winter dusk crept in through the small high windows set flush with the walls, sang high and clear a note of comforting warmth reflected in a ruddy gleam upon the smooth boards of the floor, and in the capering shadows on rough-hewn rafters and wall.

In this one room, too, was a bed. A bed of which to sing and on which to dream. A queen of beds, a matriarch of beds, monarch and throne all in one.

Four slender pointed posts, smooth and silvery from the polishing twirl of many passing hands, upheld the sturdy frame across which ran, to and fro, across the back, a network of heavy cord. On this was laid the tick, a stout casing, the centre of which was ripped open every fall after threshing was done, to disgorge the chaff and stuff it again to an almost insurmountable height with fresh straw, clean, golden, and rustling at every touch as with echoes of whispering fields.

Topping this was the feather bed, a mighty corpulence, rounded, fat, and smooth as a giant's paunch. Over this was spread a protective shroud of heavy unbleached muslin, followed by such amplitude of sheets (woven, in Adelaide's case, by her own mother), comforters, and quilts as would woo the whole hundred eyes of Argus himself to sleep. And over it all lay a marvellous counterpane to which were sewn huge pink tulips with Gargantuan leaves, such as might have been plucked from the garden of the monster whose belly they hid. At the head, propped up like the lineal but lesser relatives of the feather bed beneath, were two immense pillows whose snowy cases were religiously changed and washed every Monday morning, irrespective of whether they had been used or not. For beds like this were Company Beds. Up the ladder-like stairway that led into a loft, partitioned into separate chambers by widths of calico, the family slept (except when clemency of weather afforded the boys the freer opportunity of the barn), on beds of lesser state, but corded like the one below and also having ticks filled with straw or husks of corn.

My father and mother occupied the company bed when we visited at Adelaide's, but I slept on a trundle-bed that was drawn from beneath the big one when the evening's visiting was done, the cider and friedcakes eaten, which was sometimes as late as nine o'clock. Eight was my father's usual hour for retiring, as four in summer and five in winter were his invariable hours for rising, and such dissipation as was indulged in at Adelaide's was a matter for much ostensible yawning and a final impatient, 'Well, jiminy crickets! Ain't we *never* goin' to bed?'

Adelaide, I know it now, though few would have recognised her as such during her life, was a genius at homemaking, one of those rare souls to whom the making of a comfortable home was the whole of life's ambition. She had no other aim. I doubt if she ever even owned a pocket-book in her whole life. What need had she for one when Big Jim was known far and wide as the best 'pervider' in the county? He did, to be sure, buy calico for her dresses and Cory's in the same way that he bought sugar, coffee, tea, crackers, and muslin – wholesale, or, in this case, by the bolt, so that Adelaide and Cory wore dresses alike – and also off the same piece with which the comfortables were covered – for time on end. Or until they wore out, when another bolt would be purchased. But it would have taken more than monotony of pattern to destroy the serenity of Adelaide's existence. And certainly nothing less than genius could have accomplished all that Adelaide did, and still have leisure. For Adelaide enjoyed that priceless disposition of time which allowed her what in these facile days of efficiency is practically non-existent – leisure. The silly old rhyme about 'woman's work is never done' had no meaning for Adelaide.

The memory of hot summer afternoons, when Adelaide had, with sweeping gesture and majestic stroke, cleared the long table and kitchen of dishes and food, donned a stiff white apron gathered full about her ample waist and tied in a bow across her broad back, dipped her bare feet in a basin of water outside the door and drawn her chair to the shade at the side of the house, remains with me as the ideal of what women, if they were only as wise as Adelaide, might attain for the good of their souls. With chair tipped against the house to ease her back and elevate her knees, horny heels hooked over the rung of the chair, and calloused hands folded quiescently in her lap, she sat. Just sat. Humming a

87

restful little tune perhaps, 'On Tombigbee's River So Bright I Was Born,' or 'I'll Hang My Harp on a Weeping Willow Tree,' and smiling at Cory and me playing at her side.

Sometimes Adelaide used her leisure to the advantage of her larder, but such expeditions were always for her pleasure, never to be counted amongst her tasks. When wild strawberries were ripe, for instance, over in the field of timothy and clover, she would take a tin pail and the fingers of a little girl in one hand, and, in the other hand, those of another little girl who had a smaller pail in *her* hand, and set forth, sunbonnet on her head and nothing on her feet, in quest of the makings of a shortcake for supper. Happy hours, indeed, were these when I was allowed to stay a week or more after my folks went home; hot, fragrant, leisurely afternoons with Adelaide's bare feet plop-plopping along the cow path in the lane, and our smaller ones plop-plopping in faithful mimicry beside.

Or, again, in early spring, she would go to the woods beyond the clover field and there gather a big pail of what for want of a more learned name we called 'sponge mushrooms,' but which I afterward came to know as one of the rarest and most delicious of the mushroom family (although I believe these are not a true mushroom, but a fungus), the morel, and the like of which I have seen but once or twice since. These Adelaide stewed in their own juice with plenty of butter, and they tasted like a combination of Elysian mushroom and chicken hatched in the Garden of Eden.

Later when the redcap raspberries came and the creeping blackberries ripened along the sandy roadside, she would fare forth with her tin pail in hand to regale her family with fruits nurtured in their natural soil, ripened in the summer sun and so flavoured beyond anything known to cultivated field. She reckoned time by the sun, and could tell the hour, as most farmers could, almost to a second. When the rays of the sun slanted to a certain length she would squint at the sky and remark, ' 'Bout ha' pas' four. Time to go home and get supper started,' for she always allowed herself plenty of time and she never was known to serve a meal late, observing strictly the hours of six in the morning, twelve at noon, and five-thirty at night. This practice, it may be said in passing, was one of the secrets of her successful career.

I do not know whether the age of science has determined by any rule whether the sense of taste, to tickle the tongue, or the sense of smell, to enchant the nose, is more dear to memory, but it is my belief that remembered odours and fragrances are more poignant than those of other senses. For to these are linked a thousand other associations almost equally dominating. The odour of a cinnamon rose, for instance, brings up the picture of a little country bridge

where youthful love first breathed; the pungent odour of sage recalls a kitchen filled with sunshine and the business of preparation for festal days; a tuberose will ever be a reminder of the first anguished inroads of personal grief.

And so, with the memory of the incomparable fragrance of crushed wild strawberries as our fingers reddened with the stain is interwoven the soft, penetrating sweetness of clover as our hot bare feet trod the honey from its green-white heads, and over both these the almost unbearable sweetness of wild grapes blossoming along the fence. Odours are bound up with the deep blue sky of June, the sudden melodious call of a bobwhite from the wheat field, and the sharp honing of a whetstone against a scythe. There are memories of Adelaide's ineffable tenderness to the pale, anæmic little Cory, as she lifted the child in her own capacious arms at times to carry and cuddle against her own wide breast. Memories of my own sharp homesickness the first time I was left behind, with my father and mother disappearing in a cloud of dust, when Big Jim picked me up in his great arms and carried me off to ride on the broad flat back of the farm horses until the keenness of my woe had been assuaged. And all begirt with the sense of the endlessness of time, the security in a plentitude of days for all our industries. The feel of *leisure* with which Adelaide, in the slow, sure motion of her hands, the certainty of her powerful stride, the comfort of her full, high breast, endowed our days.

Adelaide, in her cooking, had the touch of an artist, the skill of a craftsman, the taste of an epicure – and the hand of a woman who cooked food as if she loved it. And yet, she had 'nothing to do with.' She kept her flour in a barrel – flour ground from wheat grown in their fields and not refined beyond its own gentle nature – and she dipped into it with a handleless coffee cup as she needed it. She had no sifter, no mixers or beaters. But she had thick cream, both sweet and sour, she had plenty of butter, and, more than all, she had standards. She knew a good thing when she saw it and she knew how to make it. She had no thousand and one different volumes on the art of cookery, but she had a sure knowledge of the effect she desired to reach. In this she differed considerably from many women who have all that Adelaide had not, and who hardly understand what a standard is or how to reach one. But the subject of this commentary was intended to deal with the meritorious topic of food cooked and eaten in the open air, as practised by Adelaide's ingenious brood.

My own father did not much hold with such unconventional cookery, and, while he relished with undeniable gusto the lunches my mother and I often carried to him where he worked in the fields, he preferred, as the hired man once said, to put his feet under a table and his elbows on it. Still, one of the most enjoyable events of the year, to him – although he would never admit it – was the spring visit to Adelaide's with supper down by the lake, where the fish were, as you might say, swung from hook to pan, and another was the later and similar occasion when corn was roasted practically as it stood.

Down the cow path in the lane we went, where elderberry bushes graced the stake-an'-rider fence with their flat white pancake blossoms, sweet-perfumed and rich with promise of wine and pie, and mingled with a tangle of wild grapes, high-bush blackberries, and woodbine. Over the fence on one side a field of timothy grass waved long cylindrical heads of reseda green, and from the other came the gentle whisper of young corn welcoming the evening dew. The odour from its newly escaping tassels mingled muskily with that of an occasional bush of eglantine standing straight and virginal, wrapped in its mantle of misty green and adorned with jewel-like blossoms of seashell pink.

Philly and Dan'l, suffering the penalty of being the youngest of the boys, were left on shore to build and tend the fire, a bed of embers being essential to both the frying of the fish and the roasting of potatoes to accompany them. They could paddle around close to shore in an old boat several degrees more offensive than the official craft, but since their own supper as well as that of others depended upon their attentiveness to the fire, their vigilance was distinguished by a faithfulness not altogether altruistic, while the older boys, accompanied by my father, who, in his impatience had preceded us, were already hauling in the slippery pout.

There they were then, as we arrived, Philly zealously stoking the blaze and Dan'l just pulling in with a few perch and bluegills to his credit, which, as he well knew, would give my father great delight. For while the bullhead is good solid eating – and safe, with no bones except the spine – the bluegill is one of the small lake's delicacies and peculiar to the lakes of Michigan – at least so Michigan claims – with perch a close second.

A halloa to the true fishermen brought up their anchor, and in a few minutes the cronk-cronk, cronk-cronk, of rusty oarlocks was followed by a grating on the sand and a scramble to land. The catch – twenty or more fine, big, fat bullheads (more properly known as horned pout) – was held up to our admiring gaze.

'Stinkin' mess,' my father grumbled, bursting with the pleasurable knowledge that a goodly number were to his own credit. 'Ain't worth skinnin' now 't we've got 'em.' Nevertheless, when the fish were skinned, gutted, rolled in flour, and fried in hot, sweet, pork fat his disinclination toward them seemed to have disappeared.

A white oilcloth had been spread on the grass where the land rose to a little bank, and on it the bread, a cup of butter, a pan of beans with its accompanying cruet of vinegar, a jar of pickles, and a bunch of scallions, gathered from the garden as we passed, had been placed. Tin pie plates for service were distributed, along with forks (three-tined, of steel and with bone handles) and knives. Coffee was boiled in a tin pot on the stones and drunk from tin cups.

Around this alfresco feast we sprawled, tucking our feet under us as best we could. My father, scorning such lack of dignity, betook himself to a flat-topped stump near by, while Big Jim sat on a fallen log.

Servings of the blue-white, fine-textured flesh of the horned pout, rolled in flour and fried in lard, and thinner ones of the bluegills and perch, were dispensed; blistering hot potatoes with ash-covered jackets were tossed about (literally), and the bread and beans were passed.

My father, heartily munching the hot, well-buttered centre from a roasted potato and the sweet flesh of pout, muttered that the only advantage he could see in squatting down beside a marshy lake in an uncomfortable position to eat a mess of fish that might just as well have been put on a table like civilised folks was that you could throw the bones in the fire. Adelaide's family, however, including Big Jim, who, like my father, considered it beneath his dignity to admit it, would rather eat food of their own cooking out of doors than the finest meal ever set on a table. 'Ought to give 'em a manger,' grumbled Big Jim, grinning with pride of them, 'and be done with it. Or a trough!'

Adelaide, however, humoured them. 'If they don't never want to do nothin' worse than eat out o' doors,' she argued wisely, '*I* shan't worry. They got to eat a peck o' dirt sometime, may's well begin.'

Adelaide, who loved her little joke, recognising my father's look of disappointment as no form of dessert was forthcoming, said: ' 'Lije, I know you ain't hardly been able to eat a bite without seein' pie before you, but seemed like there wasn't a single thing I could make a pie out of 't we could carry. If we'd a et at home I'd a beat up a custard pie, eggs is so plentiful now, but I'd as soon carry a greased pig as a custard pie.'

'No more'n I'd expect,' grumbled my father, 'from this fool notion of eatin' on the ground. Piece of pie on a decent table's worth more'n a mess o' fish outdoors any day.'

'Well,' drawled Adelaide, humorously, 'seein's you take it so hard I'll see what I can do for you.' Whereupon she produced from the bottom of a covered kettle which my mother had carried, having been admonished to handle it carefully, two delectable pieplant pies, separated from each other by an upturned pan.

The boys whooped. Cory cried, 'I knew it! I knew it! And I never told.' My father's mouth forgot to close. Rhubarb was one of his favourite pies. Big Jim grinned expectantly.

Clean saucers were produced for the pie, and as the knife slid through the tender crust and loosed the juice which ran like liquid rose quartz, our lips involuntarily moistened with the dew of expectancy and our eyes narrowed to the charm of colour and form. For, after all, what more pleasurable shape of pattern can meet the eye than that of a generous wedge of luscious, ambrosial pie? (See how I unwittingly lapse into rhyme at the very thought!)

My mother was loud in her praise. 'I never tasted such pieplant in my life!' she exclaimed. 'Honest, Adelaide, I never did.'

'Oh, pshaw!' Adelaide protested modestly. 'You know, 'Miry, 's well's I do, the' ain't nobody in the world can beat you makin' pie.'

'Just the same,' insisted my mother, 'this is the best I ever ate. Do you put flour in to keep it from runnin'?'

'Yes,' said Adelaide, ' 'bout a tablespoonful to a pie. I mix it with the sugar.'

'You don't skin the rhubarb, do you?' My mother was regarding the lovely coral juice in her saucer with the eye of a connoisseur.

'Not when it's young,' said Adelaide. 'The skin don't count then, but it does make it pretty. I just cut it up into little pieces, lay it on the crust, sprinkle it with sugar and flour – plenty of sugar – and then I dot it with pieces of butter. That keeps it from runnin'. Then I pinch the edges of the top crust down and moisten 'em together – same's you do.' My mother nodded her head in grave assent.

The last piece of fish was eaten, the last white mealy potato reduced to crisp, scorched skin. The saucers held only the rosy evidence of a late delicacy, and, replete to satisfaction, we sat or lay back upon the grass, content for a moment to watch the fireflies in their crazy dance over the water and the young moon dropping to tangle its pale light in the tops of tamaracks across the lake. When mosquitoes grew obnoxious we packed up our dishes and went to the house.

No, my father did not hold, so he said, with the heathenish custom of cooking and eating out of doors. But we, my mother and I, came to expect, with a reasonable degree of certainty, the annual suggestion that we make an all-night visit to Adelaide's sometime in late May (when, as everyone knows, fishing is at its best). Then along in August, when the first sweet corn was sufficiently mature to warrant plucking, my father would casually ask my mother if she would like to go to Adelaide's on, say, the coming Saturday. When we got there he would as likely as not declare that it was one of the worst times of the year to go away from home, but that nothing would do but come, because 'Miry was set on it and had talked of nothing else for weeks.

When the matter of a corn roast was broached my father would grumblingly protest against having to mix grit from the cornfield with his butter and probably find ants in his coffee, but those who knew him noted the glint in his eye and a certain stealthy wetting of the lips. Both he and Big Jim would go through the usual banter about eating more ashes than potato, and threaten to stay at home and eat their supper off the pantry shelf, but if they had been taken seriously and the roast given up because of their disinclination, they would have been both amazed and bitterly disappointed.

My father, soon after our arrival at Adelaide's upon such an occasion, was always the most eager to get started. 'Come, come,' he would fret. 'If you're going to *have* this fool roast let's get started so we won't be eating crickets in the dark.' And Big Jim, relegating the last of the chores to the hired man, was always there in time to find the most favourable spot for his long legs.

For the corn roast Adelaide provided young chickens, cornered, caught, beheaded, scalded, and dressed between the time of our arrival, around four o'clock, and the hour when we set forth for the field with baskets of provender, a jug of water, and a huge coffee-pot full of coffee ready for reheating.

The chickens she fried in a pan laid upon an improvised grille made of stones and topping the pit where corn and potatoes were roasting, and they were fried in butter – sweet in quality, generous in amount.

Adelaide's 'fryers' were the earliest of the spring chickens, and they had fed sumptuously on grain, cornmeal mash, grubs, and insects. By August they were plump and tender and full of flavour. When you picked up a leg of one of Adelaide's fryers and set your eager teeth upon it, the meat immediately parted company with the bone, and flew, so to speak, to the ardent companionship of solvent factors.

'If you want fryers to eat,' said Adelaide, 'feed 'em! Don't ask *me* to set and gnaw onto a bony, gluey thing 't ain't never had enough to eat a day in its life.'

About the time that Adelaide laid the last delicately fried wing in the heated pan reposing on the stones beside the fire, and had the coffee-pot boiling, the boys were pulling the stalks away from the fire and hauling forth the roasted ears and the crisp potatoes.

'The's certain things,' one of the hired men once observed at such a feast, 'that *ort* to be et out of doors, and corn's one of 'em. If you want to drizzle butter all down the sides of your mouth, the' ain't nobody settin' acrost the table to scowl. And watermelon's another.'

He warmed to his theme. 'Over to Miz' Sander's now, she cuts off a round piece of watermelon and then cuts *that* in two like she read in a book, and you got to eat it with a *fork*! That ain't no way to eat watermelon, you can't get the taste of it that way. You want to cut it len'thways, a good wedge of it, and then run it acrost yer mouth like a mouth organ. If you're out a doors you c'n hold yer head over'n spit the seeds out and then sling the rine away and nobody cares. Some things hadn't never ort to be brought to the table a-tall.'

94

Apropos of watermelon, this was invariably the climax to our corn roast: rich, juicy melons grown by Big Jim's boys in a sandy field well within sight of the house – for the sake of protection – and brought fresh from the vines to be laid on cool damp ground underneath a clump of ferns until time to cut them. And, needless to say, they were eaten in the fashion approved by the hired man, with a seed-spitting contest thrown in as extra flavour to the feast.

VII

The Sunday School Picnic

The social and communal life of our small world's summer centred around a few anticipated events. The Fourth of July was still looked upon as a patriotic anniversary and so taught to children. Towns large and small gave due heed to its celebration with speeches, a reading of the Declaration of Independence, much fanfare by local bands, and fireworks in the evening. This outburst of patriotic fervour, however, did not interfere with a little horseplay on the side, such as climbing greased poles, chasing greased pigs, sack races, potato races, and other primitive sports. Our neighbours, the Covells, always went to the celebration.

Scrubbed and clean, but barefooted, since, as my father said, Old Man Covell was too tarnation mean to buy shoes for them until snow flew, they piled into the lumber wagon, father, mother, children, and the hired man – theirs or someone else's who wanted a ride – with the basket of vittles, and set off soon after breakfast to see the doin's. Swinging on the gate, I watched them go, envious to the tip of my own bare toes, as the horses jogged dejectedly along in the hot sand, and the wagon trundled cumbrously off to the wonders of the proper observance of a Fourth o' July celebration. For my father did not hold with crowds, nor had he much patience with public performances. 'Caperin's' he called them, and said he had something better to do than chase off to town to see somebody show off.

As a matter of fact, he had – according to his own notions. That little ceremony of his own of fingering from the hills of his early potatoes the first small, round fruit, and plucking the first peas from the vines. These he always brought in with an air of proffering gifts *from* the gods, swaggering a little,

96

boastfully benign, as if to say, 'There! Now see what you get by staying at home and letting *me* show you how to celebrate the Fourth of July!'

He always made it a point to sow his buckwheat on this day, too, according to a tradition that was observed by many other Michigan farmers.

'Sow your buckwheat on the Fourth of July, wet or dry.'

The Sunday School picnic came next, usually somewhere between haying and harvesting. Why, in a locality where one could hardly travel three miles in any direction without coming upon a lake, the Sunday School picnic was always held in an upland grove seemed to me, for some time, a mystery; upon more serious reflection in later years, however, I supposed it was because the lake, in those days, was a useful part of the topography for fishing purposes, but beyond this it had no social interests. The boys swam in it sometimes on hot nights after work, but no one had considered developing it for recreational uses. The shores were muddy, weedy, and infested with snakes and mosquitoes. The grove, therefore, a cluster of oaks usually, with a few maples and an occasional hickory, was the chosen site for the picnic.

Previous to the given day, the big boys would go and clean out the underbrush, put up swings, build a crude platform from which 'pieces' would be spoken, with maybe a dialogue given or a tableau shown, and from which the minister would address his flock.

A long table of planks was laid on 'horses,' and seats erected at the sides for the dinner. And despite the 'programme' or any other attractions that may have been offered by teachers or pastor, it was around this long table that the chief interest centred, and it was upon this that all eyes were focused as the vehicles bearing whole families, or parts of families, drew up and disgorged both the human element and that which would provide means for its animation.

Better parents than mine or better citizens would, I believe, have been hard to find, but they were not numbered amongst the zealous in the outward semblance of religion. My mother was much more socially-minded than my father and would, I think, have been glad to lend her support to such community interests as the Ladies' Aid and the Sunday School, and did, so far as she could by contributing to any special cause. Occasionally the Ladies' Aid met with her, but my father drew the line at prayer meetings. 'Lot of carpin' ol' hens,' he snorted, 'settin' round and rippin' someone up the back and then gettin' down on their knees and talkin' t' the Lord as if He's their brother-'n-law and tellin' Him what to do.'

It was therefore not until I was about eight years old that I ever attended a

97

Sunday School picnic, and I was actually feverish with excitement for days beforehand. From the young Covells, who invariably attended this or any other function where food was plenteous, and free; from the hired man, who seemed to have pleasing recollections of similar occasions; and from what I could extract from my mother's more conservative store of knowledge, I had managed to build up an illusion of what heaven would be like, reduced to terms of a hickory grove, and a table as long as from here to town, laden with such stores as nothing short of a feast of Heliogabalus could equal.

There would be lemonade by the gallon, so quoth the Covells, 'made in the shade, by an old maid' (the humour of which doggerel I failed to see then, nor have I since), and brought by the donors in stone churns or crocks, with whole thick slices of lemon floating free for him to grab who could.

There would also be *ice cream*! This I could hardly believe, for ice cream, *real* ice cream frozen with ice, was a rarity such as no child born of these days and fairly cradled in a cone could understand. With a lake or pond on every third farm, more or less, and ice to be had for the cutting, only one farmer in a hundred, or less, had an ice house. He who did, and could have ice cream *every Sunday*, was a Crœsus amongst us.

Sometimes in winter my mother would bring in some freshly fallen snow and mix it with whipped cream or the beaten white of an egg, sweeten and flavour it. That was a toothsome sweet not to be despised, but to have genuine ice cream right in the midst of summer was too imposing a possibility to be easily adjusted to the childish mind.

The vision invoked by the tales of the hundred-and-one different kinds of cakes that would be found on that long table – even *frosted* cakes – was beyond belief, and waiting for the day became an agony and a dread. *If anything should happen!*

But nothing happened except that my father refused flatly to go.

'I *told* you I wouldn't go,' he said hotly as we sat at breakfast on the fateful morning, 'and I won't! You can take the mare and go if you're set on it,' he said, 'but you'll get bit with mosquitoes, and prob'ly sit down in poison ivy, and Stib Obart says Collins' Grove is alive with snakes.'

'Anything more?' enquired my mother, mildly derisive. 'You don't suppose the mare'll run away with us, do you, and spill the dinner?'

'Huh!' my father snorted as he shoved back his chair, took his hat, and started impatiently for the door.

'I'll leave your dinner,' said my mother, 'under a pan in the cellarway. Fried chicken and a basin of beans – but I wish't you'd go along and have some ice cream and cake –'

The door of mosquito netting slammed, after which came the sound of sturdy boots stomping their way off the stoop on to the gravel path beyond.

'He wants to go worse'n a dog,' my mother said as she cleared the table, 'but he won't give in. There never was such a stubborn man!'

Certainly he hung upon our going. Twenty times he came steaming in at the door to enquire:

'What time you goin' to get off?'

'Ain't you most ready yet?'

'You got any bakin' sody, in case you get stung?'

Once my mother ventured to urge him. 'You better come along, 'Lijer,' she said. 'You got no hay down – nothin' to hender.'

'Nothin' to hender!' shouted my father, flinging out his hands, and wheeling upon her as if she had accused him of some heinous offence. '*Why* ain't there nothin' to hender? I suppose I ain't got to – to cut around the wheat field ready for the reaper –'

'You ain't got a thing to do today that you couldn't do tomorrow,' my mother interrupted spiritedly, 'but if you don't want to go you needn't. Here, take these two baskets and put 'em in the back of the buggy.'

Silently my father picked up two baskets, seemed to study them for a moment, then went out the door. One he set down on a bench outside, the other he kept in his hand.

'Don't forget this one,' my mother called after him. 'It's got the victuals in it. That one's only got the tablecloth and dishes.'

'I'll get it,' he called back, 'when I bring up the mare.'

He harnessed the mare to the top buggy and brought her to the horse block. He hitched her to the post and went back to the barn after the linen duster for our laps. My mother and I went out and climbed into the buggy.

'Did you get both baskets in?' my mother asked, taking the reins in her hands and peering out the side.

'I put in what you handed me,' he replied shortly, and stood there looking after us as we drove away.

'He'd give his neck to be goin' along,' said my mother impatiently, 'but he just won't – stubborn ole coot!'

I looked back as we drove out of the yard, feeling sorry for my father, in whom I saw only the little-boy-left-behind, for that is exactly how he seemed. He could never bear to have my mother go anywhere without him, or to go himself and leave her behind. If it was only to town or to the mill, he wanted her along. When he came in even from the field his first word was a call for ' 'Miry,' and if she was not in sight or in hearing of his voice, 'Where's your mother?' he would demand, and set off, without waiting for reply, to find her. And now there he stood, forlorn and lonely, watching her depart for festivities in which he had neither share nor desire to share.

Sympathy for his unhappy state was clouding the brightness of my own joy in anticipation and, seeing this, my mother said:

'Now don't you worry about him. He would have come if he'd wanted to. It's just his own cussedness, so let him alone.' Her impatience was obviously tempered with tenderness for a wilful spouse, and so my heart was soothed.

Realisation brought no disappointment in the eagerly looked for fête. There was the platform with a background of branches and leaves of green. A bowery, they called it. On its floor was a piece of carpet, and there stood two chairs and a small table, 'property,' for the dialogue. There were the little girls who were going to 'speak pieces,' fluttering about in white dresses. (I had a new one myself, of dimity, smocked and ruffled, for I, too, was going to speak a piece!)

There were the swings already occupied by older girls, while some of the big boys 'ran under.' And there – there was the long table, and on it were baskets, boxes, things done up in white tablecloths, surety for that feast of delicacies so beguilingly foretold.

Women greeted my mother as we drove up.

'Don't unload your things till after the programme, Miz' Thompson,' one said; 'they're all ready to begin.'

One of the boys came and drove our horse off to unhitch and unbridle her in the shade, and give her the measure of oats my father had provided.

'You fetch our things, Johnnie, when they're ready, will you?' my mother said, and, taking me by the hand, led me over to the position of honour occupied by the performers – a bench at the foot of the platform. Others sat on stumps, blankets, or the ground.

First, the minister had to offer a prayer, and then the programme began. A quartette by the choir, a declamation by this same Johnnie Brent who had taken charge of our horse – 'Darius Green and His Flying Machine' – given with appropriate, if awkard, gestures and pantomime. Then my own name was called, and, pushed by my mother and pulled by a Sunday School teacher whom I had never seen before, I was hauled, shaking and pallid, to the platform, where I was transfixed with fright and could not, with any amount of prompting, utter one word.

Panicky and sobbing, I was allowed to stumble back to my mother's arms, where she doubtless longed to flay instead of to comfort me, as she did.

In time, however, the programme was finished. Women, whose minds had been on melting butter and drying cakes, rose hastily and proceeded to the

100

unwrapping of their stores. Johnnie was sent for our baskets – and returned with one.

'Where's the other?' demanded my mother. 'The one with the *dinner*. This is just dishes and things.'

Johnnie protested that this was the only basket in the buggy.

'But I put *two* in! That is – are you *sure*? I'll go and see myself.' She went, and returned twisting her fingers together and all but weeping.

'He never put it in,' she cried, distracted. 'He just set it down somewheres and forgot it. *All our dinner!*'

Friends consoled, assured her there was enough and plenty to spare. She must not worry.

'I'd go back and get it,' she exclaimed, 'if there was time.' But there was not time. The ice was melting in the lemonade, the ice cream must be eaten soon. Butter was softening.

'You must take hold and help set the tables, Miz' Thompson, and don't give it another thought.'

But that she was giving it all her thought, that she was chagrined, sick with disappointment, and not a little angry, was evidenced by her nervous jerky movements, the thin line of her lips and the smoulding fire in her eye. 'I don't see,' she kept saying, 'how he *could* have been so careless. I wish I'd put them in myself.' Doing a thing yourself, my mother averred, was the only way of being sure it was done at all.

Overcoming, finally, the nature shyness of the lone child, I was led off to the swings to play with other children. But not, wholly, to lose sight of the fascinating performance going on at and around the table.

Cloths of varied assortment were spread over the planks. Plates, cups, knives, forks, and spoons were laid out according to families. Then began the ceremony of placing the food. Unable longer to withstand the enchantment of the scene, I, with other children, deserted the more extraneous entertainment, and hovered about, goggle-eyed and open-mouthed, as one goody after another came to rest upon the cloth.

A whole ham boiled, as its producer pridefully announced, in cider which was just at the sparkling point, – together with a handful of raisins – until almost tender, and then skinned and baked long enough to set and brown the crust of brown sugar, mustard, and spices. The knife, cutting through the crunching crust, slipped into the rosy meat like the blade of a scythe before ripening grain, while one thin pink slice after another rolled down upon the cutting board.

Pans of beans with generous slabs of salt pork, cross-ribbed in strips of bronze, islanded in the middle.

Platters of cold chickens. 'I had two chickens,' mourned my mother, 'fried in fresh butter, and a pan of raised biscuits and – butter! I put in two pounds to have enough! It'll melt and run all over Kingdom Come.'

Mounds of hard-boiled eggs, bottles of homemade chilli sauce, pickled beets in quart jars, sweet pickles, sour pickles, loaves of sweet, fine, moist bread with crust buttered and browned.

'I'll be ashamed to eat a thing,' murmured my mother, vexed and sore, 'but my tongue just *drips*.'

'Don't think of it,' they told her. 'You always bring more'n your share. It won't hurt, once, to eat off'n others.'

When, finally, the cakes were unmasked from their covering of milk pans, white paper, or napkins, and set decoratively down the centre of the table, the suspense grew unbearable. Loaves of frosted cake; layer cakes oozing lemon cream; whipped cream cakes; rich brown chocolate which also inundated top and sides; and raisin cake.

'And *I* had a panful of sour-cream cookies,' wailed my mother, 'fit to melt in your mouth if I do say it.'

'I guess we all know about your sour-cream cookies, Miz' Thompson. I wish you'd give me the rule for 'em,' said Miz' Bouldry as they worked together setting the table.

'Why, it's simple enough,' said my mother, lifting golden doughnuts from crock to plate. 'You take a half cup of butter, and a half a cup of sugar, and beat 'em together with a spoon till they froth. Then you beat in a couple of yolks, and about a third of a cup of sour cream, with half a teaspoonful of soda dissolved in it. Then you add enough flour to roll 'em out – just enough to handle 'em, and roll 'em thin. I sprinkle some caraway over the top and stick a raisin in the middle. Who you s'pose made these friedcakes?'

'Why, le's see.' Miz' Bouldry turned the crock around, inspecting the blue scroll on one side. 'Well, I *think* that's Miz' Whittaker's crock. She makes about the best friedcakes I ever see.'

'I'd like to get the rule.' My mother arranged the last well-rounded cake upon the plate and eyed them hungrily.

'My sakes,' exclaimed Miz' Bouldry, uncovering a pan. 'Look here. You'd know who brought *that*, all right.'

My mother leaned over, inspected the contents, and curled a disdainful lip.

'*Dried apple pie!*' exclaimed Miz' Bouldry with contempt. '*This* time of year. Wouldn't you think even that Covell woman'd know better?'

'No,' said my mother shortly, 'I wouldn't. Not her. Anybody 't 'd *dry* apples nowadays wouldn't know enough not to eat 'em in July.'

'Well,' Miz' Bouldry's tones were slightly defensive, 'I wouldn't say *that*

102

exactly. *I* dry apples sometimes – they come in handy between time when the Baldwins is gone and the Early Harvests come. But I wouldn't make a dried-apple pie *now*. And look at the crust! So greasy it'll slide off the table if we don't watch it. What'll we do with it?'

'Well,' replied my mother dubiously, 'I s'pose we'll have to set it on the table somewhere. Where is she?'

'Over watchin' the men throw horseshoes. All a-twitter. What's that, Miz Taylor?' to an approaching matron.

'I said ain't you 'bout ready?' It was the generalissimo, marshalling forces. 'If you be, I'll send the boys after the lemonade.'

Miz' Bouldry and my mother were ready.

'Here, boys! Boy-*uz!*' The *charge d'affaires* lifted her voice. 'You go fetch the lemonade now, and set it here in the shade. And some of you men bring the ice-cream freezer and keep it covered with blankets. Now, *come on, folks,*' raising her voice and brandishing a long-handled spoon which she struck on a milk pan for attention, 'let's get set down and begin. These youngsters are starvin' to death.'

The lemonade was brought and served by the dipperful to a miscellaneous assortment of handleless cups, mugs and glasses. Shouts of amusement greeted Johnnie Brent, aged seventeen, as he held up a huge moustache cup for his portion.

The minister rose and made a prayer, mercifully brief. Just before he had reached the final blessing of the food to His cause, and as the last tattered remnant of patience was wrung from hankering tongue, a mighty rumbling of wheels, a clatter of hoofs, and a clank as of loose boards were heard on the rough woods road leading into the grove.

The minister hastily ended his prayer and all eyes were turned toward the sound. Over a little rise of ground appeared the heads of a span of horses – one with a star in her forehead, the other with a piebald face. There was no mistaking them. They were our horses, Star and Baldy.

My mother gasped and rose, dropping her fork while her napkin floated to the ground.

The horses approached and proved to be hitched to an empty hayrick, the timbers of which beat a tattoo upon each other like running a stick along a picket fence. In what you might call the prow of this vehicle, like some old weather-beaten figurehead braving a battling sea, sturdy legs well apart, hands gripping the reins as of fiery steeds and he guiding a chariot of war, his old straw hat pushed back on his head, his short white beard trembling a little from the unsteady action of his foothold, stood my father.

Some of the men shouted a welcome, some rose. The generalissimo crawled

103

out from the bench where she sat and started toward him, incoherently exclaiming.

My mother remained immobile, watching him. He drew his horses to a flourishing stop and sprang out. He took the missing basket from the bed of the wagon and walked around to where she sat.

'Here,' he said shortly, 'you went off and left this. I thought I better bring it even if I did have to mess up a day's work.'

My mother rose without a word, took the basket, and began to distribute its contents. My father was urged to sit.

'Might's well stay now 't you're here,' they said. And, 'Come on, 'Lije – Mert Owen and I can lick the hide off'n you pitchin' horseshoes.'

He stood uncertainly, glancing a bit wistfully at my mother. Still she said no word.

'You set right down here in 'Miry's place,' one of the women told him genially, 'and we'll fix a place for her down here.'

'Well,' said my father, becomingly hesitant, but finally convinced that he would get no encouragement from my mother, 'I s'pose I might's well now 't I've had to spoil the day anyhow.'

The only remark my mother vouchsafed was after we had arrived home, she and I having followed dutifully in the wagon's dust.

My father was standing on the stoop watching the clouds, mumbling pessimistic prognostications of rain.

'Ought never to have lost this day,' he growled, 'and wouldn't if you hadn't a gone off half-cocked –'

My mother narrowed her eyes, thinned her lips, and looking him unflinchingly in the face, said slowly, '*I noticed you took time to shave and put on a clean shirt.*'

Caught squarely in a trap of his own setting, my father grinned like the wilful old boy he was at heart, took the milk pail, and went to the barn.

VIII

The County Fair

The one great and final event of departing summer is yet, however, to take place. This is the County Fair.

Now, the County Fair was, in Southern Michigan in the eighties, still an honest and authentic stimulus to agrarian effort. Men strove to outdo each other in quality of stock, in size of vegetables, grain, and fruit. A blue ribbon was treasured as a reward for labour and skill.

Women vied with each other in housewifery arts, baked and canned goods, and needlework; loaves of bread and cakes; jars of preserves and pickles; quilts – Aunt Catherine had one which she exhibited year after year, and always winning first prize, of seven hundred and fifty tiny pieces and a marvel of quilting. 'Dangdest piece of tomfoolery I ever see,' pronounced my father when the quilt was described to him. 'Cuttin' up perfectly good cloth and sewin' it together again. Might better go out and pick potato bugs.'

He could neither be persuaded nor badgered into visiting the Fine Arts Building where quilts, aprons, bags, and knitted counterpanes hung in profusion against the wall, even though my mother had entered a Log Cabin quilt all made of silk.

'What in time I want to go and see it hung up *there* for?' he replied to my mother's suggestion, when we first arrived and plans were being made for our various sightseeing tours. 'Ain't I seen it around for a year? And anyhow, what's it good for? Old wool comf'table on my bed's worth ten of it.'

Nevertheless, when he had visited Agricultural Hall and seen, to his illy concealed pride and satisfaction, the huge pumpkin he had entered, and the stalks of corn from his field far outdistancing all others in size and height, he

105

straightway headed toward where he might expect to find my mother, and, having found her, nothing would do but she must go immediately to see how inferior were all other similar exhibited products beside his.

'Oughta see a pumpkin Frank's got in there,' he chuckled, striding across the sandy stretch between halls. ' 'Bout's big as a wash basin. He's got some dang good apples, though – Spitzenbergs.'

Uncle Frank, between whom and my father there existed an ever-present but quite friendly rivalry, and his wife, Aunt Catherine, with their two daughters, Amelia of my own age, and Saryette, older, would be at the fair today. So would Uncle Matt and Aunt Martha, still other distant cousins, and by virtue of custom and long understanding we should all meet sooner or later, and our well-victualled hampers would be combined at noon to make a picnic meal.

My mother raised no argument – having long since learned the futility of such exercise – about the relative merits of squash or corn and a Log Cabin quilt, but viewed with wifely pride the results of praiseworthy husbandry. She did, however, although unintentionally, deal a blow to his boastful spirit, when she said, 'Why, 'Lije, that's one of these new pie punkins Frank's got. See the ticket says so – "pie punkin" – and they never grow big.'

'*Pie* punkin!' my father scoffed. 'As if anybody had to raise a special kind of punkin for pie! You been makin' punkin pie out of ordinary punkins ever since we's married, ain't you?'

'Yes,' my mother agreed, 'but that's no sign they couldn't be bettered. I've heard these punkins are finer-grained and sweeter than the others.'

My father snorted. He was, in general, none too susceptible to innovations, the old order being sufficiently satisfactory to him. Fortuitously, however, we shortly ran into Uncle Frank's family and all reference to agricultural exploits were zealously avoided.

We went together to visit the stock, marvelling over the prodigious size of the hogs, the sleek hauteur of the bulls. The women, however, were soon tired of this and went back to the Hall of Fine Arts, where they pored endlessly over quilts, spreads, tidies, and other needlework, drifting from there to the shelves upon shelves and counters upon counters of preserves, jellies, jars of canned goods, and then to the cakes, pies, and loaves of bread.

Amelia and I were starving and began to pull at our respective mother's skirts and beg to know when we could eat. Saryette was doubtless hungry too, but haughtily refused to be seen too familiarly associated with the 'children,' whose appetites frankly led them to cast wistful eyes on the peanut vender just outside the door and the booth where taffy was being pulled while you waited. Besides, she was suffering, as her mother frankly and much to Saryette's adolescent embarrassment and annoyance declared, from new shoes a size too small.

'I told her,' said Aunt Catherine, in a none too confidential tone, 'when she tried 'em on (we went and bought 'em this morning), *not* to keep 'em if they hurt. But nothing would do but she must wear 'em. Go set down, Saryette, over there where the sewin' machines are, and wait till we get ready to go.'

But Saryette, hobbling stiffly and painfully in the new shoes, refused such advice and trailed miserably in the wake of women whose interest in the various exhibits, it seemed, could never be appeased.

Before long they were joined by Uncle Matt and Aunt Martha, and in a few minutes my father was seen peering into the hall, and, spying the family, he came vigorously forward with the announcement that he was hungry as a polecat and it was time to eat.

'Where's Frank?' asked Aunt Catherine, apparently to my father's surprise.

'Said he was comin' to find you half an hour ago. Come along and let's eat. It's high noon now. Frank'll find us all right.'

Joyfully Amelia and I skipped at the heels of the men, who led the way, followed by my mother, Aunt Catherine, and Aunt Martha. Saryette, the suffering in her face intensified almost to the point of tears, brought up the rear.

Dinner at the County Fair was one of the chief events of the day and second to none. Years of prearranged custom made it comparatively easy for the various families to find each other, especially as they all left their horses and 'rigs' at the same place.

The dinner would be eaten on the grass in the shade of a group of trees not far from the race track, and toward such seclusion we would make our way after gathering the provender from the various vehicles in which it reposed.

Our own conveyance was a Democrat wagon drawn by a team. Uncle Frank boasted a small carryall, while Uncle Matt and Aunt Martha had come in a top buggy. They had but one child – Julia, a young lady who would arrive with her beau after dinner, in time for the races. They would stay for the bowery dance in the evening.

'Well, 'Miry,' said my father in high good humour, anticipating the feast to come, 'I hope you ain't left your basket of vittles to home this time.'

'No danger,' countered my mother tartly, 'seein's how you was all ready to come right along *with* us today.'

Shamelessly, he chortled as at some huge joke, although he would have been hard pressed to say who the joke was on. And with great gusto he brought the baskets from our wagon, while Uncle Matt brought theirs.

'I don't see where in the world Frank is,' Aunt Catherine worried. 'You go and get our things, will you, 'Lije?'

'If he don't show up in a minute I'll go find him,' my father offered, setting her basket down along with the others, and adding, 'You got something in there

107

smells mighty good, Cathy. Smells,' sniffing hungrily, 'like roast pork.'

'Your nose don't deceive you none,' Aunt Cathy agreed complacently, 'it's pork loin. Frank killed a young hog for the thrashers, so I cooked a roast for us.'

The roast of pork was only one of the many delectable comestibles that emerged, one after another, from the napkin-covered baskets. My father stood for a few minutes, legs staunchly spread, feet planted firmly on the grass. He wore a thin alpaca coat and a hat just a few degrees better than its disreputable counterpart which was his inseparable companion from dawn to dark on the farm. He watched the cloth being spread on the grass, the six-quart milk pan full of beans, with its nicely scored and crisply browned centrepiece of pork, which Aunt Martha placed at one end of the cloth and covered with a towel.

'Don't seem to be many flies,' she remarked, 'but they're liable to come.' A jar of freshly made chilli sauce and a cruet of vinegar were stood beside it. 'Made this chilli sauce just the way you like it, 'Lije,' she added, 'lots of onion.'

With increasing torment he watched Aunt Catherine unwrapping the roast of pork which she set at the other end.

'*Crimus!*' he cried, jerking his hat forward on his head and turning squarely on a swift heel. 'We ain't goin' to *wait* for Frank. I'll go look for him, but when I come back – *we eat*. Frank or no Frank!'

The women laughed and went on with their unpacking.

'This chicken pie's hot *yet*, 'Miry; how'd you ever manage?' exclaimed Aunt Martha as her hand touched the pan.

'I didn't take it out the oven till we's all ready to start,' said my mother, 'and then I set it on a hot soapstone.'

'Well, of all things!' exclaimed Aunt Catherine. 'I'd never thought of that in a thousand years. Let's *keep* it on the soapstone so it'll stay hot.' The suggestion was accepted, and my mother went to get the stone and place it under the pan.

Now, a chicken pie, such as my mother made, seems to have gone the way of strawberry shortcake, headcheese, buckwheat pancakes, and salt-rising bread. Even I, who have striven, with the limited resources at hand, to preserve some semblance of that homely art, have seldom been able to reach that peak of perfection, that acme of culinary excellence, which my mother managed in a chicken pie as a mere matter of routine and custom. The fault, I claim, is neither in manipulation nor in any sophistication of taste, but with the chicken.

The chickens which my mother used stepped, as you might say, from coop to pan. Nothing was lost in flavour, delicacy of texture, or tenderness of flesh in that short route between block and pot. No fowl of uncertain heritage or questionable vintage could hope to lend such lickerish bouquet to creamy gravy or flaky biscuit as did those which had grown to youthful maturity under my mother's watchful eye, nourished, so to speak, in the very shade of the block which would eventually be the scene of their undoing.

Once, indeed, when living on the outskirts of a town, I raised a dozen or so Plymouth Rocks to the prescribed age, and under conditions that seemed reasonably similar to those under which my mother practised her delectable art, and as a result achieved a pie that was not too far unrelated to that familiar of my childhood. But even then the handicaps were beyond my control, for I was not able to find a milk pan of the proper size and proportion!

In my mother's chicken pie were no alien or distracting elements such as carrots, onions, or peas. Hers was a *chicken* pie! And whether or not, circumstances and conditions permitting, I could emulate her artistry and set before you a dish of such outward beauty and inward relish, I can at least tell you how she used to make it.

In the first place she selected, for such an occasion as the County Fair, two or more husky young roosters, corn-fed and ripe with oats from the field and grasshoppers from the meadow, the flesh moistened and seasoned with a spot of buttermilk from the churn.

These were killed but a day in advance of their honourable contribution to the feast, and drawn and hung up in the woodshed overnight to mellow. In the morning they were rinsed, dried, and cut up. The leg yielded drumstick and upper joint; the back, for a pie, was deftly split down the centre, leaving an 'oyster' of meat on either side. The bones helped to support the crust. The wings were disjointed, and the wishbone separated from the breast, which was left whole until after boiling, having been severed from the neck.

These parts, together with the giblets, were now put into the kettle and covered (but just covered) with boiling water. They cooked slowly until almost tender, when they were seasoned with salt and pepper. Now the cover was left off the kettle to let the water evaporate a little and so that the remaining liquid would absorb yet more flavour.

When the meat was finally done – *done*, but not dropping from the bones – it was transferred from the kettle into a pan, which was set on the back of the stove while the gravy was being made. With spring chickens there would be no grease to strain off, but when year-old hens were used, as was sometimes done for a Sunday dinner in the spring, the fat was skimmed off.

Now, to the amount of broth remaining – and there should not be over three cups at the most – add a thickening made of three tablespoons of flour mixed to a thin paste with milk. Cook until quite heavy, then add two cups of sweet cream previously warmed, and a tablespoonful of butter. Also further seasoning if needed. The giblets are reserved for another day. The gravy when done

109

should itself have the consistency of thick cream. Season with pepper and salt.

Now lay the chicken, piece by piece (the white meat cut into suitable sizes for serving and the breastbone discarded), in the pan. Over the top is spread a rich crust of biscuit dough about a fourth of an inch thick. My mother made a sour-cream biscuit dough and there is none better, but do not give up making the pie if sour cream is out of the question.

This crust is laid on as for a fruit pie, with a slit in the centre to allow for the escape of steam. Biscuits on a chicken pie are all very well if that is the kind of pie desired, but it is not a County Fair chicken pie!

In the meantime, the remainder of the food is transferred from basket to cloth, and the party assembled – all but my father and Uncle Frank.

Aunt Catherine frets. 'The pork's going to dry out, and your chicken pie'll be all cold, 'Miry. Where in *tunket* can those men be?'

I stared in shocked amaze at Aunt Cathy. 'Tunket' is my father's word, and, used by him, savours of demoniacal worlds as hinted at by the preacher or openly threatened by the evangelical exhorter who sometimes comes into the neighbourhood to stir our dormant religious natures.

My mother feels of the pan. 'It's hot yet,' she says, and adds, 'here they come now.'

My father comes striding across the lot, a grin upon his face, his eyes full of that teasing light which to my mother's experienced intuition betrays him as 'up to something,' while Uncle Frank hurries along at his heels, a nervous frown on his face. He smiled propitiatingly at Aunt Catherine as they squat before the cloth and greet the relatives they had not seen.

'Find him at the side show with the fat girl, 'Lije?' This is from Uncle Matt, who fancies himself something of a wag. 'Or pickin' out the winner over to the track?'

'I found him,' says my father with deceptive gravity, 'wrestlin' with Satan over by the merry-go-round. If I hadn't come along just when I did he'd a been straddle of a pony this minute.'

Amelia immediately sets up a howl to be taken to the merry-go-round too. She wants to ride a pony too. I have, as yet, never seen a merry-go-round, and so devote myself, a true disciple of my father, to the dinner.

A good dinner was no unique experience in the lives of these farm people, and yet a picnic of this kind, under the stimulating influence of new and exciting surroundings, the pleasant and genial spirit of relationship not too frequently renewed, the food to which conscientious and traditional cooks had given their undivided attention, and the fact that we had breakfasted as six and it was now

nearly one – all these circumstances combined made of it an occasion to point and prick the memory for ever after.

I remember as if it were yesterday the strident sound of the 'music' of the merry-go-round, a sort of calliope operated by steam, and the eagerness with which I anticipated making its acquaintance. The shouts of children as they chased pell-mell across the dusty lot toward where, my father said, the balloon was being filled; the shuffling of feet toward the race track, and the distant bellowing of bulls, lowing of cattle, and cackling of hens.

But even more clearly do I recall the taste of that chicken pie, which, with all due regard to Aunt Catherine's roast of pork and Aunt Martha's delicious pan of beans, with new, fresh chilli sauce, was the *pièce de résistance* of the meal.

The crust, as the sharp knife slid smoothly through its rich texture, parted almost flake by flake, so perfectly was it blended, crisply browned on top and unctiously mellowed on the other side with hot, steaming gravy, deeply cream in colour and with a fragrance peculiar to the most popular bird in the world. It was a crust such as must have concealed the four and twenty blackbirds which sat before the king, for only queens in their household right could make such a crust.

My father carved the pie, counting noses as he did so to be certain that none were missed. But it was a huge pie, made in the largest-sized milk pan, and goodness knows the number of chickens. On each plate, as it was set before him, he skilfully placed a triangle of crust, and on top of it a slice of white meat and a drumstick, a thigh or other bit of the dark. The usual hoary remarks about the amazing number of legs to a chicken were made; certain known favourite portions were remembered, such as 'the part that goes over the fence last' to Aunt Martha; the neck to Aunt Catherine, 'though what in time,' the carver marvelled, 'anyone wanted that piece of leather-nothin' for'; the heart to Uncle Frank, with the time-worn reminder that 'every part strengthens a part'; a wing to my mother – 'ought to be able to fly pretty soon, 'Miry – all the wings you've eaten,' and so on until the pie was properly distributed, and my father could sit back and begin the attack upon his own well-piled plate.

In the meantime Aunt Catherine had severed the pork loin into faintly pinkish-white cuts, which, with a serving of the stuffing, disseminated an odour of sage familiarly tinged with onion and black pepper.

Then the beans went round, spooned from the pan together with a thin slice of the crisp salt pork, also an extra pan of sour-milk biscuits my mother had made for those who wanted such a base on which to ladle the gravy from the pie, a contingency apparently much appreciated, judging by their rapid disappearance. Of course, when we had the chicken pie for Sunday dinners at home, there were mashed potatoes to act as absorbent matter, but the biscuits made a very satisfactory substitute, since the gravy, owing to effective contact with the soapstone, was still hot.

Aunt Catherine had brought for my father a jar of his favourite quince preserve, quince and sweet apple, palely gold and honey sweet, and edged with that peculiar perfume which only the fragrant quince can given.

'I don't see, 'Miry' – my father was savouring, taste by taste, the delectable flavour of his favourite conserve, and lifting half-closed eyes to my mother – 'why *you* don't ever make quince preserve. Cathy'd let you have quince, wouldn't you, Cathy?'

'I've made quince preserves every year but this since we were married,' said my mother coolly, 'and you know it. I told you to go and get the quinces and some Tolman Sweets and you didn't do it.'

'We got Sweet Boughs. Couldn't you use them?'

'No,' said my mother firmly, 'you can't. They're too soft. If you'd a set out a Tolman Sweet tree ten – or even five years ago –'

But when there was any sign of blame being laid at his own door, my father always found some other topic of conversation more interesting, and he did so now.

112

To top the meal we had watermelon. Not that this fruit was any particular treat, for almost everybody grew melons, but it was cool and wet and easy to carry. Uncle Matt brought, also, a basket of luscious peaches, yellow Crawfords, of which he had several acres. And there were always cookies. These, too, lent themselves to transportation. Aunt Martha was quite famous for her sour-cream cookies. Her recipe was in my mother's dog-eared, smudged old cookbook, but in these days when even sweet cream, to cook with, is practically prohibitive, it has been little used.

Repeating the recipes of those days when the art of cookery was taught by mother to daughter, generation after generation, and when each housewife, translating a neighbour's 'rule' to her own use, knew by the artistry of touch and sight just how to measure a 'cupful,' a 'heaping teaspoonful,' or a 'pinch,' is not always satisfactory. No two of them have had the same-sized cups, but if a recipe said 'one cupful' they could gauge the amount required to a nicety that would put many a modern cookery graduate to shame. It was an art, and still is amongst a great number of women, but the women of my mother's day concentrated upon it. The woman of today is, in the first place, not taught cookery along with the three R's – and even before if not instead of – as those women were. In the second place, because cookery is not second nature to her she can save time and energy at being accurate. The attempt, therefore, to follow out the rules given in this book may not always be satisfactory, although we have tried, by our own use of them, to make them reasonably translatable. In the main, however, we present both as pleasant reading.

Aunt Catherine's contribution by way of a sweet was one whose spicy breath announced its chief ingredient before even the napkin was removed from the containing tin. Ginger cookies!

'Ha!' announced Uncle Matt, sniffing. 'That's what I *came* for, Cathy. Haul 'em out.'

Now, hopeless as the case must be for most, since Aunt Catherine's ginger cream cookies call for buttermilk, again in the interests of the chosen few we will read from the book of days gone by:

You cream a cup of butter (a substitute will do, in these parlous times) with a cup of sugar. Then you add a cup of molasses, half a cup of buttermilk, into which has been stirred a teaspoonful of soda, and the yelks (*they* said 'yelks') of two eggs. Mix these thoroughly and then stir in one-half teaspoonful each of cloves, allspice, cinnamon, nutmeg, ginger, and one of vinegar. (Why these were called 'ginger' cookies with so many other pungent ingredients predominating, I do not know, but they were.) Now you add enough flour to make a dough that you can roll. Do not roll all the dough at once (in these or any other cookies), but take a piece at a time, roll it thin, cut out your cookies (you *should* have a cutter with knobbly edge), and bake them in a hot oven. *And watch the last batch.* You know how likely one is to get careless with the last batch – leave them in while you go to sprinkle the clothes or something, and let them burn.

After the cookies have cooled, you frost them. Whip the white of the eggs to a froth, boil one and a half cups of sugar until it threads, and then beat it (for ten minutes) into the egg whites.

My mother's spice cake was one of my father's favourite, and while I cannot be certain that she ever took one to the Country Fair, she *might* have and on the chance we may as well set down the recipe.

There were half a cup of butter and a cup of light brown sugar creamed together. To this was added a cup of molasses (into which a teaspoonful of soda was stirred) and a fourth of a cup of sour cream. Add three eggs well beaten, a teaspoonful of nutmeg, a half teaspoonful of cloves, one-fourth teaspoonful of salt, and half a teaspoonful each of cinnamon and mace. Then stir in two and one-fourth cups of flour.

This was poured into a biscuit tin – a shallow oblong pan, well greased – and baked for half an hour in the kind of oven that turned a white paper to a delicate brown (375 degrees).

Frosting a spice cake was something like gilding the lily, but it was often done.

Replete and content, the men lolled back upon the grass smoking their pipes, all except my father, who got up and fidgeted about until the food was packed. Then, turning to my mother, 'Well, 'Miry,' he said, 'what you folks goin' to tend to after dinner?'

'I thought prob'ly we'd all want to go to see the races,' spoke up Uncle Matt, glancing quizzically at Uncle Frank, who, as everyone knew, had a sneaking fondness for a good horse and for a good race, although his religious scruples, for which his relations had small respect, would not allow these inclinations an honest recognition.

Uncle Frank looked up eagerly, but my father was before him.

'Not Frank and me,' he said, reproachfully. 'You *know* Frank don't approve of gamblin' –'

'Well,' interrupted Aunt Martha, who liked to witness a little sport herself, 'you wouldn't *have* to gamble, would you, just to go and see a horse race?'

'You wouldn't *have* to,' my father admitted, shaking his white head sagely, 'but you might be tempted. Frank and I are going to see the stock judged.'

There were some protestations, some pooh-poohing, some speculative and curious glances at my father's imperturbable face. 'Lije was up to something, but no one knew exactly what.

114

The dinner was finished. Chicken pie, pork roast, and beans were but remnants of their original selves. Only empty jars bespoke the quince preserves, chilli sauce, and dill pickles of a few minutes before. Aunt Marthy's and my mother's cookies, Aunt Catherine's spice cakes – all were gone. The locusts had swept the plain.

As the women rose to begin the work of clearing away and packing up, my father relented.

'Well, Frank,' he said, squinting judicially, 'I don't know but we'd better go along 'th Matt, after all. Leave him by himself and he'll pick the wrong hoss, sure's shootin'.'

But Uncle Frank surprised him. 'No,' he said, slowly, pulling what my father called his 'Amen' face, 'I guess Cathy 'n' me'll go along over to Agricultural Hall where they're judgin' the vegetables. I got a pie punkin over there –'

My father snorted and marched off across the dusty field, while Uncle Matt laughed and followed.

'You girls comin' oiver?' he turned to say.

'We're going to take the children over to the merry-go-round for a while,' Aunt Marthy told him, 'and then we'll be over.'

On the way home, jogging along at a quickened pace because the horses wanted to get to their own beds and oats, my mother said curiously, 'Where'd you find Frank today, 'Lije?'

My father chuckled: 'Layin' a bet on Life-Saver.'

'Life-Saver?'

'Yes – that's Hi Wiggin's hoss – and I be danged if he didn't win.'

'Well,' my mother was not versed in sporting vernacular, nor my father, for that matter, either, 'did Frank *get* anything?'

'Got twenty-five dollars,' he said dryly. 'I stood right behind him for five minutes and he never knew it. Heard him bet five to one.'

'Did he know he won it?'

'He didn't go round there again – they went home early. But don't you worry. He'll learn it fast enough – the old Amen coot.'

IX

Father helps to entertain The Ladies' Aid

October days ushered in the cider season and the making of apple butter. Gathering windfalls and seconds into the wagon to be taken to the mill was another of those homely tasks that gave zest to the lives of country folk, for here again you reaped the fruits of your own labour, as when, for instance, you carried your own corn to mill, and took your own meal home for your own johnnycake. When you ate buckwheat cakes in winter you thought of that hot July Fourth when it had been sown, 'wet or dry.' You smelled the bee-sweet odour of small white orchid-like flowers upheld on their stout, wine-coloured stems and heard the hum of a million wings. Like God, you looked back upon your work and called it good. With your pancakes you ate sausage ground from the meat of your own hogs, and on your potatoes milk gravy made after frying salt pork out of your own pork barrel.

When you took apples to the mill you drank what special juice you preferred. My father liked the amber liquid pressed from golden russets, and when he took russet apples to the mill he got russet cider – or he knew the reason why.

And while he was at the mill he drank copiously from a tin dipper kept for customer's use, although cider, he contended, reached its perfect state just two weeks after grinding. And so he took small loads to mill, and brought small kegs of cider home. He was an exceedingly temperate man and had small tolerance for the toper. When cider began to get hard he neither drank it nor served it to his guests.

'Don't intend to make a fool of *myself*,' he said, 'and nobody ain't goin' to blame me for makin' a fool of them.'

Once the cider became unfit for sober men to enjoy it was but a content for

116

the vinegar barrel. Except in one single instance: if he got a severe cold he would draw off a pitcher of hard cider, mix with it a powerful dose of cayenne pepper and a generous quantity of rock candy, and set it on the back of the stove to simmer. At bedtime, with his feet in a pail of hot mustard water and a blanket around his shoulders, he would sip the vicious remedy to a complete routing of the disease.

Apple butter was made in our house, in a big copper (or brass – I do not remember which) kettle on the back of the stove. Some of our neighbour women made it in a huge iron cauldron in the yard. Not the largest size, in which hogs were scalded at butchering time, but a squat black wench of smaller proportions.

My mother did not make apple butter in large quantity, for my father could not abide it. 'Butter!' he snorted. 'Might's well call bran mash "butter." If I'm goin' to have butter, I want *butter*!' (And he wanted plenty of it.) 'Don't try to give me no messed-up apple sass and call it *butter*!'

Neither was I enamoured of the concoction, so my mother made up but one kettleful, which was preserved in small-sized stone jars with a film of brandy over the top to keep it from spoiling. And she made even this, I think, in order to

miss nothing of the continuity in 'picklin' and preservin'' which ran its course in all good farmhouse kitchens from the time when strawberries ripened straight through to apples.

The Covells, however, made it by gallons and ate it, spread offensively thick, on bread, biscuits, and pancakes.

It was a tedious job, making apple butter, but less so, it seems to me, when brewed out of doors, especially on an October day with the sun beating warmly down upon your neck, and crimson leaves drip, dripping from the maple trees – sometimes straight into the huge pot itself, like some jocose gamester flipping cards into a hat.

But it took time. For instance, you put ten gallons of sweet cider into the cauldron and let it boil away to half. Then you added – a quart or so at a time – three pecks of pared, cored, and quartered apples. This you let cook over a slow fire for four or five hours. Then you added (stirring all the whole with a long wooden paddle) ten pounds of sugar and five ounces of cinnamon and boiled it until it thickened, never forgetting to stir, lest it stick to the kettle.

And there you are with your apple butter, and welcome. To be out of doors on an October day with a blue sky overhead, sun on your back, and only the gentle *llp!* with which an autumn leaf breaks its loose hold upon a parent stem to mar the silence, would be a joy under any circumstances – almost. To have to stand and stir, stir, stir, for five, six, or more hours – well, I do not like apple butter anyway.

Autumn is here. The blue of October sky grows thick, is filmed with grey. The apples are picked and barrelled, to put in bins. Baldwins, selected for long keeping, Northern Spies, Greenings, Jonathans, Seek-No-Furthers, Russets, Gillyflowers, in the bins for more immediate use, or, if the cellar is unsafe in coldest weather, in the apple pit outside. Lovely names, incomparable fruit. Cider and vinegar barrels are full.

The corn is being husked. Frequently my mother and I go into the field with my father. He has made a huskin' pin for each of us – a hickory peg with a leather protection for our fingers. These are memories of my earlier years – school did not claim me until after I was seven years old, and then only in good weather. The schoolhouse was too far away.

Sometimes it is cold and there is frost on the stalks until the sun comes out to dry it off. My mother has to leave the field early enough to go to the house and get our dinner. My father and I go when she rings the bell. The bell is fastened to a pole on the back stoop. You ring it with a rope.

Mother does not want to spend much time on dinner (for not only is there need to get the corn in before cold weather comes, but she likes to work in the fields), so she has planned meals that are easily prepared or that can be cooked while she is out.

One day there is salt pork fried in batter with mashed potatoes. The slices of pork have been freshening in cold water all the morning. Four eggs (for our family of three) are beaten, and to these are added three heaping tablespoonfuls of flour, a cup of milk, a little salt and pepper.

The pork is drained and wiped, dipped a piece at a time in the batter, laid in a frying pan, and cooked slowly until brown. What batter is left is turned into the pan after the meat is taken out, and fried. It is brown and crisp and good.

Sometimes there is an Irish stew. Pieces of salt pork and small chunks of beef have been simmering all morning. When my mother goes up about eleven o'clock, the water is nearly boiled away, the meat is beginning to sizzle. She puts in potatoes cut in half, and several onions, adds a very little water, seasons with salt and pepper, perhaps a bay leaf, and lets them steam and cook. Her ear, although she is busy stirring up batter for the dumplings and setting the table, is attuned to the song of the kettle, and when she hears the meat begin to fry she adds half a cup or so of water – no more. Ten minutes before dinner she will add a little more water and drop in the dumplings. When we are called there is a piping-hot platter of lightly browned meat, potatoes, and onion, with gravy made after these are taken up – and the dumplings, light as a feather, tinted here and there with the brown of the meat, savouring of all the other ingredients, and delectable to the tongue.

To my own private brand of the stew I add a parsnip, but I shall not force parsnips down anyone's throat. Take them or leave them. I take them.

My father liked Bubble-and-Squeak. That may have been the British in him breaking out, as I understand it is an English, and not a York State or Midwestern dish. I do not know how my mother learned of it, for I never heard of it anywhere else in Michigan, but she made it, and it was one of the things that could over-cook and be none the worse. We liked our cabbage all cooked to shreds anyhow.

Making no claims to relationship with John Bull, I cannot say whether our manner of making Bubble-and-Squeak would pass muster in his wife's kitchen or not, but this is how we do it:

Half a cupful of fat, equal quantities of pork or bacon, and butter, are put into a heavy aluminium kettle (of course we had an iron kettle, black as Sambo and sooty on the bottom; I use a Dutch oven) and brought to sizzling heat.

A medium-sized cabbage has been finely shredded – probably two quarts when done – and a number of potatoes peeled and sliced. These, together, are put into the kettle, well seasoned with salt and pepper, and a cup of hot water added; the dish is then covered and set over a slow flame for from forty minutes

119

to an hour. Time is not so important to a Bubble-and-Squeak as it is, for instance, to a sponge cake in the oven.

The mixture must be stirred from time to time, especially at first. It is served in a vegetable dish with strips of bacon, slices of salt pork nicely fried, sausages, or thin pieces of boiled corned beef placed across it. We, in recent days, have even accompanied it with pats of well-browned Hamburger.

With the corn husked and in the crib we are about ready for winter. The straw stacks in the barnyard provide bedding for horses and cattle. The mows are full of hay; there are oats in the bin.

The foundations of the house have been banked against the cold. The Covells bank their house with bedding from the barns which is mixed with coarse manure and sends an offensive odour into the house, but my father uses the raked-up leaves and quantities of firm straw, weighting them with boards. When the snow comes it will pack this down and keep our floors at least warmer than they would be without.

The woodshed is full of wood – not ranged in serried ranks, stick upon stick, nosed evenly across an arched entrance facing (smugly) upon the road as in New England woodsheds. No. Midwestern farmers, spitting tobacco juice derisively, would have met any suggestion for the expenditure of time in such precise arrangement with disdainful shrugs.

'Got su'thin else to do 'sides stand there and lay up stove wood stick at a time so's to make a show fr'm the road.'

The woodshed is usually an addition, with a flooring at one end adjacent to and level with that of the kitchen, where tubs and mops and pails and churns are kept, with the wood piled (but not precisely) on to the ground in the other end. Now the sawbuck and chopping block are brought in from the chip yard, with the saw lying athwart the one, and the axe blade driven into the other.

There may not be wood enough to last through the winter (a pile of chunks for the front-room stove are still outside), but, if not, on some pleasantly thawing day along in February the horses will be hitched to the pung and a trip made to the wood lot for further supply.

Inside the house further preparations have been made. Doors have been battened, windows caulked – we do not need to worry about getting enough fresh air. The chunk stove has been set up and the drum put in the pipe that runs through an upstairs bedroom to the chimney on the roof.

Cellar and pantry are stocked. There is a barrel of wheat flour in the latter, at least a twenty-five-pound sack of white sugar, with as much of brown, and a sack of buckwheat flour, with another of corn meal. When these are used up we shall go to mill. There is molasses in a big jug, and coffee, tea, and other groceries on the shelves. And the bean barrel – we must not forget the bean barrel, for it plays no inconsiderable part in the winter diet.

In the cellar, besides the bins of apples and potatoes, the piles of squash, turnips, and cabbage lying on the uncovered ground, there are cupboards and shelves full of canned and preserved fruits. Perhaps a pan of broken honeycomb, for my father always kept a few hives of bees.

My mother (as did all her contemporaries) began this preparation for winter with the strawberry crop. When the best and heaviest pickings were over – those that brought the best price – the preserving began, until there were dozens of glasses standing back in a dark corner in order that the delicate colour might not fade.

Following strawberries came raspberries – 'rawsberries,' we called them – black caps, and red, also transmuted into jam to be eaten on freshly baked bread for supper or used in tarts; gooseberries for a 'fool' or to be served with game; currants – many, many glasses of jelly, for this makes the best jelly roll, and is the best accompaniment to the chickens, turkey, or game dinner.

Jars of cherries, plums, pears, peaches, and small stone crocks opulent and fragrant with preserves: citron, quince, gingered pears.

And pickles! No end of pickles. First of all there was a barrel of cucumbers preserved in brine. These would be taken out as needed, freshed in cold water, and then soured in spiced vinegar. There were crocks of sweet pickles, mustard pickles, chowchow, piccalilli, watermelon rind. Bottles of catsup – chilli sauce.

A little later my father would fill a barrel of sauerkraut. Sound, hard heads of cabbage were run across and across the sharp shaving board of his own making, the fine shreds falling, being poked into the barrel. The cabbage was covered with salt, stirred, packed down, and more added until the barrel was full. Then it was covered, first with a cloth, then by a board weighted down with stones.

At first there was only the odour of freshly bruised cabbage, not at all unpleasant, but as time passed and fermentation got in its deadly work, some logical doubt might have arisen in the criminologist's mind as to the contents of the barrel. A little later, however, one would afford to stifle olfactory animadversion for the sake of a savoury dish of sauerkraut stewed with pig's knuckles.

After butchering, too, there would be the barrel of salt pork, the crocks of lard and sausage, pickled pigs' feet, jars of mincemeat, with hams curing in the smokehouse, later to hang in the cold cellar.

In the attic were bags of nuts, strings of peppers, and bunches of herbs – sage and savoury, as well as those of medicinal nature. And dried apples in some!

Ah, how pungent was the air, how teasing at every turn was the odour of this provident brewing during all the days of summer and fall. How infinitely satisfactory to the housewifely eye was this cumulative show of conserved surplus, this prescient gratifaction of anticipated need, this lavish prospicience to individual and family appetite.

Not the cleverness of a well-turned verse, nor the glut of colour in a glowing canvas, can more fully slake the thirst of creation that does this rich provision for her family's needs satisfy the true home lover. And as a remedy for boredom, ennui, or a flagging spirit, I can recommend nothing more salutary than a garden for production and a cellar for preservation of its harvest.

Once, late in October, the Ladies' Aid met with my mother. 'I haven't had 'em this year,' she said in response to some derogatory remark of my father's. 'I ought to have 'em at least *once* before winter.'

'Have 'em,' retorted my father not too cordially, 'but don't expect nothin' from *me*.'

'If I can expect *nothin'* from you,' rejoined my mother doubtfully, 'I'll be thankful. You generally manage to mess up anything of that sort some way or other.'

'I'm goin' t' the barn and stay there,' my father told her tartly, adding with revived interest, 'what you goin' to give 'em to eat?'

'I'm goin' to have 'em to dinner – they all have to get home by chore time, and you can't go to the barn and stay all day. You'll have to eat.'

'I'll go to mill,' said my father with sudden inspiration. 'I'll take me a lunch. I'd rather go without any dinner,' he added belligerently, 'than be mixed up in the mudge you'll be in gettin' ready, and the bedlam after they're here.'

My mother did not reply. She went about her preparations feverishly and hoped for the best.

'I *would* like to have something a little different from what they have all the time,' she said, fingering her recipe books and frowning. But, even with a well-stocked cellar and pantry, on a farm ten miles from town, what could a housewife find to treat her friends with that they could not get at home? And even if she had got to town, supplies in the way of rarities would have been exceedingly limited. So the only hope for distinction lay in execution.

'I'm going to have eggs pickled in beet juice for one thing,' she told my father. 'I read about that in a paper.'

'*Beet* juice!' he echoed scornfully. 'What in tunket you want to spoil good eggs for, picklin' 'em in beet juice?'

'And Dutch cheese and raspberry jam. I read they was good together.' Communing with her managerial self, she paid him small attention.

'Well, what you goin' to give 'em to *eat*?' he persisted with some show of

hospitable defence. 'Eggs in *beet* juice – huh! And Dutch cheese – that's a *dinner*, is it?'

She brought far-focused eyes back from their inner vision to rest on him.

'I'm going to have *scalloped oysters*,' she said slowly, watching for the full effect of this staggering announcement on a man who considered scalloped oysters a dish short only of what angels ate, and who did not get them three times a year.

He started at her in dumb amazement. Finally, when he could speak at all, 'Where in – where you goin' to get 'em?' he asked, his usually dominant tones husky with indignant, astonished, and abused appetite.

'Jim Bouldry's goin' to get 'em. He's got to go to town tomorrow – the meetin' Friday – to take a calf he's butcherin' –'

'Where'd you find out all this?' Injured confidence all but overrode indignation.

'Miz' Bouldry was over yest'day afternoon when you's over to Covell's –'

'If the ole coot'd ever return anything he borrowed I wouldn't have to spend time runnin' after 'em –'

'– and we talked it over. She said Jim'd just as soon. I'm goin' to get two quarts.'

'*Two quarts*!' His eyes could not leave her face. He was utterly flabbergasted by the enormity of the situation. Then – 'How many women's comin'?'

Eight. The' was goin' to be –'

'*Eight*! You expect eight women's goin' to eat up two quarts of oysters?'

'Well, I couldn't tell. If the's any left –'

My father snorted, grabbed up his old felt hat, greasy from leaning against the sides of cows while milking, and stomped from the house.

This conversation had taken place on Wednesday evening. On Thursday my father maintained an aggrieved and stubborn silence, but was seldom away from the kitchen. He kept the outside door open so much of the time going back and forth that my mother finally could stand it no longer.

'For goodness sake, 'Lije,' she cried, 'either stay inside or out. You keep the oven cooled off all the time, openin' that door.'

Miz' Bouldry had come over early in the afternoon to help my mother with her preparations, and upon her my father cast malevolent glances, as, being the president of the Ladies' Aid, she might also be the root of all his evil times.

He went out, in ominous calm, but was shortly back again, ensconcing himself in the rocking-chair by the window, shielded and fortified by the weekly newspaper, the *Jackson Citizen*.

'I'm goin' to set rolls tonight,' my mother confided intently to Miz' Bouldry. 'Potato rolls. You ever have 'em?'

124

'I never even tasted 'em. That'll be a treat, I'm sure.'

My mother had to tell her how to make them.

Miz' Bouldry remarked that they sounded awfully good, but you had to start 'em early in the morning.

My mother admitted the fact. 'But,' she contended, 'you can be doing a lot of other things while these are rising.'

My father rustled his paper, crossed his legs, and then let his cowhide-booted feet clump to the floor.

'I'm settin' salt-risin' bread tonight,' said my mother, 'so it'll be fresh –'

Father slammed the paper on to the floor beside his chair, grabbed the greasy hat from its hook, and stalked out.

Friday arrives. My father, with an old felt hat, a shade less disreputable than the one he wears to the barn, pulled well down over his eyes, having break-fasted, stands for a moment eyeing my mother in her neat calico dress, stepping briskly from pantry to stove.

The eggs have been boiled, shelled, and are standing in a pickle of beet juice. The salt-rising bread is in loaves ready for the oven. It must be fresh without being hot for dinner. The potato rolls are on their second lap. Currant jelly, mustard pickles, and pickled peaches with cloves sticking in them have been brought from the cellar and await final disposition in pretty dishes. Miz' Boundry is coming early to help with the table.

My mother brings in the oysters in shiny tins and sets them on the table. She rolls crackers, brings out the butter, milk, and pan to bake them in. She almost stumbles over my father standing wistfully – and directly – in her way. The trip to the mill hangs in the balance. A word from her – but it is the wrong word.

'Your lunch is all put up,' she said absently, 'in the tin pail – there on the breakfast table.'

He turns away. His face sags. His eyes under the old hat and the bushy brows give her a last reproachful, but unnoticed look. He picks up the pail, lingers a second at the door, goes out. We hear him 'g'lang' to the horses in an unconvincing tone.

'I'd of liked him here to unhitch their horses,' Mother remarks as he clatters away, 'but he'd of been a nuisance. Anyway, they're all coming in two rigs.'

They come, unhitch their own horses, and put them in the barn. They lay their things in the spare bedroom. They sniff and smell and offer to help.

'My land, Miz' Thompson, what you *got* 't smells so good?'

They put on white aprons – lawn, muslin, starched fruit-of-the-loom, cambric – and take their sewing. They are making things for a fair.

'If the's anything I can do, you jes' holler, won't you?'

125

The table is spread. On top of the old cherry bureau where my mother kept towels and linens, and in the top drawer of which my father treasured fish lines and seed catalogues, stands the bellflower sauce dish in which are plum preserves. Beside it, the eight small sauce dishes and a plate of tea cakes.

'My, those tea cakes look good,' Miz' Bouldry exclaims on one of her many trips to the dining-room, bearing a large glass dish filled with a cabbage salad made with sour-cream dressing. 'You must of made them this morning, too.'

'They're nothing to make,' disclaims my mother modestly. 'Just break an egg in a teacup and fill it up with sugar and heat it. You have to turn it into a bowl to beat it. Then you add a cup of sour cream and a teaspoon of soda and a little salt and some nutmeg and flour enough to stiffen it. I baked 'em in patty pans. They baked in between the bread and the rolls.'

The ladies put up their work. They file into the dining-room, again exclaiming over aromatic odours and tickling sights.

I am relegated to the kitchen with a hot roll, a tea cake, and earnest promise of more to come. The door is almost closed between, but not quite. I hover near to tease my nose and accommodate my ear.

The dinner proceeds with much treble of laughter, clamour of talk, and rattle of dishes. Hours, it seems, pass. I am but recently accomplished in telling time

126

and I do not believe my eyes, which try to convince me that hardly more than ten minutes have passed.

In the confusion even I do not hear an arrival. Presently, however, just outside the door I am startled from a tantalising reverie by my father's voice.

' 'Miry! Hey – 'Miry!'

Silence in the room. A chair is pushed and my mother comes out, a frown on her flushed face. She opens the outside door.

'What you – what in the world –'

'You got a bird cage, 'Miry?' It is my father's most sanguine voice. My mother's face clouds with suspicion.

'No, you know I ain't got a bird cage. What you got there?' He is secreting something under his coat.

'I got a bird. I'll show you.' He steps inside, in full view of the dining-room door, and takes from underneath his coat – a baby skunk, a little black and white cunning thing. He sets it on the floor. The ladies scream, shove back their chairs, hold up their skirts, babble. Miz' Lizzy Martin, always slightly hysterical, springs to the seat of her chair.

My mother stamps her feet. Tears of rage are in her eyes.

' 'Lije Thompson, you take that animal out of here! You hear me? You take it *out!*'

My father shoves back his hat, opens his eyes, stares at her in grieved surprise.

'Why, 'Miry!' he said mildly – *too* mildly. 'I brought it to Delly. I won't hurt nobody. Baby skunks ain't got no smell yet.'

I am enamoured of the funny, waddling, nosy little creature and I bend to it.

'Don't you *touch* it!' cries my mother. 'And if you don't get it out of here, 'Lije Thompson, *this minute*, I'll – I'll –'

Without a word my father picks up the offending – but not offensive – little creature and goes out the door, I tagging.

Outside I glance at him. He is snickering. My father! Actually snickering. He puts the skunk down and it waddles away.

'Found it out by the barn,' he chuckles. 'Took it along with me – for a ride. I thought they'd like to see it. Don't *you* think it was pretty, dawtie?'

I do, but I do not know what to make of my father. He swore he would not come inside the house while the Aid was there, and now he brings a baby skunk – to amuse them.

We go to the barn, unhitch the horses, feed them, linger.

'Jininy Christopher!' exclaims my father, looking longingly towards the house. 'I'm hungry. Ain't you?' I am. Starving. Pretty soon we see my mother coming.

127

'You come along into the kitchen, both of you,' she scolds, 'and eat your dinner. And I hope you're satisfied, 'Lije Thompson. You about spoiled everybody's appetite.'

We slink into the kitchen. The table, apparently, has been cleared. There is an unexpectedly generous amount of scalloped oysters left. Plenty of cabbage salad, some eggs, mashed potato, bread and rolls.

The ladies, considerably subdued, are having their dessert and tea.

My father and I bend to our enjoyment. We do not talk much. We just eat.

And then on a warm, blue-gold day in the very last of October, we take our final walk through the garden – my father and I. The last – until another year.

The strawberry bed and raspberry shrubs are loosely mulched with leaves and straw. Rhubarb and horse-radish, their brown frost-bitten leaves lying flat and withered upon the ground, are also given light protection.

Stalks from the garden sweet corn are gathered and thrown to the cattle. The ground where so recently vegetables grew lush and full of colour has been raked free of frost-killed vine and leaf. Summer is over. The garden has conceived and borne, and suddenly we remember Old Wart! Old Wart and the Stri-pud Family, and all the guards and guardians, benefactors and friends, whose gay and glad, or dumb and silent, offices contribute to the final accomplishment of our purpose. And, somewhat to our dismay, we are confronted with a great silence. There are no robins busily engaged with leaf or twig, or rebellious worm. A few jays are noisily conspicuous as the grey cat which follows at our heels is sighted, but their cries are less vociferous. There are no young now to protect.

The Stri-pud Family, long since grown dull of hue and slothful in disposition, has gorged itself upon mole and meadow mouse preparatory to a long fast – and disappeared.

X

Breakfast, Old Style

'Jumping Christopher!' I heard my father say. 'What do you mean by setting pap down in front of me? Where's *breakfast?*'

I do not remember what it was that provoked this outburst, but it must have been some experimental item of the menu, a faintly suggestive forerunner, perhaps, of the orange juice, cereal, toast, and coffee which have now become the standardised American breakfast.

My father came to the breaking of his night's fast after a preliminary hour's wrestling with chores, and he went from the table to a day's work in which fields had to be ploughed, seed sown, hay cut, grain reaped, corn husked. To men like him, breakfast meant meat and potatoes – the chief staples around which the meal revolved. And meat usually meant pork in one form or another, commonly salt. Variations there were, to be sure. In the butchering season there was fresh pork, and liver; later on there would be sausages, or smoked ham and shoulder; in early spring and summer, eggs. After a rainy day, when the men had not been able to work in the fields, there might be fish. But always there were potatoes. Sometimes they were boiled, with an accompaniment of milk gravy or creamed codfish; again they were sliced and crisply fried; or they might be baked, with pink slices of home-cured ham and gravy.

Our home-cured ham was like nothing I have seen or tasted since. The difference between commercially smoked hams and those cured in the little slant-roofed brick shanty out behind our house is traceable, I suspect, to the fact that the former were not smoked with corncobs. Some of the commercial houses burn hickory sticks, yes, but no corncobs. If you have ever smelled freshly shucked corncobs burning, you can imagine what that odour did to a ham.

Breakfast, Old Style

When it came to cooking the ham for breakfast, my mother sliced it about one fourth of an inch thick and freshened it in cold water brought to warm on the back of the stove. It was then drained and wiped dry. In its own firm border of fat it was fried slowly to sweet perfection, and then removed to a hot platter. The remaining fat was allowed to reach a smoking heat (an additional amount being added if necessary from a surplus store), and into this my mother sifted flour to a bubbling paste, stirring while it seethed and browned. When enough flour was added to absorb the fat, warmed milk was stirred in gradually and evenly to make a gravy having the consistency of heavy cream. It was then salted and peppered to taste.

Our breakfasts did not begin with fruit or fruit juices. If we had fruit at all, it was eaten with friedcakes and cookies; but in general fruit was reserved for supper, fresh in season, preserved the rest of the year.

My father liked eggs for breakfast – two or three, at least – and he wanted them fried or boiled. If boiled, they must be boiled hard. But a hard *fried* egg was his abomination.

Few women can fry an egg as my mother could. Her technique was perfect, and the result was no leathery mass of frizzled white and broken yolk, but an intact globule of filmed yellow set in a circle of delicately congealed albumen. She fried eggs in the fat from bacon or ham, whichever happened to be in use. This fat was made hot – sizzling but never smoking; if it was too hot, it was drawn to the back of the stove until there was no danger of browning the thin edge of the white before the yolk was cooked.

Each egg (taken from the nest the night before) was broken separately and gently into the sizzling fat, and never were so many introduced into the spider at one time that their edges mingled. Then my mother stood by, spooning the hot fat over them until the whites were coagulated but not hardened. They were then, at the exact moment of perfection, taken from the spider with a pancake turner and laid on a warm platter along with the ham, rosily tender and faintly browned, or bacon, done to a curl but never to a crisp. An egg fried in this fashion, its qualities and virtues instantly sealed within it by a hot, sweet coating of honest fat, cannot be too great a tax upon the digestive machinery. Numberless were the fried eggs my father consumed, and he bore up under them until well past his eighty-fifth birthday.

A poached egg is another dish apparently difficult to achieve, but it was not beyond the scope of my mother's culinary art. The water, she maintained, should be at the hard-boiling point when the eggs are slid into it, one at a time, and after that it must be allowed only to bubble. This is accomplished by drawing the pan to one side of the stove, while the bubbling water is spooned over the eggs until the yolks are filmed and the whites 'set.'

For the more inexperienced housewife we might add that a teaspoonful of vinegar will help to keep the white of the egg in shape and does not affect the flavour. But it is care and attention that bring the perfect result.

'You have to stand over things,' my mother said, 'to make 'em right.' She was none too fond of housework, often preferring a day in the garden or field, but she was extremely conscientious and 'stood over' her cookery until she herself, a critical epicure, could pronounce it good. Then she felt reasonably sure that my father would at least find no flaws in it. He was a man of just if not equable nature, but little given to praise.

'If you think a thing's good,' I have heard my mother say, 'why can't you say so?'

'If I don't say it *ain't* good,' was his reply, 'you'll know it is.'

Salt mackerel was one of my father's favourite dishes. It came in a 'kit' or small wooden pail and smelled to heaven when it was opened. For breakfast a fish was

washed, scraped on the inside, put in cold water the night before, and set on the back of the stove (in which there would be no fire) to freshen. In the morning the water was changed and the frying pan ('spider,' we called it) brought forward to heat slowly. When everything else was ready to serve, the water was drained off (we said 'dreened' off) and the fish allowed to pan-broil for about ten minutes. Transferred to a platter and dotted with butter, it made a most palatable accompaniment to boiled potatoes. Nowadays it would not be considered acceptable unless the platter were cluttered up with a few sprigs of parsley, an embellishment that would have been lost upon my father, to whom 'weeds' by way of garnishing were a matter for ribaldry.

With our modern conveniences I have found that after rinsing the fish in the morning, to wipe it, brush it with melted butter, sprinkle it with pepper, and broil it, is perhaps an improvement on the old spider method, although I feel a twinge as of treason in admitting this.

Fried mush came along in the fall, after the first harvest of winter corn and before the pancake season set in, and again in the spring when the batter pitcher was washed and put away. Fried mush for breakfast followed a preceding supper of mush and milk. My mother made her mush by sifting yellow corn meal, fresh from the mill, into an iron kettle of boiling salted water; with one hand she sifted the meal while with the other she stirred it with a wooden spoon. It was then drawn to the back of the stove to bubble and sputter and spurt for an hour or longer – and woe to you if it happened to spurt on to bare hand or arm while stirring.

Whatever mush was left over after supper was packed into a greased bread tin. In the morning this was sliced and fried in hot fat, and eaten with butter and syrup.

We did not often have maple syrup. There were a few maple trees on our place and my father would occasionally tap them to get enough sap for a drink; or, as a special treat, my mother would sometimes boil down a little sap into sugar. Although other farms about us boasted a 'bush,' and maple syrup was not an unknown luxury in Southern Michigan, it was not common as it is now. Instead, we had sugar syrup – white and brown sugar boiled together in a small amount of water – and it answered the purpose very well. And, of course, the covered glass dish of honey – honey in the comb and fresh from the hive – was as customary an accessory to the breakfast table as the butter dish.

Frequently there were hot breads. Usually sour-milk biscuits, since there were always sour milk and sour cream on hand. Both of these are a considerable luxury, but in my humble opinion no baking-powder biscuit yet devised can compare with the 'sour milk and sody' kind.

The few suggestions that I shall make for hot breakfast breads are but variations of what I had in my mother's home and in the homes where, a few years later, I taught country school.

For cinnamon rolls I take the usual baking-powder biscuit recipe (two cups of butter, four teaspoonfuls baking powder, half teaspoonful of salt, two tablespoonfuls of shortening, and about three-fourths of a cup of milk), add another tablespoonful of butter, roll it out into a sheet about one-fourth of an inch thick, and brush it with soft butter. Over this sprinkle a mixture of brown sugar and cinnamon. Roll it up like a jelly cake and cut into slices an inch in thickness. Lay these in a greased pan and bake as you do biscuits.

Another variation of the same biscuit dough is to make drop biscuits by adding about three tablespoonfuls of milk to the rule, beating well, and dropping from a spoon into greased muffin tins. Sprinkle a little sugar over the top, put a raisin in the centre, and bake.

My mother made a coffee cake with yeast that required raising, but I found the following very satisfactory: Mix together a fourth of a cup each of butter and sugar. To this add the yolks of three eggs, the juice and grated rind of a lemon, a tablespoonful of water, and beat. Stir in two cups of flour into which two teaspoonfuls of baking powder have been sifted, and, last of all, add the beaten white of eggs and mix thoroughly. Spread not too thickly in a rectangular biscuit tin and sprinkle over it with a mixture of one-half cup sugar and one teaspoonful of cinnamon. Then add finely chopped nut meats and bake.

Now if you want to make an apple cake of it and have it for tea, use the same rule, but, instead of spreading sugar and cinnamon, first brush with soft butter, then cover with thinly sliced apple, and sprinkle with the sugar and cinnamon.

The 'sour milk and sody' biscuits my mother made called for two cups of flour, one teaspoonful of soda, one-fourth teaspoonful of salt, three tablespoonfuls of shortening (half lard, half butter), and a cup of thick sour cream. The soda and salt are sifted with the flour, and the shortening worked into this. Use a mixer, or finger it lightly. The heat of fingers melts the shortening and forms a paste, whereas shortening should be mixed *with* flour, not into it. Add the sour cream, knead lightly, pat or roll out, cut into rounds about three-quarters of an inch thick, lay in a greased pan, and bake quickly.

For Sunday-morning breakfast (because they require longer cooking) nothing could be better than popovers, and the following is a good rule (but I never saw a popover in my mother's house!). One cup of flour, one-half teaspoonful of salt, one cup of milk, two eggs. The eggs are beaten until very light and the milk added, then the flour and salt sifted together. Now beat again (these modern contraptions do have their uses) until very light and then pour into *hot* greased iron muffin tins or glass baking cups. The oven should be very

133

hot (450 degrees) for twenty-five minutes. Then lower to 300 degrees for twenty minutes. This is a small recipe – about enough for three reasonably hungry people.

Then of course there was johnnycake, but for this you *must* have buttermilk. A pint of good rich buttermilk, three eggs, two tablespoonfuls of butter (melted), a pint of corn meal (yellow), a teaspoonful of salt, and one of soda.

Beat the eggs, whole, until very light and then stir in the buttermilk, corn meal, and the soda, which has been dissolved in a tablespoonful of hot water. Now add the salt and butter, mix it all well together, and pour into a rather shallow baking tin, well greased. Lard is better for greasing tins than butter.

Friedcakes were always, month in and month out, as much a part of the first meal of the day as coffee. I think my father would have considered it a personal affront to ask him to make a breakfast without friedcakes. He did not 'dunk' them, and he did not hold with men who dunked them. I remember his once reproving a hired man who had the habit. 'Well, Curt,' he said, 'see you been hobnobbin' with the Lunkers.' (The Lunkers were a family that lived down on the crossroads and were known for their slovenly habits.) I felt a little sorry for the man, who laughed awkwardly and soon after left the table.

Cookies, too, were a regular addition to the breakfast menu – molasses cookies and sugar cookies, which more favoured children than I were allowed to 'soak.' Soaking a cookie is not the same as dunking it. Dunking is accomplished by holding one portion of the friedcake while dipping the other, but soaking is crumbling the cookie into a partly finished glass of milk and eating it with a spoon. To this my father also objected. 'If you want *dough*,' he said, 'lick the dish. If you want cookies, *eat* cookies. Don't spoon 'em.' I ate cookies at the table, but spooned them when the occasion allowed. I also licked the dish.

In winter, breakfast took on new meaning, for then the fried mush, johnnycake, or ordinary plain bread gave way to buckwheat cakes. There were differences in taste regarding the lacing of these cakes. Some insisted that the only proper sauce was butter; others preferred sugar and thick cream; still others liked to pour over their cakes the hot brown fat from fried ham or pork. But the general preference was for butter and syrup. If maple syrup could be had, so much the better.

After the buckwheat crop was harvested, my father, never a patient man, could hardly wait for the pancake season to open. My mother did not like to begin too early, for, like other habits, once started it was difficult to break, and the routine lasted until spring, without respite. This meant added details in an already crowded day of petty tasks: the cakes had to be 'set' the night before, and while the rest of us were at breakfast she had to stand over a hot fire to cook them, for she would not compromise with her belief that buckwheat cakes should be eaten direct from the griddle, a theory in which my father upheld her to the teeth. Ours was not a large family, but there was often a hired man, frequently a visiting relative, sometimes the itinerant preacher, a seamstress, or perhaps the ragman spending the night. And my father himself was no light eater. So, if my mother seemed to dally about beginning the ritual, she had good cause.

My father, however, was not one to let excuses stand in the way of the execution of his desires. 'It's about time to get the batter going, ain't it?' he would remark on a frosty night of late October. Each time my mother offered some reasonable objection to explain why that particular night was not the proper occasion. This went on into early November, my father growing more and more impatient. I remember once when, after he had repeatedly raised the pancake question without effect, he attempted to take matters into his own hands.

My mother was frequently called upon to sit up with some sick neighbour, and it was on one of these occasions that he tried to speed the pancake season. Unfortunately he had small knowledge of the chemistry of food and absolutely no imagination with which to offset his lack. I, being a very small child, was put to bed before my mother left the house, and it was not until next morning that cataclysmic noises in the kitchen warned me that sometime untoward was afoot. I rushed in to find the whole top of the stove covered with a greyish, foaming mass which had gushed from the mouth of the batter pitcher to overflow upon the floor in rivulets, pools, friths, firths, lagoons, narrows, guts, and whatever other forms a seething fluid may take. Over it all stood my father, a heroic figure with bald head flushed, fringe of white hair and beard awry, steel-grey eyes snapping with temper and dismay.

At that moment my mother appeared. She opened the outer door and stood speechless on the sill.

My father faced her in belligerent but wordless challenge. Finally he exploded: 'How many yeast cakes do you *put* in the dang things?'

Without answering, she stepped inside the door and took from him the mop with which he had been trying to clean up the mess. 'Go along out,' she said tersely, 'and tend to things you know something about.'

He went, and when he had gone my mother burst into gales of laughter that fairly rocked the now-empty batter pitcher standing on the stove. 'He must have put in a dozen yeast cakes,' she gasped, and then, more soberly and not without some measure of scorn, 'serves him right! Meddling with things he's got no business with!'

135

But it seemed to me that, however right it served *him*, it was she who bore the brunt of his unhappy venture.

That night after supper, while my father was doing his chores, my mother busied herself with the ingredients that go into buckwheat cakes. When we were finally seated about the lamp for the evening, my father perusing the weekly *Citizen*, my mother with her mending basket near, she remarked casually, with a gleam of mischief in her mild eye: 'I set the cakes tonight.'

'Time!' said my father, and the incident was closed.

Sausage was a frequent accompaniment of buckwheat cakes. Its odour and flavour still haunt me, proof that some mysterious ingredient in its making has been lost to mankind. As I pondered this culinary conundrum, the answer suddenly came to me. It was the *sage*. The whole secret lay in the sage. We grew our own in a neat little row along the garden's edge, picked and dried it, and crumbled it – aromatic, fresh, and pungent – into the meat. But, on second thought, perhaps the pepper may have had something to do with it, too. For my mother ground her own pepper in a little wooden mill that she held in her hand or on her lap – a little mill made, I should think, of maple, with a tiny drawer underneath to hold the piquant, pungent spice. Yes, certainly it is the pepper

and the sage that have grown tame along with too much time- and labour-saving propaganda. These deserve, it seems to me, a place on the shelf of whetting memories.

What did children eat at those breakfasts of meat and potatoes and pancakes? Why, we ate meat and potatoes and pancakes. We drank quantities of milk, ate acres of bread, consumed butter by the pound, and we also ate doughnuts and cookies by the dozen. My pleasantest memory is of breakfast in a nice warm kitchen on a cold morning, with my little glass mug of milk (it had 'A Good Girl' printed on it in gold), a huge slice of bread all buttered at once (there was not a single book of etiquette in our community), some little pancakes cooked just for me, and my eye on the cookie plate.

And some of us, at least, lived and throve. I think doubtless we should have been the better for more fruit, less fried food. On the other hand, we were husky urchins living mostly out of doors, breathing fresh air night and day. Those old enough to go to school had often to fight their way through drift and sleet for a mile or more, exercise quite likely to aid in the assimilation of any amount of breakfast fuel. Smaller children were bundled into leggings, as I was, arctics, coats, mittens, and hoods, and sent out to roll in the snow with the dog, or wallow back and forth with their fathers to barn, fold, pen, coop – shovelling paths, bedding the horses and cattle, giving fowls fresh water, feeding the sheep. And all of us, big and little, had chores to do.

Children were ill – no attempt was made to avoid the routine which they were supposed to weather, mumps, measles, whooping cough – and usually survived through good luck and sometimes good nursing. More dread diseases – diphtheria, scarlet fever, and 'lung fever' – over which there was an appalling cloud of ignorance, brought too frequently fatal results. But from the consequences of our hearty breakfasts we seldom suffered. And on a winter's day we were never sent off to school or play on a sketchy and hastily swallowed meal of cold cereal and cold milk, as children often are now. If to eat a hearty breakfast meant getting up at six o'clock, or even before, we got up, and ate with the family, and went out sustained by both good cheer and good food.

Men, too, in those days certainly lived by their breakfasts, but not by breakfasts alone. Supper was the least important of the day's three meals, because by then the rigours of the day were done, but dinner – at noon – was a 'fillin' ' meal, designed to sustain the menfolk through a lusty afternoon's work in the fields.

The dinner menu varied with the seasons. The best time of the year seemed to be in the fall. Then, after butchering, we would have fresh meat – spareribs, pork shoulder, loin, liver. And a little later in the season one neighbour after another would kill a 'beef critter,' a sheep, or a calf, sharing with each other and thus continuing the succession of fresh meat as long as possible. In a good many homes the shotgun, fish line, and trap contributed to the fresh meat supply.

In winter our diet was more monotonous, but we had the cellar to draw upon, as I have already described. At that time women did not know enough about canning to preserve any great quantity of fresh vegetables except tomatoes. Between Christmas and the first 'greens' of spring our only vegetables were Hubbard squash, cabbage, 'beggies,' and such others as could be kept in the cold cellar or root house. A few years later carrots were recognised as fit for human consumption, and my father raised celery and parsley, but in general farm vegetables were of the coarser type.

I spoke of the monotony of winter meals, but as I re-read the foregoing paragraph and recall the roster of the shelves as given in a preceding chapter, I cannot work up much compassion for our sad state. Within the past few years I have seen times when to have stepped into cellar or pantry such as we knew then would have seemed like entering Aladdin's cave of treasure. To be sure, we lacked the fresh vegetables which are abundantly available today in almost every market the year round, but, if we now have them, we do not have the generous supply of butter fresh from the churn with which to dress them, or the bread fresh from the oven to accompany them. And, altogether too frequently, we do not have the money with which to buy them.

My mother and her contemporaries were as stubbornly partial to certain utensils in which they cooked their favourite dishes as my father was to the iron 'kittle' in which he insisted doughnuts must be fried. It made no difference, for example, that the iron spider was heavy and unwieldy, and that its handle was so short and got so hot that an inadvertent touch without a holder would sear the flesh as quickly as the fire itself – all frying *had* to be done in the spider. Used as it was over a wood fire, the outside was encrusted with burned-on soot, but the inside was as smooth as the softest satin.

Every housewife of that day had such a spider, and she treasured it in the same way she did her pie tins after they had been slightly burned and browned. You could not, so my mother said, bake a good pie in a brand-new tin, so the tins were used for this and that until they were properly tempered and seasoned.

Then there was the iron kettle in which *only* could a proper Irish stew be made; and the well-seasoned dripping pan, into which went, in turn, the turkey for Thanksgiving, perhaps a goose at Christmas, and, at odd times between, spareribs, a roast of beef, or a whole pig with an apple in its mouth. Like the spider, these utensils were tempered by long use and smoothed by frequent scourings.

Cleanliness was a fetish with my mother. There were few commercial cleaners on the market when I was a small child, but there was the brick board on to which dust from a fine brick was shaved with an old knife, and with this and a piece of soft cloth the steel knives and forks for the table, as well as the kitchen cutlery, were scoured. Wood ashes were used to clean the spider when fish was fried – to remove the odour – and were generally employed for other purposes as well. Soft soap also had its part in keeping chopping bowls, cutting boards, and wooden-topped tables clean. Of course all housewives made all their own soap, except, perhaps, an occasional fancy perfumed cake for the spare bedroom. Baking soda was used to remove stains from the inside of tea and coffee-pots, and to sweeten milk pails and pans.

Keeping things clean in that day was a task not to be lightly undertaken. Water was heated in the tea-kettle (also of iron, pot-bellied and black as night) and in the reservoir at the back of the stove. You had to use it sparingly. The sink, if you had one, was of iron, with wooden drainboards reduced to the splintery stage by much scrubbing. There was no smooth enamelware, no lightweight aluminium. Utensils were black, ugly, heavy, and unwieldly. Dripping pans, saucepans, and kettles had rolled edges under which grease and dirt could collect if allowed.

In spite of all this, my mother's creed was firm. 'Things *must* clean,' she said, 'or food won't taste good. Don't think the coffee's to blame when it's the pot.'

The hired help in those husky days were almost always the social equals of the family itself. There were few 'furriners,' and although a good many hired men drifted into the country from cities where work was scarce, especially during haying and harvesting, they were almost always American born. The hired girl came from some neighbouring family where girls were plentiful enough so that one or more could 'go out to work.' They were trained by their mothers and grandmothers in housewifery ways, and there were few of the daily tasks, indoors or out, that they could not perform. They could not only make a shirt, but they could also wash, iron, or mend it as the need arose, and sometimes they married the man who wore it.

The hired girl and the woman she worked for were always on equal terms. They worked together, sat and sewed together, and sometimes took turns in going to the little country church. They confided in each other and praised each other.

'Your bakin'-powder biscuits is always just a *mite* lighter'n mine, Miz' Eddy, and I don't know how you do it. I use the same rule to a T.'

'Mebbe it's the oven, Marthy. But if they are, your piecrust's flakier'n mine. I just can't get a flaky piecrust the way you do.'

When the 'girl' married one of the boys in the family, the two would set up their own housekeeping on a rented farm or in a small house on one of the parental acres. Sometimes a beau came wooing from another farm, to meet with jest and joke from the boys on *her* farm. Sometimes she never married, but just stayed on and on, cooking, washing, cleaning, attending her friend the mistress through childbirth, and nursing the children. And sometimes she nursed her friend the mistress through a final illness and then married the widower. If so, it was a satisfactory arrangement all around, and one approved by the neighbours. She was used to the house, the children were used to her, and a man with a family had to have someone – so why not her? Marriage, however won, was built on the solid foundation of *home*, in tradition and example. Divorces were few and unpopular.

Equally friendly were the relations with the hired man, although he was a little less likely to marry into the family. Just the same, he ate with the family on all occasions; he washed in the same basin and used the family comb. He held the baby, played with the older children, teased the girls, commented freely on family affairs, and asked to have his favourite dish cooked. In short, the hired man was just as good as anybody else, and did not hesitate to remind the family of this fact if they chanced to forget it.

My Uncle Frank was what the neighbours called 'a little nigh.' He not only hated waste, as did all thrifty farmers, but he was a shade less than generous in all his dealings than most. His wife set a bountiful table, for Uncle Frank was a hearty man, and, while he was exceedingly hospitable in urging food upon his guests, he viewed the greediness of children with disfavour and the robust appetite of the hired man with hostility.

The hired man was particularly fond of butter. One day at dinner Uncle Frank watched him for some time as he plastered one knifeful after another on to bread, potatoes, and whatever else happened to be on his plate. At last Uncle Frank could contain himself no longer, and said, casually but pointedly: 'Tom, I see butter's gone up to twenty-five cents a pound.'

Tom, undismayed, affected a lively interest in the fact. He looked over at the depleted butter dish, and, reaching across the table, took half of what was left on to his own plate, then remarked with the air of a connoisseur: 'Well, Frank, it's wuth it. That's danged good butter your womern makes!'

XI

Little Runt

Thanksgiving was the day of days, after my father's birthday, for intimate family gathering and unstinted feasting. There were times when my mother resented the invasions of my father's numerous relatives, but on this day she welcomed numbers. Only numbers could provide suitable scope for her prowess as a cook. A meagre family of three, even though augmented by a hired man, was no excuse for the array of meats, vegetables, cakes, cookies, pies and puddings and bread, and the orgy of preparation which, on this day, were her great delight.

Such preparations were sometimes in progress far ahead of the eventful date, as in one particular instance when Aunts Hanner and Sophrony, Uncle Frank and Aunt Catherine, with Amelia and Saryette, their daughters, and Uncle Matt and Aunt Martha, who were all within reasonable visiting distance, were invited to partake of the Thanksgiving dinner.

That year a young sow mistook, in the exuberance of her youth, the proper season for mating and, in early fall, presented herself with a lively litter of thirteen husky pigs. All but the thirteenth. The thirteenth was one too many for the calculations of nature and he, being shrivelled and feeble, was rooted out of place by the others and repudiated by his mother. My father brought him into the house, scrawny, unable to stand on his little spindling legs, blear-eyed and livid, and laid him on my mother's lap.

'Runt,' he said succinctly. 'Thought maybe you'd like to put him in a box or something.'

My mother placed an old apron on a chair and laid Little Runt upon it. Then she warmed some milk, stuck a finger in it, and let the little creature suck it off.

This he did repeatedly until, satisfied and warmed, he fell asleep.

In a few days a bottle was substituted for fingers, and in a week Little Runt not only had a chance but was well on the way to normal pig life. He was given a small box near the kitchen door, and all day his contented grunts, and more demanding squeals as mealtimes drew near, were heard.

It became my duty to dump the box, give him fresh straw, and see that he had water.

'Fat him up,' said my father, eyeing Little Runt speculatively, 'and we'll have him for Thanksgiving dinner. I've always wanted roast pig for Thanksgiving.'

My mother reminded him that he had had roast pig once some years before at Uncle Frank's house and that he had not liked it. In fact he had pronounced the whole dinner an utter failure because he had not liked the pig.

'Fed on sour milk,' retorted my father tersely. 'Flabby and tough. Frank's too tarnation stingy to feed a pig fit for roasting. Feed the critter up,' he advised, 'on sweet milk and corn-meal mush, get him nice and fat, and we'll ask the old curmudgeon over here Thanksgiving and show him what a roast pig's like.'

So Little Runt was fed on sweet milk, fresh corn meal and vegetables, and he throve to a state of porcine beauty beyond all rightful expectation, considering his early stage.

He was tolerated by Shep, who, after eyeing him for a few weeks with cold disfavour, finally accepted his presence around the yard with mild lenience, and even allowed him to sprawl full belly-wise in the sun.

He tagged at my mother's skirts when she looked for eggs and when she fed the hens, always sniffing at everything in his path, continuously expressing his affection, gratitude, and general satisfaction in life, with cheerful little ungh-ungh-unghs or a high-pitched protesting squeal.

He allowed me to wash and scrub him until his skin was pink and smooth and firm as that of any buxom farmer's child, and made no serious objection to the still pinker ribbon sometimes tied about his neck. With his little round quirking nose, his small bright watchful eyes, and his upcurled wiry tail, Little Runt was a pig to be proud of – and one to warrant the growth of an affection on the part of the family which without doubt he appreciated and returned.

My father watched the process of his growth with evident approval. He was not as large as the other members of his immediate family, but he was well proportioned, and his contours were such as to stimulate the imagination of the gourmet.

'Going to look pretty good spread out on a dripping pan 'long about the twenty-ninth,' observed my father early in November, sitting on the back stoop and watching Little Runt nuzzle the cats away from their rightful pan of milk.

Mother made no reply, and as for myself I looked at my father with positive distaste. How could he be so unfeeling, actually smacking his lips at the thought of Little Runt spread out in a dripping pan! Poor Little Runt! I ran and grabbed him up and held him, kicking, squealing, protesting, on my lap, glowering at my father as at an ogre of bloodthirsty proclivities.

'Just how,' queried my father at another time, as Little Runt grew in stature and rotundity, 'do you make the stuffing for roast pig?'

For quite a few moments my mother did not reply. Her face reflected none of the gustatory fervour that lightened my father's, and she even turned her head away from where he was scratching Little Runt's back with a stick. The subject seemed to lack favour with her as it grew in the approval of my father.

Surprised at her silence, he set his penetrating eyes upon her and said, 'Huh?'

'Stuffing?' she repeated with apparent reluctance. 'Oh, I make it 'bout the same as for turkey. Little more sage, maybe.'

'Umm-m!' My father made pleasant reminiscent sounds in his throat. 'Sage! You picked the sage yet?'

'Yes,' she replied, 'long ago. Savoury, too, and all the herbs.'

143

'Put any onion in it?' With the pertinacity of the obstinate mind, he seemed intent upon teasing his always latent appetite.

'Yes,' said my mother, shortly, 'plenty of it.'

After an interval of silence in which Little Runt kept up a running commentary on the salubrious effect of back-scratching, he asked solicitously, 'You begun to save up dried bread yet?'

My mother lifted her hands impatiently. 'Good gracious!' she exclaimed irritably. 'What do you think that pig's goin' to be – an elephant?' With which crushing remark she left the room.

And then, all of a sudden, Little Runt took to following my father about, his nose close to the heel of the man whose favour he seemed to think it vital that he should gain. At first he was merely tolerated, with much berating and execrations bordering upon the profane.

'Get out of the way, you dod-rotted, blame little ole fool,' my father would exclaim, accompanying the admonition with a thrust of the boot designed to caution rather than to harm. But within a short time, as Little Runt, with porcine stupidity, ignored his master's indifference and increased his noisy attentions, the companionship seemed to be encouraged.

'Come along then, you old cuss-fool,' he would invite leniently, 'you get under foot and you get your tarnation nose knocked off.'

But Little Runt, with the assured experience of all the dumb brethren of the farm in the futility of my father's pretentious bluster, trotted close to heel and thrust his pink nose curiously into the pit his master was digging for winter vegetables, or pried into whatever task he was about.

And into my father's voice crept an extra note of bravado when he referred to the succulent dish so soon to be served upon his plate.

'You goin' to have anything besides roast pig?' he asked of my mother in what was intended for a casual tone, but which certainly bordered upon the anxious.

'Potatoes,' replied my mother promptly, 'and squash, and boiled onions –'

'I mean any – any other – *meat?*' he persisted in a manner strangely hesitating for one of his forthright spirit. 'I didn't know as just the – the – pig'd be enough.'

'Well,' said my mother judicially, 'I didn't know as 'twould be, myself, seein' how your mouth's waterin' for it. So I thought I'd roast a turkey. Old Tom's good and fat.'

My father's face lightened unwarrantably.

'May be's well,' he replied carelessly. 'When you want him killed?'

'Anyway, not yet,' replied my mother shortly. 'You can kill him when you butcher the pig.'

144

My father rose and went outside, where we heard him vociferously greeted by Little Runt, with his own response made in loud and threatening tones. My mother smiled with her eyes, but her lips were tightly shut as she went about her work of clearing away supper. After that he talked loud and often of the Thanksgiving feast so rapidly approaching. He asked my mother if she was going to put a raw apple or a cooked one in Little Runt's mouth. He enlarged the daily rations of meal and milk and even gave him a few small ears of corn. He cut up pumpkins and fed him bit by bit. He stood by the pen (Little Runt now had a shelter all his own, so, as my father said, he 'wouldn't run the fat off') and scratched his back and talked to him, always loudly and truculently of his approaching fate when anyone was within hearing.

My mother grew tight-lipped and stern. She listened to his enthusiasm concerning the succulency of young pork flesh in stony silence, and refused to discuss with him the details of the dinner as his apparently sadistic tendency grew. As for me, I mourned for Little Runt and avoided my father. I likened him to the giant of fe-fi-fo-fum fame, and prayed something would happen to save Little Runt. I even opened his pen and let him out, adjuring him to escape before his day of doom, but the little fool would always follow back to the pen, ungh-unghing and wee-weeing in stupid conceit.

With the imminent approach of the festal day, my father haunted the kitchen. He watched the filling of the cookie jars – grey stone for sugar cookies and a brown glazed one for molasses. He sampled each batch of doughnuts as it came from the kettle and said they were not quite up to my mother's usual standard. He took, at my mother's invitation, repeated tastes of the mincemeat under preparation and with the air of a connoisseur suggested the addition of a *lee-tle* more boiled cider, just a *speck* more of allspice, and, finally, with a tentative glance at my mother's face, just a *touch* of brandy. Adding and mixing and stirring and tasting, together they brought the concoction to what both were satisfied was a state of perfection.

One Saturday about two weeks before Thanksgiving my father came into the kitchen where my mother was making mince pies.

'You know this old receipt book,' he said genially, holding it up and tapping the cover lightly with his spectacles.

'Yes,' said my mother, eyeing him with suspicion, 'it was my mother's. What of it?'

'You use any of these receipts?' he queried in unctious tones.

'Sometimes. What you want?' she asked bluntly.

'Why, I don't want anything, 'Miry. What makes you ask that?'

'Because,' she said witheringly, 'when you talk smooth like that you're generally up to something.'

'I found a receipt,' pursued my father, sitting down in the rocking-chair by the window and adjusting his spectacles, 'I thought maybe you'd like – unless you've seen it.'

'I guess I've seen pretty near everything in that book several times over,' she told him coolly. 'Which one is it?'

He cleared his throat and read: 'English Way of Roasting Pig.'

'Huh!' exclaimed my mother, pinching down the edges of her crust with a competent thumb. 'You don't need to read me anything about English ways of roasting pigs. American ways are good enough for me.'

'Still,' persisted her obstinate spouse, 'this is different. You listen.'

She listened.

' "Put some sage, a large piece of saltish bread, salt and pepper in the inside and sew it up. Observe to skewer the legs back [That's a queer way to put it, ain't it – 'observe to skewer the legs back'] or the under part will not crisp. Lay it to a brisk fire [Must have been one of these hearth fires they used to have] till thoroughly dry; then have ready some butter in a dry cloth and rub the pig with it in every part. Dredge as much flour over it as will possibly lie, and do not touch it again till ready to serve; then scrape off the flour very carefully with a blunt knife, rub the pig well with the buttered cloth, and take off the head while at the fire; take out the brains and mix them with the gravy that comes from the pig." Gosh, 'Miry, sounds like some heathen performance!'

'So it is,' interrupted my mother sharply, 'and nobody but a heathen'd set and gloat over it!' And, hastily wiping her hands on a towel that lay near, she made an excuse to go to the buttery. My father waited with unwonted patience until she returned and then resumed:

' "Then take it up and cut it down the back and breast, lay it into the dish and chop the sage and bread quickly as fine as you can [Seems as if they could have done that before], and mix them with a large quantity of fine melted butter that has very little flour. Put the sauce into the dish after the pig has been split down the back and garnished with the ears and the two jaws. Take off the upper part of the head down to the snout. [I thought we'd cut off the head once.] In Devonshire it is served whole, if very small, the head only being cut off to garnish with as above." '

'Well!' observed my father, closing the book and rising, 'if that's the way they roast a pig in England I'm glad I'm a Yankee.'

And all the time Little Runt was innocently wee-weeing as my father approached his pen with the tri-daily rations, and sniffed and sniffed his fat content as he stuffed his little pink hide to his own doom.

146

Two days before Thanksgiving my father beheaded Old Tom, filled the big brass kettle with boiling water, scalded and plucked him. The wing tips were cut off whole for brushing the hearth and the tail feathers were finally gathered up and tied together in the form of a duster. He was then handed over to my mother with the somewhat ostentatious remark, 'There's your turkey. I'll fetch the pig in tonight. Stib Obart's goin' to butcher him for me.'

Turning in the door as at an afterthought, my father continued, '*You* don't want his head cut off, do you, 'Miry? The way that book said the English do?'

I never saw my mother roused to a pitch of real anger in all her life. Her sense of humour was keen and her understanding of my father was deep, and as for *throwing* anything, she never so much, I believe, as tossed a ball. And yet for a moment I thought that, certain as the world, she was going to throw the bowl of suet she was crumbling full at his head. So did he, I think, for he made a quick exit.

The bowl came down heavily on the table and my mother lifted a corner of her apron to wipe her eyes. As for me, I was openly bawling. No miracle had happened, no ram in the bushes to save Little Runt. Stib Obart and his hideous knife stood, a menacing shadow, in the too near future.

As for my father, there was no understanding him. He had seemed, especially in the last few weeks, to love Little Runt. He had fondled him, scolded him, even called to him when not in sight. He had scratched his back, and now he talked callously about cutting off his head.

After supper that night he set off with Little Runt, squealing, kicking, protesting, in a box in the back of the pung, it having snowed enough during the day to warrant the use of that vehicle.

My mother and I sat close together in the sitting-room by the evening lamp, she mending, I playing half-heartedly with paper dolls. Our ears were strained to catch, in imagination only, since the Obarts lived a mile or so away, the shrill, harsh cry of fear and pain, our eyes seeing crimson splotches on the sweet new snow.

Along about nine o'clock my father returned. He put the horse in the barn and then came stomping up to the door – the back kitchen door where a light had been left burning.

'Where you want him?' he called lustily.

'Put him down cellar,' my mother replied. 'On the table.'

She did not rise, she made no enquiries. She took me off to bed and sat with me until I slept.

My mother always stuffed her meats at least twenty-four hours before roasting, so for one day Old Tom hung head down in an outer room to cool, while the little pig lay supinely upon the mahogany table in the cellar. I crept down once for a peep at him, but the sight of the now too-white form sticking stiff, inglorious feet in the air was too much for me. I ran whimpering upstairs to the comfort of my mother's arms.

Early in the morning of the day before the feast a big bowl of stuffing was prepared – sage, savoury, marjoram, and thyme crumbled between the fingers into well-moistened bread; onion chopped and added; salt and pepper, and lastly the generous half cup of melted butter, with frequent tastings as the rite proceeded.

When it was finally enriched to my mother's satisfaction, the turkey's ample cavities were filled and sewed. The wings were trussed, the neck bent back; and then, dipping her hand in the moist stuffing, my mother rubbed the entire exterior of the bird with the savoury dressing. Over this paper-thin slices of fat salt pork were laid, and the bird, now in the roaster, was again consigned to the cold room to await his final call to glory.

On Thanksgiving morning the family were early astir. There was much to be done. The company would begin to arrive before eleven and my mother wanted to make progress before they came.

'Once your Aunt Catherine gets here, and your Aunt Hanner, there'll be so much talk I shan't be able to think.'

The little pink carcass was brought up as soon as breakfast was over, and at sight of it I burst into tears, and fled the kitchen, but could not remain long away. And neither could my father.

Immediately after the early breakfast and the completion of his morning's chores he had shaved, scrubbed his bald pate until it shone, and brushed the fringe of silvery hair and short white beard to a state of bristling order. He put on a clean white shirt and over it a fresh blue 'wamus,' a sort of short coat made of denim which, with him, took the place of a house coat. He was then ready for the festivities and began to watch the clock as well as the progress of affairs in the kitchen.

Particularly he was interested in the preparation of the pig for roasting.

'You *do* rub it with butter, don't you?' he demanded with eager interest.

'Who said I didn't?' countered my mother a shade tartly, as well she might with a small girl following her about, tiptoe with excitement, and a restless, curious man under her feet when she had a thousand things to do.

More irritable than I had ever seen her she seemed as she rubbed the tender flesh with the buttered cloth and sprinkled it with flour, and especially impatient she seemed with my father, who watched her every move with avid eyes.

And when he asked her if she was going to 'observe the skewer the legs back' she lost patience with him entirely. 'I wish you'd get out of the kitchen, 'Lije Thompson,' she told him hotly, 'and go and *do* something. Fill up the woodbox and the water pail, and *stay* out.'

He went, and so did I, for I could bear neither the sight of Little Runt in his defenceless state of abrogation, nor my mother's face as she bent over him. I shared her unhappiness in this sacrifice of what seemed like one of the family to man's baser needs, and together we held an unspoken but united animosity toward my father's apparently heartless concern for Little Runt.

The elevated oven, as I remember it, was a monstrous affair, but I cannot recall whether both the turkey and the pig were roasted at the same time, or whether first one was baked and then the other, but I do most definitely know that the odours, as my mother opened the door to baste the browning meats, were such as neither the voluptuous nose of my father nor my own ever-susceptible palate could withstand, and soon we were both back sniffing greedily at the redolent air.

Holidays and company-coming were usually the occasion for exuberant spirits on all our parts, for excited anticipation, chatter, and comment, but today my mother's grim face cast a shadow upon the day and there was small pleasure in the prospect of a bountiful table, the *pièce de résistance* of which was to be our so recent companion.

Time, however, is no respecter of emotion, and as the hours wore on the tempo of activity increased. Potatoes were pared and left in a kettle of cold water that they might not discolour. My father brought a huge Hubbard squash up from the sand pit in the cellar, and broke it into small pieces with the axe. He was not a handy man when it came to household procedures, but on this day he seemed unusually eager to make himself useful. Indeed, as I look back upon it now with mature judgment, I recall that his manner was, for a man of his independent and somewhat truculent disposition, singularly prop-itiatory.

After chopping the squash into parts, he scraped out the seeds and loose pulp, emptied the waste, and stacked the green and golden sections neatly on the kitchen table.

'Anything more I can do, 'Miry?' he enquired solicitously, only to meet with a suspicious glance from my mother.

'Yes,' she said shortly, 'you can peel the onions.' This was more than he had bargained for, but his quick, rather shocked look into her face brought him no quarter.

'They're in the butt'ry,' she said tersely, 'and you better peel 'em all.'

149

To my certain knowledge, my father had never up to this time peeled an onion or any other vegetable in his whole life. Nor had he ever washed a dish or in any other way shown any inclination toward self-preservation so far as the preparation of food was concerned. My mother often said that if he were left alone he would probably starve to death before he would cook himself a meal. And now there he was standing at a kitchen table peeling onions and surreptitiously wiping his weeping eyes, while my mother stepped briskly from room to room, her hands filled with one delectable dish after another, her lips grimly set, her eyes unsmiling and hard.

The onions peeled and standing in a pan of water, my father scrubbed his hands in the tin basin, wiped them on the roller towel hanging on the back of a door, and then, without a word or a glance in my mother's direction, put on his hat and escaped.

To a little girl accustomed to basking in the warmth, the approval, the impregnable security of a united family life, there was something oppressive and sinister in the atmosphere of this morning. Still, there was assurance in the wealth of delicacies stored against the day.

In the buttery were the pumpkin pies that had been baked earlier in the morning, the ruffled edges of their biscuit-brown crusts encircling smooth plaques of yellow custard coated with a thin, almost transparent veil of dappled russet and bronze.

From these were exhaled a most flavoursome odour reminiscent of autumn days when the lusty vine strewed its golden fruit wantonly against the corn, mingled with the spicy fragrance of cinnamon, nutmeg, ginger, and all-spice.

Alongside these were the mince pies baked a week earlier, stored in cold and now brought out to be warmed at the last moment on the oven top. Marked with an 'M' they were, and through the delicate tracery of the letter one caught tantalising whiffs of meat preserved in heavenly juices, apple, currant, and raisin all welded into one sweetly tart aroma, itself bathed in the effluvious bouquet of rich old brandy, such aroma as the Olympian gods may have dreamed of but never met.

Here, too, arranged in glass sauce dishes, pickle dishes, preserve dishes that were the possessions of but ordinary women, but which are now elevated to the high estate of the rare, were pickled peaches with the pointed ears of cloves dotting their amber sides; mustard pickles to neutralise the too-rich content of the young pork; bowls of crimson cranberry sauce, globules of currant jelly for those who did not favour the fruit of the bog; long, green sections of cucumber pickle standing upright in the crystal dish swinging censerlike in its silver frame with hanging fork beside.

150

And then, here was the comp'ny! Uncle Frank and Aunt Catherine with the two third cousins, Saryette and Amelia. Amelia, fat-faced and smug, the known possessor of a cigar box filled with candy hearts (the kind that said, 'Will you be my girl?') which, upon the occasion of a return visit, she would let me look at but never touch; and Saryette, who had been known to faint away upon being unduly chided. A talent openly cultivated, my father declared, and one that a good sound spanking in more formative years would certainly have prevented. And not too late yet.

The horses having been attended to, and greetings exchanged, Uncle Frank and my father betook themselves to the front room, where the round chunk stove sent vibrations of heat quivering upon the air. Aunt Catherine unfolded a voluminous apron from her sewing bag, tied it around her ample waist, and laid capable hands to the setting of the table. By the time Aunt Hanner and Aunt 'Phrony had arrived with the remainder of the guests, the table was dressed in its long white linen cloth, the tall silver caster and its five crystal bottles as a centerpiece, and the various relishes, jellies, and preserves clustered about it.

At two o'clock the family were seated around the board, the turkey, his crisp juicy skin bursting here and there in the plenitude of his stuffed insides, before my mother at one end of the table, and the rosy-brown, crackling-coated, well-rounded porcine frame before my father. The little pig's legs, now untied, squatted wantonly beneath his well-padded hams and shoulders, his golden belly crouched upon the table.

Scorning what the English recipe was pleased to describe as garnishing, my mother had left the head intact, with upstanding ears and truculently extended snout. In his mouth was a beautiful red apple, polished (for I saw him do it) on the sleeve of my father's wamus, and inserted by him, at my mother's request, into the open mouth after the pig was placed on the table. Over his haunches a small crisp tail upcurled with a realism seldom equalled in culinary lore.

A beautiful creature he certainly was, smoking, steaming, reeking of succulent juices, and rich with fragrance of herbs sun-ripened in our own garden.

'How do I carve him?' enquired my father with suspicious alacrity, poising his instruments above the plate before him, and ignoring the expectant silence with which my mother always recognized the religious tendencies according to Uncle Frank. Dismissing the too-previous question as unheard, my mother turned in the direction of her guest and politely enquired if he would like to ask a blessing.

Uncle Frank, knowing my father's contempt for an attitude that he considered lacking in sincerity, waved dismissal of the courtesy.

'Best way to thank the Lord,' observed my father benignly, slipping the razor-edged knife well under the skin of the succulent pig and watching with round eyes the free rich juices run, 'is to fall to and eat. Pass up your plate, Cathy, for some of the best roast pig you ever tasted in your life. 'Miry'll tend to the turkey.'

One by one he filled the huge plates – a slice of well-done pinkish-white young pork, a bit of crackling brown skin, a spoonful of mashed potatoes whipped with cream and butter to a very froth of delectable flavour, a spoonful of the stuffing. My mother, brooding eyes intent upon the work before her, was carving the turkey – a thin piece of white meat rimmed with chestnut-brown, a bit of the dark, laying the pieces on the side of the platter and transferring them to the plates as they reached her.

Finally all were taken care of except Mother, and Father, holding his knife above the riddled carcass, said with odd gusto, 'Now, 'Miry, I'm going to cut *you* a nice juicy slice.'

My mother, struggling to control herself, said, 'I don't care for any, thank you,' and burst into tears.

We all with one accord turned to look at her, the guests in astonishment, I with streaming eyes and sobbing breath, and my father in consternation and apparent anger.

'Well!' he said with what would seem to be a righteous indignation. 'I been wonderin' if you was goin' to show some signs of feelin', 'Miry. Wait a minute.'

He threw down his napkin, shoved back his chair, dashed through the kitchen, snatched his hat from a nail as he went – all, it seemed, in one whirlwind of motion, his guests staring after him in rooted amazement.

My mother wiped her eyes, and in a shamed and shaken voice said, 'It was Little Runt. I fed him by hand – he t-tagged us around – I didn't see – h-how he *could* – I d-don't know what he's up to –'

But her tearful, broken apology was interrupted by a confusion of the strangest sounds – a mingling of the sharp, staccato squeals of a struggling pig, snuffles and grunts, my father's voice raised in affectionate abuse, the back door opening.

'Hol' your tongue, you tarnation fool-cuss' – and there he was, white hair flying, hat awry, and in his arms, legs kicking, snout wrinkling, small pink body squirming, was – sure as you live – Little Runt!

'There!' said my father, wheezing a bit from exertion. '*Now* what you think?'

Every chair had been pushed back. Food was cooling on the plates. I had flown from my chair to greet Little Runt and pull him into my lap.

'Why!' cried my mother, gasping. 'What – where –!'

'Well,' said my father, flinging off his hat and smoothing hair and beard, and beaming with satisfaction in his own exploit, 'when I see you [addressing my mother] was really *bent* on roast pig for dinner [my mother lifted her hands,

152

opened her mouth, and remained silent], I thought I'd have to fix it some way to save Little Runt's hide. You see,' he now turned eagerly to the dumbfounded guests, 'this was a runt we raised by hand and he took to following me round, so when it came time I didn't have the heart to – so I took one of the others over to Stib Obart's instead.' Then, with a swift turn from the still silent table, he addressed the contented, adventuring pig.

'Come along now,' he said, and, executing a flank movement, caught Little Runt by his hind leg and hoisted him to his arms, admonishing him sonorously.

'Thanksgiving for *you*, all right, you fool runt, you, but hogs don't celebrate it in the house,' and in an uproar of squeals and protesting kicks Little Runt was borne away.

' 'Lije,' said Uncle Frank sententiously in his absence, 'always was a sentimental old fool.'

'Let me,' urged my mother politely, ignoring the remark, 'give you some of the turkey.'

Almost immediately my father was at his place washed and brushed, passing the squash, asking for the cranberries, urging second helpings where the first were hardly touched. He made complimentary and utterly absurd remarks about Aunt Catherine's fine looks, joshed Uncle Frank about a horse trade he had recently made, and otherwise disported himself as the benignant and genial host. To my mother he was especially considerate, but could not at the last deny himself the pleasure of a subtle thrust which would reflect upon his own clever scheming.

'Well, 'Miry,' he said handsomely as the guests, replete with food and hospitable content, drove away in the dusk and blue-white snow and creeping night, 'ain't you glad *now* that I done something about Little Runt?'

'You better go feed him,' said my mother dryly, which he did. And, so far as I can remember, Little Runt may have lived to a fat old age and died in his pen.

XII

A Simple Christmas

Christmas, in the days of my childhood, was not the occasion of the orgy of spending and sophisticated entertainment that it now is. Santa Claus was to me neither a real person nor a dominant myth. He was supposed to have had a hand in fashioning the renewed wardrobe of Annette, the only doll I ever owned, a mature and haughty creature with china head and elaborate chignon. But there was a certain familiarity about the fabrics from which her garments were made that was reminiscent of my mother's piece bag, a fact quite logically arousing some childish doubt.

An orange in the toe of the stocking, a well-polished apple oddly resembling those in our own cellar, a stick or two of pep'mint, cin'mon, or horehound candy, constituted the contents of the average stocking, and quite satisfying they were, too, to a generation of children not sated with useless, destructible, and often soul-destroying junk as are ours of today.

Christmas Day was lifted, in our home, only a few degrees above the plane of any other simple holiday. We had company, certainly, but because of the imminence of New Year's Day, my father's birthday, when the clan would congregate, this was confined to such relics of our immediate community as were likely to fare worse. Such, for instance, as Miz' Lou Esty, the itinerant seamstress who went from house to house to sew and mend, and who, after the unlamented demise of her husband some years before the time of my own memory, had no home other than a room in the Bouldry house, where she went, as she herself said, to catch her breath between seams.

Miz' Esty was an interesting person because of her intimate acquaintance with neighbourhood affairs, but not a woman of superstitions, as proved by her

154

own related experience.

Someone of the neighbours had broken a mirror and Miz' Esty, who had been present at the time, flouted the consternation of the family and their trembling apprehension of the prophesied seven years of bad luck.

'*I've* broken mirrors,' said Miz' Esty with complacent assurance, 'and *I* never had no bad luck. I remember one time we was moving; there was a big dresser in the back to the wagon and it bumped into something and the glass smashed to pieces.'

My mother, to whom, with my father, she was relating the incident at the supper table, said:

'And you didn't have any bad luck?'

'Nothin' I can remember. Of course,' she added negligently, 'Esty died that fall, but I wouldn't count that.'

'Neither would I,' my father agreed when, later, he and my mother were laughing over Miz' Esty's evaluation of misfortune. 'Knowing Hod Esty, *I* wouldn't.' For Hod Esty, as all the neighbours knew, was a shiftless, worthless toper, refusing to work, and spending, when he could get his hands on it, the money which Miz' Esty earned. Justified, as anyone would feel, was her curt summary of the situation.

Old David H. was another derelict whom I remember sitting at our Christmas board upon at least one occasion when Miz' Esty was also a guest. David H. was a first-rate carpenter but one whose itching foot had become entangled in the treacherous vine, and whose wife, her endurance finally exhausted, had turned her back upon his bed and board, taking their one child, a little girl, with her.

My father was utterly intolerant of drunkenness, and, but for the mellowing influence of his own approaching anniversary, would probably never have listened to my mother's gentle plea for David H. as a Christmas guest.

'What in tunket you want that old sot around on Christmas Day for?' he demanded indignantly. 'You already *got* Miz' Esty. If you want more company, why don't you ask the Covell young-uns and give 'em a square meal?'

To his surprise and apparent consternation, my mother took up the challenge.

'I'm glad you thought of it, 'Lije,' she said genially. 'I'll ask 'em today.'

And ask them she did, four half-starved little Covells, all girls, ranging in age from five to twelve, who stared greedily when my mother told them they were to come to dinner, and appeared on the eagerly anticipated day scrubbed and brushed and dressed in their poor best, two hours ahead of time.

Nevertheless, David H. was also invited, but my father himself did the asking. 'Met old David H. down the road,' he informed my mother largely one

155

day, as having devised a creditable plan. 'Asked him to dinner, Christmas. Keep him sober *one* day, anyway.'

David H., aside from being a man of skill in his craft, was a considerable character. He had some degree of education, was well spoken, and he had a mind. Pursued by propagandists of teetotalism, as he frequently was, he would shake his head and say, referring always to himself in the third person:

'No, David H. ain't goin' to sign no pledge. When David H. puts his foot down *hisself*, he'll quit drinking. *But – David H. ain't goin' to put his foot down!*' However he came soberly to Christmas dinner, sleekly shining, pomaded, and proud.

On the day before Christmas my father came home with a large, fat goose, dressed and drawn, dangling its long neck around his feet. The goose was singed, pinfeathered, and washed. Not merely rinsed with a dash of cold water, but put into a large dishpan of quite hot suds and scrubbed with soap and baking soda. A proceeding my mother accorded to most fowls, especially the large ones, turkeys, geese, and ducks.

'They're oily,' she explained, 'and then they wallow in the dirt. Nothing but soap and hot water'll get 'em clean.'

From the soapy water, the goose was rinsed in hot and then cold water, which plumped her up and gave the skin a youthful appearance.

I once knew a spinster lady of uncertain but reasonably predictable years who, having set her heart upon gaining the attentions of a man considerably younger than herself, tried the same treatment upon her face.

'You take an old hen,' she said, quite seriously, 'and you dip her first in hot water and then in cold, and she'll plump up and her skin'll look fresh as a daisy. I don't see,' she added ingenuously, 'why it wouldn't work on a human as well.'

Apparently it did, for the nuptials were not long after announced.

My mother's reason for the hot and cold rinse, however, was not so much to give the semblance of youth, as to cleanse and freshen the skin.

The stuffing for the goose which was my father's favourite was made of mashed potato and onion. About a cupful of chopped onion was lightly fried in a piece of butter as big as a walnut, with salt and pepper, and added to the mashed potato which had been generously treated to a seasoning of cream, butter, pepper, and salt. It must not, however, be mushy. The cavities were stuffed with this and sewed; wings, legs, and neck were trussed. And then my mother mixed together salt, pepper, and a little finely crumbled sage, and with her fingers rubbed this over the surface of the fowl.

If the goose was over a year old it was parboiled or steamed before roasting. If a spring goose, it was put in the roasting pan with a cupful or so of water and some butter and frequently basted. The giblets were cooked seperately, chopped, and added, with the water in which they were cooked, to the gravy made from the juices in the roasting pan *after* the excess fat had been poured off.

Of course this fat was saved and treasured, for 'goose grease' was an invaluable remedy for cold-on-the-lungs, and equally useful as a lubricant for shoes that had been wet with snow.

Sundry herbs were grown in our garden as they were in most farm gardens. The leaves were picked when full grown, dried and kept, to be finely crumbled as used. These were doubtless less convenient than the small containers of today and belong to that pleasant past when an attic garlanded with herbs and festooned with peppers was part of the accepted preparation for winter, but there are still those who believe in their greater potency, and a row of sage, savoury, bay, marjoram, and thyme I would also urge, flanked by chives, shallots, scallions, mint, and parsley in every garden. With these and a few cloves of garlic at his hand, and an old, well-seasoned chopping bowl for his use, even the most finical gourmet should be able to fashion at least a few dishes to his liking.

157

Miz' Lou Esty came early to help with the dinner. Under my mother's direction she prepared a dish which was in our family a prime favourite chiefly as an accompaniment to roast pork, but which proved equally acceptable as an accessory to the dinner of roast goose. This was a combination of apple and onion, and for which I have no other name.

To make this you first gauge the amount of onion by your fondness for that vegetable, but as my family was – and is – what you might call onion-minded, we are never chary of that lusty bulb.

In my own practice I use a cast aluminium saucepan in lieu of the heavy iron spider which my mother had, and into this I put perhaps two tablespoonfuls of fat – depending on the amount I am making – either salt pork or bacon fat with another of butter. When this is hot, place a generous layer of thinly sliced onion on the bottom and let it cook until soft but not browned. This is salted and sprinkled with pepper. Now over the onion goes a thick layer of tart apple, unpeeled to keep the shape, cored and sliced across. This is sprinkled with sugar, the dish is covered, and the whole cooked until the apples are tender and the onions slightly browned on the bottom. If there is any danger of scorching, the dish must be stirred, of course, which will break the apples, but the taste will not be impaired. This can be used as a garnish or served separately.

Boiled onions there were too, for in spite of the apple combination, as well as the flavour of the stuffing, no poultry dinner would have been complete in our home without the dish of silvery cloves dressed with a little cream, butter, and seasoning.

The table was spread with the second-best cloth of white linen, the best being reserved for the later, and greater, occasion of my father's birthday. Miz' Esty laid the plates one at each place, the way she said they were now doing in town, where she had recently been sewing, instead of piling them chin high before the server as was the usual country custom. We did not even use the gold-banded china for Christmas, but the sprigged rose pattern that my mother had bought not so long ago with carefully hoarded egg money.

The steel three-tined forks and knives with ivory handles lent their elegance. The bellflower goblets, sugar and creamer, the spoon holder, as well as the sauce dish of stewed cranberries (picked by my father in a neighbouring bog), sparkled like jewels. Into the goblets Miz' Esty stuffed the napkins rolled cornucopia-fashion, another innovation from the city. That was one advantage in having Miz' Esty come – she brought new fashions, new customs and styles, into our more remote homes.

The centrepiece I remember well, for I had rubbed and polished every apple – Northern Spies, Jonathans, and Greenings – to a shining splendour, and heaped them in the latticework fruit dish of white glass.

A tumbler of wild grape jelly quivered upturned upon a small glass plate – wild grape because of the muskier tang. Pickled watermelon rind – translucent pink shading to opaque green – drenched in a luscious syrup of citron and lemon flavour reposed on a small dish shaped of two graceful hands (severed at the wrists) of alabaster white. Bread, moist, fresh, and creamy white, was piled on a round glass plate which had a sheaf of wheat in the centre, and the words, 'Give Us This Day Our Daily Bread,' embossed around the edge. A blue glass plug hat held toothpicks.

We knew nothing of salads, now considered indispensable, and we ate our nuts sitting around the evening fire instead of having them shelled and salted at the table. But even so I cannot feel that our table lacked in zestful relishes or accessories. Instead, I have a vision of plenty, appetisingly prepared.

Dessert, of course, on Christmas Day, consisted on plum pudding, and plum pudding only. On Thanksgiving there were pies – pumpkins and mince. On New Year's there would be pies, mince and apple and pumpkin, but on Christmas the pudding stood alone, a monarch amongst desserts.

It had been made weeks before, in fact at the same time that the mincemeat for Thanksgiving pies was in preparation. Contrary to her usual custom, my mother had a rule for making her plum pudding. In general her cookery was of so simple an order, consisting of dishes frequently repeated, as to need no rules, but this pudding was made but once a year, and so when the time came for its concoction she took down from its place beside the clock an old cookbook and opened it to a page slightly discoloured from a tracing finger rich with fruity contact.

I think, perhaps, she also liked to read the words, for she spoke them aloud, and I can remember seeing my father draw his chair within hearing distance, adjust his spectacles, craftily lift a newspaper before his face, and give ear to the rich phrasing which fell alluringly upon the air:

' "Take of cold beef suet one pound, string it, and crumble into a wooden bowl and chop very fine. Mix with one cup of brown sugar. Into an earthen bowl put half a pound of currants, an equal amount of raisins, seeded; one-fourth pound each of candied citron, lemon, and orange peel, sliced to transparent thinness with a very sharp knife on a board; one ounce each of cinnamon, ginger, nutmeg, cloves; one teaspoonful salt (or more); cover these with one pound of flour and stir with fingers until fruit is coated.

' "Now add two cups of fine bread crumbs, four eggs well beaten, one cup of milk, one-half cup of brandy. Mix and stir to a stiff dough. Now set this aside to *assimilate flavours* for two hours or more.

' "Have ready a large flannel pudding bag, square in shape. Wet this, wring

159

as dry as possible; lay the cloth on the table, butter the centre, and sprinkle with flour. Place this over a bowl and pour in the pudding. Tie firmly with string, leaving a little room for the swell but not much. Put a plate in bottom of a large kettle of boiling water, set the pudding on it, and let boil for seven hours. Serve on a round platter with a small amount of brandy poured over, to which a light is applied after the room is darkened. A sprig of holly adds to its tastiness. This pudding (*if not eaten*) will last for weeks and is as good cold as it was hot." '

Could anything afford pleasanter reading than that? Is it any wonder that my father's newspaper dropped and sagged, or that his spectacles were pushed inpatiently to the top of his head, the better to hear?

Upon one occasion I remember his remarking to my mother as her voice dropped, regretfully, the last phrase, 'We might try that "applying a light" sometime, maybe, 'Miry, huh?'

'Yes, and likely burn the whole pudding up,' was her unsympathetic retort.

When the pudding, after the proper 'assimilation of flavours,' was finally consigned to the pot, the kitchen became of all rooms that could be imagined the most desirable. Every corner, every inch and ell, was permeated with the rich bouquet of 'assimilated' raisins, currants, lemon, ginger, citron, and spice borne upon a cloud of steam, while the pudding on its plate, with its woolly ears protruding above the boisterous, ebullient seas of darkening water, danced and bubbled, puffed and swelled, in its own juices. Perhaps it would last for weeks 'if not eaten,' but its chances for longevity beyond the date set for its proper consumption were slim indeed.

Awaiting its cue, then, for entrance upon the Christmas scene, the pudding had sat during the intervening time upon the pantry shelf, closely covered in an earthen jar.

My father was no great reader, but his attention had been known to wander from the weekly *Citizen* while my mother was reading aloud to me the *Christmas Carol*, as she did on the eve of the day I am recalling. The enchanting picture of the Cratchits' dinner obviously aroused in him a certain envy, for on one of his too-frequent visits to the kitchen in the midst of feverish activities, he said to my mother, 'What's a quartern, 'Miry?'

My mother, intent upon her culinary affairs, had lost all connective thread and looked up in surprise.

'I don't know,' she said. 'Where'd you get it?'

'Out of that story – Cratchits.' The pudding "blazed in half a quartern of brandy." '

'Huh!' said my mother flatly, and pursued her tasks.

A few minutes later my father, who was constantly in and out of the room, remarked:

'You got any brandy around, 'Miry?'

My mother looked up sharply. 'Yes,' she said briefly. 'You sick?'

'No,' he replied shortly, 'course not. I just thought maybe we could do like they say – blaze the pudding, you know, and bedight it with Christmas holly.'

'Yes,' said my mother in a scornful but muffled tone, since the guests had already arrived, 'and maybe bedight David H. too. I'm goin' to put some in the sauce and that's enough.'

If the Covells had not been his own unintentional contribution to the occasion and David H. a guest of his own asking, my father would doubtless have had something to say regarding the imposed restrictions, but as it was he seemed robbed of argument and obliged to content himself with the prospect of only the usual hard sauce as accompaniment to his pudding.

David H. himself, however, had preconceived ideas about a Christmas pudding, due, perhaps, to his own cultural pursuits. Of a sudden my mother discovered him standing at her elbow in the pantry, where she was moulding butter, sugar, and the yolk of egg into a foamy mass. Beside the bowl stood a generous bottle of brandy. David H. was licking his lips. 'I'm glad to see, Miz' Thompson,' he said genially, ' 't you know how to dousel up a sauce. Nine women out o' ten 'd stick in a little essence o' vanilla bean and think they'd flavoured it. Pudding sauce calls for *brandy*, Miz' Thompson,' he declared fervently, *'and it don't call for nothin' else.'*

My mother, at the avidity in his eyes and the ardour in his voice, grew somewhat alarmed. Surreptitiously she slid the bottle inside the cupboard door, and tactfully edged David H. back into the front room, where the Covells sat stiffly upon upright chairs. My father had been out upon some last-minute chore, but, appearing at that moment, was haled by my mother into the pantry, the door pushed to.

'You keep David H. out o' here,' she admonished him sharply. 'I thought he 's goin' to grab the brandy bottle 'fore I could get it out of sight.'

'Huh,' said my father unreasonably, 'if you'd a listened to me you wouldn't had 'im around – old coot!'

'You asked him yourself,' twitted my mother. 'Now you keep him out the kitchen.'

But keeping David H. out of the kitchen with a Christmas dinner under way was not so easily accomplished. In spite of my father's attempts to engage him in conversation, he shortly appeared at the door.

'My!' he exclaimed. 'It cer'nly does smell good here. 'Bout how long,' he enquired ingratiatingly, 'do you think it'll be afore we set down?'

'If you'll go into the front room; David H.,' my mother told him not too patiently, 'and keep out the way, it'll be about ten minutes.'

161

'I'll jes' set this dish back in the cupboard,' he said, picking up an unwanted pitcher that he had officiously brought out, 'and then you won't hear another word out of me.' With that he dashed into the pantry, where he was plainly heard rattling amongst its contents. With a grim determination my mother started toward the door, which was suddenly thrown open to catapult David H. tempestuously almost into her arms. He was visibly shaken, but bowed, scraped a foot, and begged her pardon.

'Hurrying,' he explained volubly, 'to get set down and out the way.' My father appeared in the door.

'What in tunket's all this noise?' he wanted to know. 'And how long before dinner's ready?'

'Dinner's ready now,' my mother announced testily, 'if you men'd stay out long enough to let us take it up. You may's well set down. Go 'n tell the Covells.'

'Allow *me*! Pray – allow *me*!' Before anyone else could make a move, David H. had dashed through the door, and while we continued to stare stupidly in the direction he had gone, he had lifted the oldest Covell girl literally from her chair with one hand, and the littlest one with the other. The baby he tossed to his shoulder, and with the older girl's arm tucked underneath his own he came tripping back, the girl's feet dragging awkwardly beside his, the two others following.

My mother stood with the dish of mashed potatoes upraised in her hands, the goose already upon the table. Miz' Esty was bringing the other dishes, while my father, his white hair bristling, looked as if he were about to bellow.

'Here we are!' cried David H. gaily. 'Ol' Bob Cratchit, young Tim Cratchit – *all* the Tim Cratchits – God bless us every one!'

He deposited the youngest in the high chair placed for her, set the eldest down in hers, and, again bowing deeply to my mother, drew her chair for her.

Mechanically the dinner proceeded. The goose which graced this particular Christmas dinner of which I write was garnished with small spiced red crab apples, a flight of fancy on my mother's part which subjected her to derision.

'What in tunket you got these *crab* apples strung around on the platter for, 'Miry?' my father wanted to know. 'You think David H. and I want to play marbles?'

David H. rose to their defence. 'They look right pretty, Miz' Thompson,' he said. 'I think if things look pretty they taste better.'

'What do you *do* with 'em?' my father insisted, as he poked them to one side. 'Do you *eat* 'em, or play ball with 'em?'

'Don't pretend you never saw spiced crab apples before,' my mother admonished him tranquilly. 'Of course you eat 'em. Put one on each plate and hurry up.'

162

My father served slices of hot, juicy goose, spoonfuls of mashed potato, onions, squash. Cranberries and jelly were passed. Not much was said. The Covells were plied with food. My mother made conversation with Miz' Esty. She discoursed upon the dinner. The squash was not as dry as some we had had. The onions were a mite too salt. The room, she thought, was terribly warm. She got up and opened a door. In a few minutes my father got up and shut it. He looked unhappy.

David H. ate with gusto, but absently. He seemed to be sunk in thought. No one talked. The Christmas dinner party was not turning out well. Tears were near my mother's eyes. Finally she and Miz' Esty got up and cleared the table. My mother brought the pudding, round and richly brown, with little puckers and creases where the cloth had been tied around the top. It steamed and smelled – well, it smelled for all the world like a Christmas pudding 'sweetened with syrup, tinctured with spice.' It bulged with raisins, citron, and the candied peel of orange. And she bore it proudly as one bringing a gift that should appease even the spleen of sullen men. She set it down before her and served it. Then she passed the sauce.

As the heady odour of brandy blended with golden egg and frothing butter reached her nose, her hand paused. Conscience and her responsibility as a cook held a moment's war. My father's shrewd questioning eyes were upon her. Her lips tightened. David H. glanced up at her with a curious dawn of comprehension on his face. He rose, bowed.

'Miz' Thompson,' he said, and at the deep seriousness of his voice all eyes were turned upon him, 'I c'n see 't you're bothered. You don't know whether you ort to pass that sauce to me or not. I'll tell you. I got to apologise to you. I went into your pantry and I found that bottle. I all but took a drink. *I couldn't hardly put the bottle down.* But – I says to myself, David H. may be a drunkard, but David H. ain't no sneak. It made me kind of weak. That was when I bumped into you. But I didn't touch it. So you can pass me the sauce, Miz' Thompson, and no harm done. And if the' was more women like you, David H.'d put his foot down.'

He sat down and the sauce was passed. David H. helped himself – liberally. Miz' Esty surreptitiously wiped her eyes, for what reason I do not know. My mother beamed. Her Christmas dinner was not a failure after all. 'If you *should* ever put your foot down, David H.,' she said warmly, 'I know you'd never lift it up again.'

My father chuckled. His keen eyes dwelt leniently upon the sinner. 'Like to see you put your foot down, David H.,' he said indulgently, 'but I'd hate to see you put it down *that* hard.'

The dinner was over. The little Covells were eager to go. Their mittened

163

hands were full of gifts my mother had made them, cookies, apples, and a jar of mincemeat for pies ('although they'll probably come and borrow lard to make 'em with,' she told Miz' Esty afterward), their stomachs full of food. Awkwardly and shyly they murmured their thank-yous and good-byes and hurried away.

Miz' Esty stayed to help with the dishes. She might even stay all night, since there was no sewing to be done until after New Year's.

David H., his worn old overcoat collar pulled up about his ears, his rusty coonskin cap in hand, stood to say good-bye. He had had the best Christmas dinner he ever tasted. He thanked my mother for his repast, my father for asking him. He put his thin, none too steady hand upon my head.

'David H. – had a little girl – once,' he said huskily, and, opening the door hurriedly, was gone.

The day was drawing to its early close. The skies were lowering, grey and threatening. It would snow before night set in. My father went to the front room to nod and doze. My mother and Miz' Esty returned to the kitchen and lighted the lamps. The work was not quite finished. Miz' Esty, with a full-gathered gingham apron tied over an equally full-gathered and many-gored woollen skirt, washed the dishes while my mother dried and put them away. The room smelled pleasantly of food mingled with the odour of geranium leaves and damp earth. My mother had been pouring tea on her plants. A cat crouched over a plate near the door. Another cat could be seen stretched at length upon my father's knee. The dog, Shep, lay just outside upon the step, hopefully waiting for snow.

The women talked softly together. Their voices drifted in and out of the warmth of the room, the shadows from the lamp, the homely fragrance. The fire burned low in the stove. My mother opened the lid and thrust in a couple of sticks. It would be allowed, later, to go out for the night. We would eat bread and milk for supper.

It had been a good day, after all. Nothing to make history, but good to live, good to remember.

The Recipes for Today's Cook
by Mary Norwak

Apple and Onion (for roast goose)
Page 158

1 lb/450 g/1 lb onions
1 lb/450 g/1 lb crisp eating apples
1 oz/25 g/2 tablespoons butter
1 oz/25 g/2 tablespoons bacon fat
2 oz/50 g/¼ cup granulated sugar
salt and pepper

Peel the onions and slice them thinly. Do not peel the apples but core them and then slice across thinly. Heat the butter and bacon fat in a heavy frying pan and cover the bottom of the pan with onions. Cook over low heat until soft but not browned. Salt and pepper generously and cover with apples. Sprinkle with sugar and cover the pan. Cook gently until the apples are tender and the onions are slightly browned. If necessary, stir gently to prevent burning, but try not to break the apples. Use to garnish a roast goose, or serve separately.

Apple Butter
Page 118

8 pints/4.8 1/10 cups sweet cider
6 lb/2.7 kg/6 lb apples
2 teaspoons ground cinnamon
½ teaspoon ground cloves
½ teaspoon ground nutmeg
granulated sugar

Put the cider into a large pan and simmer until the liquid has been reduced to half. Peel and core the apples and cut into large pieces. Add to the cider and simmer for an hour until soft and thick. Weigh the pulp and allow 12 oz/350 g/1½ cups sugar to each lb/450 g pulp. Stir the spices and sugar into the apple pulp over low heat until the sugar has dissolved. Cook gently, stirring frequently until no surplus liquid remains and a spoon leaves a mark behind it when drawn across the pan. Pour into hot jars and cover.

Apple Butter may be made with any type of apple, or a mixture of cooking and eating varieties. The result should be smooth and slightly sharp-flavoured.

Apple Dowdy
Page 38

1 lb/450 g/1 lb eating apples
2 oz/50 g/¼ cup light soft brown sugar
¼ teaspoon ground cinnamon
¼ teaspoon ground nutmeg
pinch of salt
1 oz/25 g/2 tablespoons butter
4 fl oz/100 ml/½ cup warm water

Baking Powder Crust
4 oz/100 g/1 cup plain flour
1 teaspoon baking powder
1 oz/25 g/2 tablespoons butter
¼ teaspoon salt
4 fl oz/100 ml/½ cup milk

Peel and core the apples and slice them into a pie dish. Sprinkle with sugar, spices and salt. Cut the butter into flakes and arrange on top of the apples. Pour in the water. Sieve the flour and baking powder together. Rub in the butter until the mixture is like fine breadcrumbs. Stir in the salt and mix to a soft dough with the milk. Roll out on a floured board to ¾ in/1.75 cm thick and place on top of the apples, pinching the edges between finger and thumb. Bake at 300°F/150°C/Gas Mark 2 for 1½ hours. Serve with whipped cream, lightly sweetened and flavoured with ground nutmeg.

Apple Pie
Page 70

8 oz/225 g/2 cups plain flour
½ teaspoon salt
4 oz/100 g/½ cup lard
4 tablespoons iced water
1½ lb/675 g/1½ lb cooking apples
4 oz/100 g/½ cup sugar
¼ teaspoon ground nutmeg, allspice or cinnamon
½ oz/15 g/1 tablespoon butter

Stir the flour and salt together. Work in the lard with the fingertips until the pieces of fat are about the size of a pea. Mix in water with a fork, and lightly form into a ball. Wrap in a piece of foil and chill for 30 minutes. Roll out half the pastry and line an 8 in/20 cm pie plate. Peel and core the apples and slice thinly. Place in the pie plate. Sprinkle with sugar and spice. Cut the butter into flakes and put on the apples. Roll out the remaining piece of pastry and cover the apples. Seal the edges together and pinch them between finger and thumb. Cut a slit in the centre of the lid. Bake at 450°F/230°C/Gas Mark 8 for 10 minutes, then at 350°F/180°C/Gas Mark 4 for 30 minutes. Serve warm with a piece of cheese.

Baked Beans
Page 21

1 lb/450 g/2 cups haricot beans
8 oz/225 g/½ lb salt belly pork
1 medium onion
2 teaspoons mustard powder
1 teaspoon salt
1 teaspoon black pepper
1 tablespoon vinegar
2 oz/50 g/¼ cup dark soft brown sugar

Soak the beans overnight and drain well. Cover the beans with fresh water and simmer for 30 minutes. Drain and rinse in cold water. Cover with fresh water and add the piece of pork and onion. Cover and simmer until the outer skins of the beans burst. Drain well and mix with the mustard, salt, pepper, vinegar and sugar. Place in an ovenware dish. Slash the rind of the pork into small squares and place on top of the beans. Bake at 300°F/150°C/ Gas Mark 2 for 1½ hours. Serve the beans hot or cold with the pork cut in slices.

Baked Ham
Page 101

10 lb/4.5 kg/10 lb ham
3 pints/1.8 1/7½ cups dry cider
1 oz/25 g/¼ cup seedless raisins
3 tablespoons dark soft brown sugar
2 teaspoons made English mustard
½ teaspoon ground cloves
½ teaspoon ground ginger

Soak the ham overnight in water to cover. Drain well and put into a pan with the cider and raisins. Bring to the boil, skim and cover. Reduce to simmering point, and cook gently for 3 hours. Lift out of the cooking liquid and strip off the skin. Place the ham in a roasting tin. Mix the sugar, mustard and spices and spread over the fat. Bake at 350°F/180°C/ Gas Mark 4 for 40 minutes. Serve hot or cold.

Baking Powder Biscuits
Page 133

8 oz/225 g/2 cups plain flour
2 teaspoons baking powder
½ teaspoon salt
1 oz/25 g/2 tablespoons butter
6 fl oz/175 ml/¾ cup milk

Sieve the flour, baking powder and salt together. Rub in the butter until the mixture is like coarse breadcrumbs. Add the milk and work together lightly to make a soft dough. Roll out on a floured board to ¾ in/1.75 cm thick. Cut into 2–3 in/ 5–7.75 cm rounds with a cutter and place close together on a greased baking sheet. Prick lightly with a fork. Bake at 450°F/230°C/ Gas Mark 8 for 12 minutes. Cool on a wire rack and serve freshly baked.

Boiled Dinner
Page 38

4 lb/1.8 kg/4 lb salt beef
1 lb/450 g/1 lb salt pork
1 cabbage
1 swede (rutabaga)
2 parsnips
1½ lb/675 g/1½ lb potatoes

Soak the beef and pork for 2 hours in cold water and drain well. Put the beef into a large heavy pan and cover with cold water. Cover and simmer very gently for 1½ hours. Add the pork and continue simmering for 30 minutes. Cut the cabbage into quarters (or eighths if very large) and add to the pan. Peel the swede (rutabaga) and cut into ½ in/1.25 cm slices. Add to the pan with the cabbage and continue simmering for 20 minutes. Peel the parsnips and potatoes. Cut the parsnips into chunks but leave the potatoes whole unless they are very large. Put into the pan, cover and continue simmering for 45 minutes. To serve, slice the beef and pork thinly and arrange in alternating slices round the edge of a warm serving dish. Place the cabbage in the centre, surrounded by the other vegetables. Serve with the cooking liquid as gravy, and with mustard pickles or horseradish sauce.

Brown Betty
Page 13

4 oz/100 g/2 cups fresh breadcrumbs
2 oz/50 g/¼ cup butter
1½ lb/675 g/1½ lb eating apples
2 oz/50 g/¼ cup light soft brown or
*   granulated sugar*
½ lemon
¼ teaspoon ground nutmeg or cinnamon
4 fl oz/100 ml/½ cup hot water

Put the breadcrumbs into a bowl. Melt the butter and mix lightly with the crumbs. Peel and core the apples and slice them thinly. Mix together the sugar, grated rind and juice of the lemon, and the spice. Grease an ovenware dish and cover with one-third crumbs. Spread on half the apples and sprinkle with half the sugar mixture. Repeat the layers and top with the remaining crumbs. Pour over the hot water. Cover and bake at 350°F/180°C/ Gas Mark 4 for 20 minutes. Remove the lid and continue baking for 25 minutes. Serve hot with cream.

Bubble and Squeak (Michigan-style)
Page 119

1 medium cabbage
1 lb/450 g/1 lb potatoes
2 oz/50 g/¼ cup bacon fat
2 oz/50 g/¼ cup butter
salt and pepper
½ pint/300 ml/1¼ cups boiling water

Shred the cabbage finely. Peel the potatoes and slice them. Heat the bacon fat and butter in a heavy pan and add the vegetables. Season well with salt and pepper and stir well. Pour over the water. Cover and simmer very gently for 45 minutes to 1 hour until the vegetables are very tender and the liquid has been absorbed. The vegetables should be stirred gently from time to time. Serve hot with grilled or fried bacon or slices of fried salt belly pork, or with sausages or thin slices of boiled salt beef.

Cherry Pie
Page 82

8 oz/225 g/2 cups plain flour
½ teaspoon salt
4 oz/100 g/½ cup lard
4 tablespoons iced water
1½ lb/675 g/1½ lb Morello (sour) cherries
4 oz/100 g/½ cup sugar
1 tablespoon plain flour

Stir the flour and salt together. Work in the lard with the fingertips until the pieces of fat are about the size of a pea. Mix in water with a fork, and lightly form into a ball. Wrap in a piece of foil and chill for 30 minutes. Roll out half the pastry and line an 8 in/20 cm pie plate. Stone the cherries, saving all the juice. Put the cherries into the pie plate. Sprinkle with sugar and flour, and then with reserved juice. Roll out the remaining piece of pastry and cover the cherries. Seal the edges together and pinch them between finger and thumb. Cut a slit in the centre of the lid. Bake at 450°F/230°C/Gas Mark 8 for 10 minutes, then at 350°F/180°C/Gas Mark 4 for 30 minutes. Serve warm with cream.

Cherry Pudding

Page 82

1 lb/450 g/1 lb canned black cherries
8 oz/225 g/2 cups plain flour
1 teaspoon baking powder
2 oz/50 g/¼ cup caster (fine) sugar
pinch of salt
1 egg
8 fl oz/225 ml/1 cup milk
1 oz/25 g/2 tablespoons butter

Sauce
4 fl oz/100 ml/½ cup syrup from cherries
2 fl oz/50 ml/¼ cup of water
2 fl oz/50 ml/¼ cup red wine
1 tablespoon cornflour (cornstarch)
4 fl oz/100 ml/½ cup double (heavy) cream

Drain the cherries very well and reserve the juice. Stone the cherries and divide them between 4–6 greased individual ovenware dishes. Stir together the flour, baking powder, sugar and salt. Beat in the egg, milk and melted butter. Divide the mixture between the dishes. Bake at 357°F/190°C/Gas Mark 5 for 30 minutes.

While the puddings are baking, make the sauce. Put the cherry syrup, water and wine into a pan and heat gently. Mix the cornflour (cornstarch) with 1 tablespoon water and add a little of the hot liquid. Mix well and add to the pan. Stir over low heat until thick and creamy. Take off the heat and stir in the cream. Turn out the puddings and pour the sauce over them.

If preferred, the pudding may be made in one large dish, when it is best to allow 10 minutes' extra cooking time. Do not turn out, and hand the sauce separately.

Chicken Fricassee

Page 76

4 lb/1.8 kg/4 lb chicken
1 slice onion
1 celery stick
1 bay leaf
4 black peppercorns
1½ pints/900 ml/4 cups water
3 oz/75 g/6 tablespoons butter
2 oz/50 g/½ cup plain flour
4 fl oz/100 ml/½ cup double (heavy) cream
salt and pepper
Baking Powder Biscuits (p 169)
Mashed Potatoes

Cut the chicken into 10 pieces (2 wings, 2 leg joints, 2 drumsticks, 4 pieces of breast). Put into a pan and cover with boiling water. Add the onion slice, chopped celery, bay leaf and peppercorns. Cover and simmer for 45 minutes until the chicken is tender. Drain the pieces and keep on one side. Strain the chicken stock and then simmer until reduced to 1 pint/600 ml/2½ cups. Melt half the butter and cook the chicken pieces over low heat, turning them frequently, until golden-brown but not crisp. Lift out the chicken pieces and keep warm in a serving dish.

Add the remaining butter to the
pan and work in the flour. Cook and
stir for 1 minute and add the chicken
stock. Stir over low heat until smooth
and creamy. Take off the heat and
stir in the cream, and season well.
Warm Baking Powder Biscuits and
split them in half. Arrange round the
chicken and pour over the hot sauce.
Serve with Mashed Potatoes.

Chicken Pie
Page 109

4 lb/*1.8 kg/4 lb chicken*
salt and pepper
3 tablespoons plain flour
3 tablespoons milk
¾ pint/450 ml/2 cups double (heavy)
cream

Baking Powder Dough
8 oz/225 f/2 cups plain flour
2 teaspoons baking powder
½ teaspoon salt
2 oz/50 g/¼ cup butter
6 fl oz/175 ml/¾ cup milk

Cut the chicken into pieces with
2 wings, 2 leg joints and
2 drumsticks. Leave the rest of the
chicken on the carcase. Put into a
pan and just cover with water. Cover
and simmer for 1 hour until the meat
is tender. Season with salt and
pepper and uncover. Simmer for
10 minutes to concentrate and
flavour liquid. Put the wings and leg
joints into a pie dish. Remove the
remaining meat from the carcase

and cut into neat pieces. Mix these
with the chicken joints. Mix the flour
and milk and stir into the chicken
stock. Simmer for 15 minutes.
Remove from the heat, stir in the
cream and season well. Pour over the
chicken. To make the dough, sieve
the flour, baking powder and salt
together. Rub in the butter until the
mixture is like coarse breadcrumbs.
Add the milk and work together
lightly to make a soft dough. Roll out
on a floured board to ½ in/1.25 cm
thick. Put on top of the chicken and
cut a slit in the centre. Bake at 400°F/
200°C/ Gas Mark 6 for 35 minutes.

Cinnamon Rolls
Page 133

8 oz/225 g/2 cups plain flour
2 teaspoons baking powder
½ teaspoon salt
3 oz/75 g/⅓ cup butter
6 fl oz/150 ml/¾ cup milk
2 oz/50 g/¼ cup light soft brown sugar
2 teaspoons ground cinnamon

Sieve the flour, baking powder and salt together. Rub in the butter until the mixture is like coarse breadcrumbs. Add the milk and work together lightly to make a soft dough. Roll out on a floured board ½ in/1.25 cm thick. Mix the brown sugar and cinnamon and sprinkle all over the dough. Roll up firmly and cut into 1 in/2.5 cm slices. Place on greased baking sheets, allowing room for them to spread. Bake at 425°F/220°C/ Gas Mark 7 for 15 minutes. Lift on to a wire rack to cool.

Coffee Cake
Page 133

2 oz/50 g/¼ cup butter
2 oz/50 g/¼ cup granulated sugar
3 eggs
1 lemon
1 tablespoon water
8 oz/225 g/2 cups plain flour
2 teaspoons baking powder

Topping
4 oz/100 g/½ cup granulated sugar
1 teaspoon ground cinnamon
2 oz/50 g/⅓ cup chopped mixed nuts

Preheat oven to 350°F/180°C/ Gas Mark 4. Grease a 7 × 10 in/ 17.5 × 25 cm tin. Cream the butter and sugar until light and fluffy. Separate the eggs and add the yolks to the butter. Add the grated rind and juice of the lemon, and the water, and beat well. Sieve the flour and baking powder together and fold into the creamed mixture. Whisk the egg whites to soft peaks and fold in. Spread lightly in the prepared tin. Mix the sugar and cinnamon until evenly coloured and sprinkle over the top of the cake mixture. Sprinkle on the chopped nuts. Bake for 25 minutes. Leave in the tin until just cold. Cut into squares and serve freshly baked.

Apple Cake

Prepare the basic cake and place the mixture in the tin. Brush the top lightly with 1 oz/25 g/2 tablespoons melted butter. Cover with 8 oz/ 225 g/½ lb peeled and sliced eating apples. Sprinkle with 4 oz/100 g/ ½ cup granulated sugar mixed with 1 teaspoon ground cinnamon. Bake for 30 minutes.

Cold Fried Chicken

Page 48

4 lb/1.8 kg/4 lb chicken
1 small onion
1 bay leaf
salt and pepper
1 pint/600 ml/2½ cups of water
2 oz/50 g/¼ cup butter

Cut the chicken into 10 pieces
(2 wings, 2 leg joints, 2 drumsticks,
4 pieces of breast). If preferred, an
equivalent quantity of chicken joints
may be used such as all drumsticks
or wings. Put the chicken into a pan
with the onion, bay leaf, salt and
pepper. Cover with water and cover
the pan. Simmer for 45 minutes until
the chicken is tender. Drain well (use
the chicken stock for soup), and
leave the chicken until cool. Melt the
butter and fry the chicken gently
until golden brown. Cool completely
and serve with sweet cucumber
pickles and thin slices of bread and
butter.

Corned Beef Hash

Page 40

1 lb/450 g/1 lb cooked salt beef
1 lb/450 g/1 lb cooked potatoes
salt and pepper
6 tablespoons single cream
2 oz/50 g/¼ cup butter
chopped fresh parsley or green pepper

Dice the beef and potatoes finely.
Mix them together lightly but do not
mash. Season well and mix with

cream. Put the butter into a thick
heavy frying pan and melt over low
heat until just hot. Add the beef
mixture. Stir well and spread to
cover the base of the pan. Cook very
gently for 45 minutes until crisp and
brown underneath. Fold over and lift
carefully on to a warm serving dish.
Sprinkle with parsley or finely
chopped green pepper. If liked, serve
with poached eggs.

Cornmeal Mush

Page 132

1½ pints/900 ml/4 cups water
6 oz/150 g/1 cup yellow cornmeal
pinch of salt

Put the water and salt into a heavy
pan. Bring to the boil and then
dribble in the cornmeal while
stirring well. Cook on low heat for
1 hour, stirring frequently. Serve hot
with milk.

Fried Mush
Pack any leftover mush into a well
greased loaf tin. Cover and leave
until very cold and firm. Cut in ½ in/
1.25 cm slices and coat lightly with
flour. Fry in butter or bacon fat over
low heat until crisp. Serve with
maple syrup.

Cream Cake
Page 49

4 eggs
8 oz/225 g/1 cup sugar
2 oz/50 g/¼ cup butter
8 oz/225 g/2 cups plain flour
2 teaspoons baking powder
4 tablespoons milk
1 teaspoon lemon juice

Filling
½ pint/300 ml/1¼ cups soured cream
8 oz/225 g/1 cup caster (fine) sugar
3 oz/75 g/½ cup chopped pecans or walnuts

Frosting
1 lb/450 g/2 cups sugar
¼ pint/150 ml/⅝ cup water
2 egg whites

Grease and base-line three 7 in/
17.5 cm sponge sandwich tins.
Preheat oven to 350°F/180°C/ Gas
Mark 4. Whisk the eggs until thick
and pale. Cream the sugar and
butter together until light and fluffy.
Lightly fold the eggs into the
creamed mixture. Sieve the flour and
baking powder and fold into the
creamed mixture. Stir in the milk
and lemon juice. Spoon into the
prepared tins and bake for
30 minutes. Turn on to a wire rack to
cool.

Put the cream and sugar into a
thick pan. Blend the nuts until fine
and add to the pan. Heat gently,
stirring well until the sugar has
dissolved. Leave until cold and use
to sandwich the cakes together.

Put the sugar and water into a pan
and heat gently until the sugar has
dissolved. Boil to a temperature of
240°F/114°C (when a little mixture
dropped into a cup of cold water will
form a soft ball). Whisk the egg
whites to stiff peaks and pour on the
sugar syrup gradually, whisking all
the time until the mixture is thick
and almost cold. Pour quickly over
the cake as the mixture sets quickly.

Cup Cakes
Page 51

2 oz/50 g/¼ cup butter
4 oz/100 g/½ cup caster (fine) sugar
2 eggs
4 fl oz/100 ml/½ cup milk
few drops of vanilla essence
6 oz/150 g/1½ cups plain flour
1½ teaspoons baking powder
pinch of salt

Filling
8 oz/225 g/1 cup sugar
2½ tablespoons plain flour
grated rind 2 lemons or oranges
4 tablespoons lemon or orange juice
1 egg
1 teaspoon butter

Frosting
4 oz/100 g/½ cup icing (confectioners')
*   sugar*
lemon or orange juice
coloured sugar crystals

Place 15 paper cases (paper cups) on a baking sheet. Preheat oven to 350°F/180°C/ Gas Mark 4. Cream the butter and sugar together until light and fluffy. Separate the eggs and beat the yolks into the creamed mixture. Mix the milk and vanilla essence. Sieve the flour, baking powder and salt. Add the milk and flour to the creamed mixture alternately, beating well between each addition. Whisk the egg whites stiffly and fold into the mixture. Divide between the cases (cups) and bake for 20 minutes. Cool completely on a wire rack.

To make the filling, put all the ingredients into a bowl over a pan of hot water. Cook over a gentle heat until the mixture reaches boiling point, stirring well. Cool completely. Cut a thin slice from the top of each cake and keep to one side. Scoop out a hollow and fill each cake with the lemon or orange filling. Replace the tops. Sieve the icing sugar and add just enough lemon or orange juice to make a thick icing. Spread over the top of each cake and sprinkle with coloured sugar crystals.

Drop Biscuits
Page 133

8 oz/225 g/2 cups plain flour
2 teaspoons baking powder
½ teaspoon salt
1 oz/25 g/2 tablespoons butter
½ pint/300 ml/11¼ cups milk
1 tablespoon granulated sugar
seedless raisins

Sieve the flour, baking powder and salt together. Rub in the butter until the mixture is like coarse breadcrumbs. Add the milk and beat well. Grease 18 deep tartlet tins with butter. Drop in spoonfuls of the mixture. Sprinkle with a little sugar and put a raisin in the centre of each one. Bake at 425°F/220°C/ Gas Mark 7 for 15 minutes. Cool on a wire rack and serve freshly baked.

English Roast Pig
Page 146

1 suckling pig
2 large onions
6 oz/150 g/¾ cup melted butter
8 oz/225 g/4 cups breadcrumbs
1 lemon
2 teaspoons dried sage
2 eggs
salt and pepper
olive oil
1 red eating apple

Chop the onions finely and cook in half the butter until soft and golden. Add to the breadcrumbs with the remaining butter. Add the grated rind and juice of the lemon, sage, eggs and plenty of salt and pepper. Stuff the pig and sew up the cavity with thin string or button thread. Score the skin with a razor blade diagonally on each side from the backbone so that the marks join and point forward like an arrowhead. Rub olive oil over the skin and sprinkle lightly with salt. Place on its side on a rack in a roasting tin. Roast at 375°F/190°C/ Gas Mark 5 for 1¼ hours. Turn the pig carefully on to the other side and continue roasting for 1¼ hours. Lift on to a serving dish and place the apple in the pig's mouth. Serve with gravy made from the pan drippings from which excess fat has been removed, to which stock and a glass of white wine or dry cider has been added.

Fig Layer Cake
Page 49

2½ oz/65 g/⅓ cup butter
8 oz/225 g/1 cup caster (fine) sugar
2 eggs
7 oz/200 g/1¾ cups plain flour
pinch of salt
2 teaspoons baking powder
4 fl oz/100 ml/½ cup milk
few drops of vanilla essence

Filling
4 oz/100 g/1 cup dried figs
4 oz/100 g/⅔ cup seedless raisins
3 oz/75 g/⅓ cup of sugar
4 fl oz/100 ml/½ cup water
2 egg whites

Frosting
2 egg whites
6 oz/150 g/¾ cup caster (fine) sugar
few drops of vanilla essence

Grease and base-line two 8 in/20 cm sponge sandwich tins. Preheat oven to 350°F/180°C/ Gas Mark 4. Cream the butter and sugar until very light and creamy and work in the eggs gradually, one at a time. Sieve the flour, salt and baking powder. Add the dry ingredients alternately with the milk, beating well between each addition. Flavour with vanilla essence. Divide the mixture between the cake tins. Bake for 30 minutes. Turn on to a wire rack to cool.

To make the filling, chop the figs finely and put into a pan with the raisins. Add the sugar and water and simmer until thick. Cool to lukewarm. Whisk the egg whites to stiff peaks and fold in the fig mixture.

Put the cake layers together with this mixture, and place the cake on a serving plate.

To make the frosting, whisk the egg whites to stiff peaks. Gradually add the sugar, beating all the time until the mixture stands in stiff peaks. Flavour with vanilla essence and spread all over the cake.

Fried Ham and Milk Gravy
Page 130

4 smoked gammon (ham) slices
2 tablespoons plain flour
½ pint/300 ml/1¼ cups of milk
salt and pepper

Put the gammon (ham) slices into a shallow dish. Cover with boiling water, drain well and dry on kitchen paper. Remove rinds and snip the fat at intervals to prevent curling. Put into a thick frying pan and heat gently until the fat runs. Continue cooking gently until lightly browned and cooked through. Lift out of the fat and keep warm on a serving dish. Make up the fat in the pan to 1½ tablespoons with a little more bacon fat or butter. Work in the flour and cook for 1 minute, stirring well. Gradually add the milk, stirring well, and cook gently until smooth and creamy. Season to taste and pour over the gammon (ham) slices. Serve with boiled or baked potatoes.

Fried Salt Pork
Page 119

1 lb/450 g/1 lb slices salt belly pork
2 eggs
4 fl oz/100 ml/½ cup milk
3 oz/75 g/¾ cup plain flour
salt and pepper
oil or lard for frying

Soak the slices of pork for 2–3 hours. Drain very well and trim off the skin. Cut each slice into three pieces. Beat the eggs, milk, flour, salt and pepper into a batter. Dip in the pork pieces and fry slowly in hot oil or lard until crisp and golden. If there is any batter left, fry spoonfuls in the hot fat until crisp. Serve with Mashed Potatoes (p 182).

Ginger Cream Cookies

Page 113

4 oz/100 g/½ cup butter
4 oz/100 g/½ cup light soft brown sugar
6 oz/150 g/½ cup black treacle (molasses)
2 egg yolks
4 tablespoons milk
1 teaspoon vinegar
1 teaspoon bicarbonate of soda
12 oz/350 g/3 cups plain flour
½ teaspoon ground cloves
½ teaspoon ground cinnamon
½ teaspoon ground nutmeg
½ teaspoon ground ginger

Frosting
12 oz/350 g/1½ cups sugar
6 tablespoons water
2 egg whites

Preheat oven to 375°F/190°C/ Gas Mark 5. Cream together the butter and sugar until light and fluffy. Work in the black treacle (molasses). Beat in the egg yolks and then the milk, vinegar and soda. Sieve the flour with the spices and work into the mixture. Knead well to make a firm dough. Roll out thinly on a floured board and cut into shapes. Put on to lightly greased baking sheets and bake for 8 minutes. Lift on to a wire rack to cool.

To make the frosting, put the sugar and water into a pan and heat gently until the sugar has dissolved. Boil to a temperature of 240°F/114°C (when a little mixture dropped into a cup of cold water will form a soft ball). Whisk the egg whites to stiff peaks and pour on the sugar syrup gradually, whisking all the time until the mixture is thick. Spoon quickly on to the biscuits, as the mixture sets very quickly.

Irish Stew (Michigan-style)

Page 119

4 oz/100 g/¼ lb salt pork
1½ lb/675 g chuck steak
1 lb/450 g/1 lb potatoes
3 medium onions
1 bay leaf
salt and pepper

Dumplings
4 oz/100 g/1 cup plain flour
1 teaspoon baking powder
pinch of salt
2 oz/50 g/¼ cup shredded suet

Soak the salt pork for an hour, drain and cut into small pieces. Cut the chuck steak into cubes. Put the pork into a thick saucepan or casserole and heat until the fat runs. Add the beef and continue cooking over low heat until lightly browned. Cover with water and bring to the boil. Cover and then simmer for 1 hour. Peel the potatoes and onions. Cut potatoes in half and quarter the onions. Add to the pan with the bay leaf and seasoning. Add just enough water to cover. Cover and simmer for 45 minutes.

Make the dumplings by stirring together the flour, baking powder, salt and suet and add just enough cold water to make a firm dough. Form into 8 balls. Put in the pan, cover and simmer for 20 minutes.

Jelly Roll
Page 49

4 eggs
8 oz/225 g/1 cup caster (fine) sugar
1 tablespoon cold water
1 tablespoon lemon juice
3 oz/75 g/¾ cup plain flour
1 oz/25 g/¼ cup cornflour (cornstarch)
1 teaspoon baking powder
pinch of salt
few drops of vanilla essence
6 tablespoons redcurrant jelly
1 tablespoon icing (confectioners') sugar

Line a swiss roll tin with greaseproof paper. Brush the paper and sides of the tin with butter. Preheat oven to 350°F/180°C/ Gas Mark 4. Separate the eggs and whisk the egg whites to stiff peaks. Gradually beat in 4 tablespoons sugar and keep on one side. Add the water and lemon juice to the egg yolks and beat until very thick and pale. Beat in the remaining sugar. Fold the egg whites into the yolks very lightly until the mixture is evenly coloured. Sieve the flour, cornflour (cornstarch) and baking powder with the salt. Fold into the egg mixture very lightly and flavour with vanilla. Spread the mixture lightly but evenly in the prepared tin. Bake for exactly 12 minutes. Turn out on a damp cloth lightly sprinkled with caster (fine) sugar. Remove base paper and use a sharp knife to trim off thin strips from the ends and sides of the cake. Spread quickly with the jelly. Roll up lightly but firmly and leave covered with a clean cloth until serving time. Just before serving, sprinkle with sieved icing sugar.

Johnnycake
Page 134

¾ pint/450 ml/2 cups milk
3 eggs
6 oz/150 g/1 cup yellow cornmeal
1 teaspoon salt
1 teaspoon bicarbonate of soda
1 tablespoon hot water
1 oz/25 g/2 tablespoons butter

Grease a 7 × 10 in/17.5 × 25 cm tin with lard. Beat the milk and eggs together well until evenly coloured. Beat in the cornmeal and salt. Dissolve the soda in hot water and beat into the mixture with melted butter. Pour into the prepared tin. Bake at 350°F/180°C/ Gas Mark 4 for 30 minutes until crisp.

Marble Cake
Page 48

2½ oz/65 g/⅓ cup butter
8 oz/225 g/1 cup caster (fine) sugar
2 eggs
7 oz/200 g/1¾ cups plain flour
pinch of salt
2 teaspoons baking powder
4 fl oz/100 ml/½ cup milk
few drops of vanilla essence
2 oz/50 g/2 squares plain chocolate
½ teaspoon ground cinnamon
pinch of ground cloves

Grease and base-line an 8 in/20 cm round tin. Preheat oven to 350°F/ 180°C/ Gas Mark 4. Cream the butter and sugar until very light and creamy and work in the eggs gradually, one at a time. Sieve the flour, salt and baking powder. Add the dry ingredients alternately with the milk, beating well between each addition. Flavour with vanilla essence. Melt the chocolate in a bowl over hot water and add the cinnamon and cloves. Put about one-third of the cake mixture into a bowl and beat in the chocolate. Spoon a layer of the white cake mixture into the tin. Spoon in some of the chocolate mixture, leaving gaps between and add spoonfuls of the white mixture. Continue until all the chocolate mixture is used and finish with a layer of white mixture. Bake for 45 minutes. Cool in the tin for 5 minutes and turn on to a wire rack to cool.

Mashed Potatoes
Page 76

1½ lb/675 g/1½ potatoes
3 tablespoons double (heavy) cream
2 oz/50 g/¼ cup butter
salt and pepper
finely chopped parsley or chives or paprika

Peel the potatoes thinly and boil until done but not broken. Drain very well and return to the pan. Mash until the potatoes are free from lumps. Add the cream and 1 tablespoon melted butter beating lightly with a whisk or wooden spoon. Season well to taste with salt and pepper, and beat until light and fluffy. Pile into an ovenware serving dish, but do not press down. Sprinkle with parsley, chives or paprika. Cut the remaining butter into flakes and dot them over the potatoes. Put into the oven at 325°F/160°C/Gas Mark 3 for 5 minutes. Serve at once.

Parsnip Stew
Page 56

8 oz/225 g/½ lb salt pork
1 lb/450 g/1 lb parsnips
8 oz/225 g/½ lb potatoes
salt and pepper

Soak the salt pork for an hour, drain and cut into cubes. Put into a heavy pan and cover with water. Bring to the boil, skim, cover and simmer for 45 minutes. Peel the parsnips and potatoes and cut into cubes. Add to the pan and if necessary add just enough water to cover the vegetables. Cover and simmer for 1 hour until the liquid has just evaporated. Season to taste and serve with Johnnycake (p 181).

Plum Pudding and Pudding Sauce
Page 159

1 lb/450 g/2 cups shredded suet
8 oz/225 g/1 cup dark soft brown sugar
8 oz/225 g/1¾ cups currants
8 oz/225 g/1⅓ cups stoned raisins
12 oz/350 g/2 cups chopped mixed candied peel
1 lb/450 g/4 cups plain flour
1 teaspoon salt
1 teaspoon ground cinnamon
1 teaspoon ground ginger
1 teaspoon ground nutmeg
1 teaspoon ground cloves
6 oz/150 g/3 cups fine breadcrumbs
4 eggs
8 fl oz/225 ml/1 cup milk
4 fl oz/100 ml/½ cup brandy

Pudding Sauce
4 oz/100 g/½ cup unsalted butter
4 oz/100 g/½ cup caster (fine) sugar
1 egg yolk
4 tablespoons brandy

Mix together suet, sugar, dried fruit, flour, salt, spices and breadcrumbs. Beat together the eggs, milk and brandy and work into the dry ingredients to make a stiff mixture. Leave to stand for 2 hours. Take a large piece of thick cotton or linen (an old tea-towel will do well) and soak in cold water. Wring out very well and place on a flat surface. Butter the centre of the cloth and sprinkle with flour. Place over a large mixing bowl and put in the pudding mixture. Tie firmly with string, allowing a little room for swelling. Put a large saucer upside-down in the base of a large saucepan, and fill the pan half-full with boiling water. Put the pudding on the saucer, cover and boil for 7 hours, adding more boiling water from time to time. Turn out on to a serving dish and flame with brandy.

To make the *Pudding Sauce*, cream the butter and sugar until light and fluffy. Work in the egg yolk and then the brandy. Chill for an hour before serving.

Popovers
Page 133

4 oz/100 g/1 cup bread flour
¼ teaspoon salt
2 eggs
8 fl oz/225 ml/1 cup milk

Grease 10 individual ovenglass
dishes or deep Yorkshire pudding
tins very well. Preheat oven to
450°F/230°C/Gas Mark 8. Sieve the
flour and salt into a bowl. Beat the
eggs until very light and fluffy and
then beat in the milk. Stir into the
flour and beat hard for 2 minutes
until very light. Heat the dishes or
tins until very hot. Pour in the batter
so that the containers are one-third
full. Bake for 20 minutes. Reduce
heat to 350°F/180°C/Gas Mark 4
and continue baking for 15 minutes.
Remove immediately from
containers and eat at once.

Pumpkin Pie
Page 22

8 oz/225 g/2 cups plain flour
½ teaspoon salt
2 oz/50 g/¼ cup butter
2 oz/50 g/¼ cup lard
4 tablespoons iced water
1½ lb/675 g/1½ lb pumpkin
2 oz/50 g/¼ cup light soft brown sugar
2 oz/50 g/¼ cup granulated sugar
1 tablespoon black treacle (molasses)
1 teaspoon ground ginger
½ teaspoon ground allspice
½ teaspoon ground cinnamon
½ teaspoon salt
2 eggs
8 fl oz/225 ml/1 cup single cream

Stir the flour and salt together. Work
in the butter and lard with the
fingertips until the mixture is like
coarse breadcrumbs. Mix in water
with a fork, and lightly form into a
ball. Wrap in a piece of foil and chill
for 30 minutes. Roll out and line a
9 in/22.5 cm sponge sandwich or
flan tin. Peel the pumpkin and
remove the seeds and pith. Cut into
small pieces and steam until tender.
Drain well and beat the pulp until
smooth. Beat in the sugars, black
treacle (molasses), spices, salt, eggs
and cream. Pour into the pastry case.
Bake at 425°F/220°C/Gas Mark 7
for 15 minutes. Reduce heat to
350°F/180°C/Gas Mark 4 and
continue baking for 30 minutes.
Serve warm with single cream.

Rhubarb Pie
Page 93

8 oz/225 g/2 cups plain flour
½ teaspoon salt
4 oz/100 g/½ cup lard
4 tablespoons iced water
1 lb/450 g/1 lb young rhubarb
4 oz/100 g/½ cup sugar
1 oz/25 g/2 tablespoons butter
1 tablespoon plain flour

Stir the flour and salt together. Work
in the lard with the fingertips until
the pieces of fat are about the size of a
pea. Mix in water with a fork, and
lightly form into a ball. Wrap in a
piece of foil and chill for 30 minutes.
Roll out half the pastry and line an
8 in/20 cm pie plate. Cut the
rhubarb into ½ in/1.25 cm lengths
and put into the pie plate. Sprinkle
with sugar. Arrange small pieces of
butter on top and sprinkle with flour.
Roll out the remaining piece of
pastry and cover the rhubarb. Seal
the edges together and pinch them
between finger and thumb. Cut a slit
in the centre of the lid. Bake at
450°F/230°C/Gas Mark 8 for
10 minutes, then at 350°F/180°C/
Gas Mark 4 for 30 minutes. Serve
warm.

Roast Goose with Potato Stuffing
Page 157

14 lb/6.25 kg/14 lb goose
8 oz/225 g/½ lb onions
2 lb/900 g/2 lb potatoes
2 oz/50 g/¼ cup butter
4 fl oz/100 ml/½ cup single cream
salt and pepper
2 teaspoons dried eggs

Chop the onion finely and fry in half
the butter until soft and golden. Peel
the potatoes and boil them. Drain
very well and mash with the
remaining butter and cream. Add
the onions and season well. Stuff the
goose, and place in the roasting tin.
Crumble the sage and mix with a
little salt and pepper. Rub all over
the bird. Roast the goose at 450°F/
230°C/Gas Mark 8 for 20 minutes.
Reduce heat to 350°F/280°C/Gas
Mark 4 and continue roasting for
3 hours. There is a great deal of fat in
a goose, and it is a good idea to place
the bird on a rack in a roasting tin. If
the skin is pricked when the heat is
reduced, the fat will run out more
freely. As a lot of fat accumulates in
the roasting tin, remove some into a
bowl two or three times during
cooking. The fat is excellent for
frying and should be saved in the
refrigerator. Serve the goose with
gravy made from stock in which
giblets have simmered and the pan
juices from which excess fat has been
removed.

Roast Turkey with Herb Stuffing
Page 148

10 lb/4.5 kg/10 lb turkey
1 large onion
8 oz/225 g/4 cups breadcrumbs
½ pint/300 ml/1¼ cups milk
1 tablespoon sage
1 tablespoon marjoram
1 tablespoon thyme
salt and pepper
4 oz/100 g/½ cup melted butter
8 oz/225 g/½ salt belly pork

Chop the onion finely. Soak the crumbs in the milk for 20 minutes and then squeeze out excess moisture. Mix the onion, crumbs, finely chopped herbs, salt, pepper and melted butter. Fill the turkey with the stuffing, reserving one-quarter of the mixture. Place the turkey in the roasting tin and rub the reserved stuffing all over the bird. Slice the pork very thinly and arrange over the bird. Roast at 350°F/180°C/Gas Mark 4 for 1 hour. Reduce heat to 350°F/160°C/Gas Mark 3 and continue roasting for 2½ hours.

Salt-Rising Bread
Page 65

Starter
1 medium potato
2 tablespoons white or yellow cornmeal
1 teaspoon sugar
½ teaspoon salt
12 fl oz/350 ml/1½ cups milk

Dough
starter (see above)
4 fl oz/100 ml/½ cup hand-hot water
4 fl oz/100 ml/½ cup hand-hot milk
1 tablespoon melted butter
1 teaspoon salt
¼ teaspoon bicarbonate of soda
1¼ lb/565 g/5 cups bread flour

Rinse a large bowl with boiling water. Put in the grated potato, cornmeal, sugar and salt. Bring the milk just to boiling point and add to the bowl. Cover and put into a bowl of boiling water and then cover this with a piece of polythene and a blanket or quilt. Leave to stand for about 24 hours until the mixture foams. The process can be helped by putting the starter ingredients into a large vacuum jar; or the covered bowl may be placed in a very low oven. The starter can be used when the foam is about 1 in/2.5 cm thick.

To make the bread, add the starter mush to the water, milk, butter, salt and soda. Stir in half the flour and beat until very smooth. Add the remaining flour gradually and knead to a soft dough. Knead for 10–15 minutes until the dough is smooth. Cut the dough in half and shape into two loaf tins which have been well-greased. Brush the tops with a little melted butter, cover and leave in a warm place for at least 5 hours until doubled in size. Bake at 375°F/190°C/Gas Mark 5 for 45 minutes. Cool on a wire rack. Eat freshly baked.

This is an extremely old type of bread, popular with pioneering families as the starter or raising agent could be prepared from everyday ingredients when yeast was not available. The bread has two disadvantages, apart from the length of time involved in its preparation. The starter develops a very strange smell, and the bread is very temperamental and only works well about one in four times.

Sauerkraut
Page 121

6 large white cabbages
cooking salt
cooking apples

Remove outer leaves from cabbages and cut the cabbage in quarters. Cut out and discard the thick stems. Shred the cabbage finely. Pack the cabbage into a large barrel or crock by putting a 4 in/10 cm layer in the base and sprinkling with 3 oz/75 g/ ⅜ cup salt and 1 finely chopped apple. Continue in layers, pressing very hard so that moisture is released

and the cabbage is covered in brine. Fill the container, leaving enough space for swelling and fermenting without overflowing. Cover with whole cabbage leaves and a thick layer of salt. Cover with a cloth and a piece of wood which fits into the top of the container. Put on a heavy weight. Keep in a warm place to ferment. After two weeks, remove scum and put on a clean cloth. Wash away any scum from the lid and sides of the container. Replace the lid and weight. Store in a cool place, each week washing the lid and sides of the container and putting on a clean cloth. The sauerkraut may be used 3–4 weeks after fermentation has ceased.

To keep sauerkraut for a long period, it is best to sterilize it in preserving jars. Drain off the liquid and bring to boiling point. Add the cabbage and bring to simmering point. Pack into hot sterilized preserving jars. Screw on lids and turn back one-half turn. Put into a pan of boiling water to cover the lids and bring to boiling point. Reduce to simmering and keep at the same temperature for 25 minutes. Remove from water, screw on lids tightly and cool before storage.

Scalloped Potatoes
Page 54

1½ lb/675 g/1½ lb potatoes
4 oz/100 g/½ cup butter
salt and pepper
1 tablespoon plain flour
4 fl oz/100 ml/½ cup single cream
1 pint/600 ml/2½ cups milk

Peel the potatoes and slice them very thinly. Put into iced water and leave for 1 hour. Drain well and dry in a clean cloth. Arrange one-third of the potatoes in a large shallow overware dish. Cover with half the butter cut in thin flakes. Season well with salt and pepper and sprinkle with half the flour. Put on half the remaining potatoes and cover with remaining butter. Season again and sprinkle with remaining flour. Top with the remaining potatoes. Mix the cream and milk and pour into the dish. Cover with a piece of foil and bake at 300°F/150°C/Gas Mark 2 for 1½ hours. Remove foil and continue baking for 30 minutes until the liquid has just been absorbed and the potatoes are richly golden-brown.

Sour Cream Cookies
Page 102

4 oz/100 g/½ cup butter
4 oz/100 g/½ cup sugar
3 fl oz/75 ml/⅓ cup soured cream
½ teaspoon bicarbonate of soda
2 egg yolks
8 oz/225 g/2 cups plain flour
2 teaspoons caraway seeds
2 tablespoons seedless raisins

Preheat oven to 375°F/190°C/Gas Mark 5. Cream the butter and sugar until light and fluffy. Beat in the soured cream, soda and egg yolks and work in the flour. Mix well to a soft dough. Take small pieces of the dough and roll into balls about the size of a walnut. Place on lightly greased baking sheets. Press down each ball lightly with a fork dipped into cold water. Sprinkle with caraway seeds and press a raisin in the centre of each one. Bake for 8 minutes. Lift carefully on to a wire rack to cool.

Sour Milk and Sody Biscuits
Page 133

8 oz/225 g/2 cups plain flour
1 teaspoon bicarbonate of soda
¼ teaspoon salt
1 oz/25 g/2 tablespoons butter
½ oz/15 g/1 tablespoon lard
8 fl oz/200 ml/1 cup soured cream

Sieve the flour, soda and salt together. Rub in the butter and lard until the mixture is like fine breadcrumbs. Add the soured cream and work together to form a dough. Roll out lightly on a floured board to ¾ in/1.75 cm thick. Cut into 2–3 in/ 5–5.5 cm rounds with a cutter. Place on a greased baking sheet. Bake at 450°F/230°C/Gas Mark 8 for 12 minutes. Cool on a wire rack and serve freshly baked.

Spice Cake
Page 114

4 oz/100 g/½ cup butter
4 oz/100 g/½ cup light soft brown sugar
6 oz/150 g/½ cup black treacle (molasses)
4 fl oz/100 ml/½ cup soured cream
2 eggs
8 oz/225 g/2 cups plain flour
1 teaspoon bicarbonate of soda
1 teaspoon ground nutmeg
½ teaspoon ground cloves
½ teaspoon ground cinnamon
½ teaspoon ground mace
¼ teaspoon salt

Grease a 7 × 10 in/17.5 × 25 cm tin. Preheat oven to 350°F/180°C/ Gas Mark 4. Cream the butter and sugar until light and fluffy. Gradually work in the black treacle (molasses) and soured cream. Beat the eggs lightly. Sieve the flour, soda, spices and salt. Add the eggs and flour alternately, beating well between each addition. Stir in the remaining flour. Put into the prepared tin and bake for 35 minutes. Leave in the tin for 5 minutes, then turn on to a wire rack to cool. Cut into squares and serve.

Stewed Rhubarb
Page 81

1 lb/450 g/1 lb young rhubarb
water
2–3 oz/50–75 g/¼–⅓ cup sugar

Do not peel the rhubarb but trim the tops and bases of the stalks. Cut into 2 in/5 cm lengths. Put into a pan and only just cover with water. Simmer for about 10 minutes until tender but unbroken. Stir in sugar to taste.

Strawberry Shortcake
Page 69

8 oz/225 g/2 cups plain flour
2 teaspoons baking powder
½ teaspoon salt
1 tablespoon sugar
3 oz/75 g/⅓ cup butter
6 fl oz/150 ml/¾ cup milk

Filling and Topping
2 oz/50 g/¼ cup unsalted butter
1 lb/450 g/1 lb strawberries

Grease a 7 in/17.5 cm sponge sandwich tin. Preheat oven to 450°F/230°C/Gas Mark 8. Sieve the flour, baking powder and salt together. Stir in the sugar. Rub in the butter until the mixture is like coarse breadcrumbs. Mix to a dough with the milk. Divide the mixture into pieces. Roll very lightly on a floured board and put one piece into the prepared tin. Melt half the unsalted butter and brush over the surface. Place the other half of the dough on top. Bake for 15 minutes. While the shortcake is baking, crush the strawberries lightly. If liked, add sugar to taste. Turn out the shortcake and split in half at once. Spread the interior of each half with the remaining butter. Put the base on a serving dish and quickly cover with half the strawberries. Put on the other piece of shortcake and top with remaining strawberries. Serve warm with cream.

Switchel
Page 71

1 pint/600 ml/2½ cups iced water
3 tablespoons cider vinegar
2 tablespoons light soft brown sugar
½ teaspoon ground ginger

Stir all the ingredients together until the sugar has dissolved, and serve chilled.

Tea Cakes
Page 126

1 egg
3 oz/75 g/⅓ cup sugar
5 tablespoons soured cream
4 oz/100 g/½ cup plain flour
1 teaspoon bicarbonate of soda
¼ teaspoon ground nutmeg
pinch of salt

Grease 15 individual tart tins with butter. Preheat oven to 350°F/180°C/Gas Mark 4. Beat the egg and sugar until light and creamy. Add the cream and continue beating until smooth and fluffy. Sieve together the flour, soda, nutmeg and salt. Fold into the creamed mixture. Spoon into the prepared tins. Bake for 15 minutes. Turn on to a wire rack to cool.

Vegetable Soup
Page 32

1 large beef bone with marrow
6 pints/3.6 l/15 cups water
3 large onions
6 potatoes
6 medium carrots
4 celery sticks
1 parsnip
8 oz/225 g/½ lb cabbage
4 oz/100 g/⅔ cup pearl barley
sprig of parsley
salt and pepper

Ask the butcher to chop the bone in two or three pieces. Put into a large pan with the water. Bring to the boil, skim, cover and then simmer for 3 hours, adding boiling water from time to time to make up the quantity of stock. Peel the vegetables. Chop the onions, potatoes, carrots, celery and parsnip roughly and add to the pan. Cover and simmer for 30 minutes. Shred the cabbage finely and add to the pan with the barley, parsley, salt and pepper. Cover and continue simmering for 1 hour. Remove the parsley. Take out the bone pieces and remove any meat and the marrow. Chop finely and add to the soup. Adjust seasoning to taste and serve at once.